NATIONS UNITED

How the
United Nations
is Undermining
Israel and the West

Alex Grobman

First Printing: October 2006

ISBN-13: 978-0-89221-674-1
ISBN-10: 0-89221-674-3
Library of Congress Catalog Number: 2006935625

Printed in the United States of America.

For information regarding author interviews, please contact the publicity department at (870) 438-5288.

Please visit our website for other great titles:
www.newleafpublishinggroup.net.

Balfour
Books

A Division of New Leaf Publishing Group

Dedicated to
Bud Levin
and
Rose Mattus

ABBREVIATIONS

AJC	American Jewish Committee, Jacob and Hilda Blaustein Library
ADL	The Anti-Defamation League of B'nai B'rith
CMIP	Center for Monitoring the Impact of Peace
C.S.S	Intelligence and Terrorism Information Center at the Center for Special Studies
CZA	Central Zionist Archives, Jerusalem
F.I.N.	*Fortnightly Intelligence Newsletter* — Headquarters British Troops in Palestine
IMRA	Independent Media Review and Analysis
JTA	Jewish Telegraphic Agency Daily News Bulletin
MEMRI	Middle East Media Research Institute
NYT	*The New York Times*
NYS	*The New York Sun*
PMW	Palestinian Media Watch
SRI	Stephen Roth Institute for the Study of Anti-Semitism and Racism, Tel-Aviv University
T.N.A.	British National Archives

ACKNOWLEDGMENTS

Throughout the course of writing this book, a number of institutions and individuals assisted me. Their help has been invaluable. Anne and Jerry Gontownik, friends and community leaders, have been very supportive of my work. They began a unique mentoring program, beginning with Josh Suskewicz, a recent yeshiva high school graduate, who worked with me as a research assistant for three years while he was a student at Harvard College. I want to thank Ari Gontownik, Josh Strobel, and Benjamin Berman who also served as research assistants.

I am extremely grateful for the generous financial support from Angelica Berrie and the Russell Berrie Foundation, Maurice and Yvette Bendahan, Rose Mattus, David Messer, and Gitta and Jack Nagel. I have always benefited greatly from Susan Rosenbluth's insightful suggestions and assistance.

A number of people read the manuscript and offered their very helpful insights: Professors Harris O. Schoenberg and Yohanan Manor, Annie Korin, Bennett Ruda, Chaim Lauer, Josh Suskewicz, Bud Levin, Rachel Eliahu, and Sharon Hes.

Working with my sons, Ilan and Ranan, has been an especially gratifying experience. They have provided profound advice, encouragement, and constructive criticism.

I am grateful to Eli Hertz, the publisher of *Myths and Facts*, for providing the maps for this book and for his ongoing insights and advice.

I would also like to thank a number of my friends and colleagues for their help and encouragement: Rabbi Ely Allen, Gila and Joseph Alpert, Rabbi Bruce Block, Rabbi Yale Butler, Shoshana Cardin, Dr. Ben Chouake, Dr. Joel Fishman, Malcolm Hoenlein, Lyn Karpo-Lance, Ilan Kaufthal, Neri Levy, Rabbi Simcha Lyons, Tiki Lyons, Dr. Lawrence Platt, Dr. Aharon Rabin, Jerrold Rapaport, Sheri and Stanley Raskas, Kevin Rosenberg, Rachel Scheinerman, Dr. Billy Spivak, Malky Tannenbaum, Dr. Arnold Yagoda, and Rabbi Arthur Hertzberg (a"h), who was my friend and mentor. My friend and colleague, Jim Fletcher, suggested the title for this work and has guided its publication and distribution.

No one could ask for better editors than Jeanette Friedman and Dr. Philip Sieradski. Their exceptional skills in editing, their clear understanding of the Israeli/Arab conflict, and their dedication and commitment to this study made the process a more productive one.

CONTENTS

INTRODUCTION

This book traces the transformation of the United Nations (UN) from an organization that voted to partition the former British Mandate of Palestine into Jewish and Arab states — making Israel a nation state — and then passed a Zionism=Racism (Z=R) resolution to delegitimize and dehumanize that nation.

AN ABBREVIATED HISTORY OF ZIONISM

Zionism — the Jewish national renaissance movement — is one of the most misunderstood examples of modern nationalism. Part of the reason is that Zionism is founded on a paradox. In an attempt to transform the Jewish people into becoming like all the other nations of the world, Zionism sought a contemporary solution to the "Jewish problem" by returning Jews to their ancestral homeland.[1] Although secular Zionist thinkers drew upon sacred Jewish traditions of rebirth and restoration, they discarded or recast anything not connected to restoration, especially religious rituals. Zionism is therefore, again, paradoxically an endeavor to restore the Jew to his historical roots through national revival while at the same time "rebelling against Jewish history"; an effort to re-establish Jewish tradition while redefining Jewish practice and ritual; an effort to enable Jews to live in their own land like every other nation, while stressing the distinctive elements in their history, culture, and society.[2]

Those who initially immigrated to the *Yishuv* (Jewish settlement in Palestine before the establishment of the State of Israel) were motivated by a desire for self-determination, liberation, and identity within the context of the liberalism, secularism, modernism, and nationalism unleashed by the French Revolution and the Declaration of the Human Rights of Man.[3] The Enlightenment, an intellectual utopian movement of the 18th century, posited that were logic and reason to reign in society, they would overcome superstition and hatred. As it pertained to Jews, it was supposed to free them from their old ways and enable them to acquire roots in their adopted lands.

The idea that it would usher in an era where bigotry and prejudice would be replaced with tolerance and moderation turned out to be a fantasy. For Jews, it was an especial failure because in the 18th century Jews still lived behind ghetto walls, essentially cutting them off from society at large. Their dress, religious practice, and ways of thinking made them appear peculiar and parochial, and set them apart. Even after the ghetto walls no longer existed, masses of European Jews maintained their Jewish traditions instead of assimilating.[4]

Though Jews had pined for the land of Zion for millennia, Zionism itself did not develop before the 19th and 20th centuries because it was much more than just a response to antisemitism. It was an attempt to create a new Jew based on Enlightenment ideas,[5] but a Jewish return to Zion was more than the emigration of a people to a new land. Zionist settlers did not seek to go to Palestine to dominate another people and exploit the area's natural resources for export. They came to establish settlements and to develop the country. The future State of Israel would have no towns or villages named New Warsaw, New Lodz, New Moscow, New Minsk, or New Pinsk — unlike the New World, where settlements were named for old cities (e.g., New London, New Orleans, New York, New England, and New Madrid).[6] Furthermore, by rejecting Europe and by creating the modern Hebrew language, the Zionists tried to create their own intellectual and cultural energy without imitating or transplanting the old ways. Using biblical (Hebrew) names to affirm control over their geography, they did not consider themselves outsiders or conquerors. Their settlements were tangible manifestations of the Jewish return to the homeland.[7]

Those Jews who settled in the *Yishuv* came to a land that was sparsely populated and economically underdeveloped, with sizable regions of desert, semi-arid wilderness, and swamps. Before the British arrived in Palestine at the end of World War I, the authorities in the Ottoman Empire had practically no involvement in regulating land use, health and sanitary conditions, or controls on the construction of private and public buildings. Except for a few roads and a rail line that projected the Ottoman Empire's imperial power, there were few public works projects. Resident Arabs, traditional in outlook, had no interest in new plans for their communities either. Thus, for Herzl and other European Zionists, in addition to its being the ancestral homeland, Turkish Palestine was inviting because of its lack of government accountability, absence of local Arab initiative, and the "empty landscape."[8]

At this point in history, post-World War I, political pressure caused the international community to endorse the Jewish desire for national self-determination and accepted that the Jewish people had a justifiable claim to return to their homeland.

Significantly, in this recognition, the Balfour Declaration and the Mandate under the League of Nations make no mention of Palestinians as a separate and distinct people with their own national rights. The indigenous people were regarded as residents whose political identity was connected to the larger Arab nation.[9]

For the British, the matter was quite clear: Palestine was not a state but the name of a geographical area. This had been reinforced by the indigenous Arabs themselves.

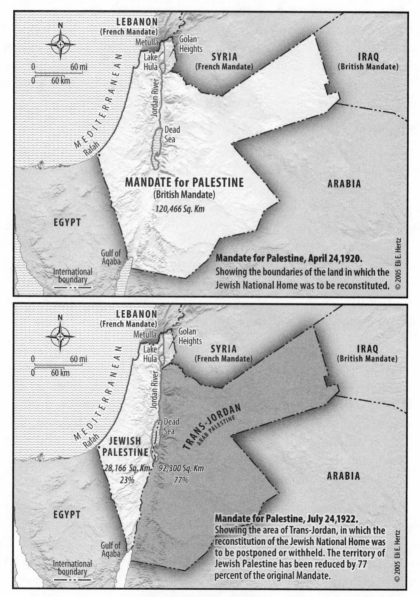

(Courtesy of Eli Hertz.)

When the First Congress of Muslim-Christian Associations met in Jerusalem in February 1919 to select Palestinian Arab representatives for the Paris Peace Conference, they adopted the following resolution: "We consider Palestine as part of Arab Syria, as it has never been separated from it at any time. We are connected with it by national, religious, linguistic, natural, economic, and geographical bonds."[10]

The purpose of post-World War I's League of Nations was to prepare those liberated from the Turks for independence. Once the indigenous populations demonstrated their ability to assume control, the mandates given to the war's victorious superpowers were supposed to be self-terminating. For the international community, justice for the Arabs meant guaranteeing their economic, civil, and religious rights. Awarding the Arabs any form of self-government within Palestine was precluded by British commitments to the Jews under the Balfour Declaration, which had been incorporated in the mandate of the League of Nations.[11]

THE JEWISH CONNECTION TO THE LAND

Culturally, during the 18 centuries of Jewish life in the Diaspora, the connection to the land of Israel played a key role in the value system of Jewish communities and was a basic determinant in their self-recognition as a group. Without the connection to the land of Israel, the people who practice Judaism would simply be a religious community, without national and ethnic components. Jews were distinct from the Muslim and Christian communities in which they lived because of their religious beliefs and practices and the eternal link to the land of their forefathers. That is why Jews considered themselves — and are seen by others — as a minority living in exile.[12]

As Abraham Joshua Heschel, professor of Jewish Ethics and Mysticism at the Jewish Theological Seminary, explained:

> For the Jews and for them alone [the land of Israel] was the one and only Homeland, the only conceivable place where they could find liberation and independence, the land toward which their minds and hearts had been uplifted for a score of centuries and where their roots had clung in spite of all adversity. . . . It was the homeland with which an indestructible bond of national, physical, religious, and spiritual character had been preserved, and where the Jews had in essence remained — and were now once more in fact — a major element of the population.[13]

The Jews did not publicly challenge the occupation of their land by the empires of the East and West. They did so in their homes, sanctuaries, books, and prayers. Religious rituals were instituted to remember the destruction of the temple and the subsequent exile. During times of joy and sorrow, Zion is always part of a Jew's thoughts and liturgy. At least three times a day, observant Jews pray for the redemption of Zion and Jerusalem and for her well-being.[14]

Arthur Balfour
British Foreign Secretary
(Courtesy of Michael Duffy)

When the Muslims invaded Palestine in 634, ending four centuries of conflict between Persia and Rome, they found direct descendants of Jews who had lived in the country since biblical times. Rabbinical leaders there continued to argue about "whether most of Palestine is in the hands of the Gentiles," or "whether the greater part of Palestine is in the hands of Israel." (Such a determination was essential, since according to *halacha* [Jewish law] if Jews ruled the country, then they were obligated to observe religious agricultural practices in one way, and in another if they were not in control.)[15]

As Muslim hegemony prevailed, major Arab contributions to history originated in Damascus, Mecca, Cairo, and Baghdad. Little came from Jerusalem, indicating the low regard the area held for its captors and its minimal occupation by

Arabs. Similarly, while the land of Palestine was two percent of the Arab-controlled land-mass, to the Jewish people it was forever the fount of their religion, their homeland.[16]

David Ben-Gurion, Israel's first prime minister, pointed out that more than 3,000 years before the Mayflower left England for the New World, Jews fled from Egypt. Jews even slightly cognizant of their faith know that every spring Jews commemorate and remember the liberation from slavery and the Exodus from Egypt to the land of Israel. Those who observe the *seder* (the Passover meal and retelling of the exodus from Egypt), end it with two sentences: "This year we are here; next year we shall be in [Jerusalem] the land of Israel. This year we are slaves; next year we shall be free."[17]

Though bound to its religious foundation, a Jewish State also means "Jewish security. Even in countries where he seems secure, the Jew lacks a feeling of security. Why? Because even if he is safe, he has not physically provided safety for himself. Somebody else provides for his security. The State of Israel provides such security."[18]

ANTI-ZIONISM BECOMES INTERNATIONAL IN SCOPE

For more than 20 years after the establishment of the State of Israel, anti-Zionism was a regional phenomenon — a clash between Arab and Jewish national movements in the Middle East. In the Soviet Union and in Eastern Europe, the Soviets exploited antisemitism for political purposes, but it was rarely part of international debate until after the Six-Day War in 1967. By the end of the 1960s, and since 1975, anti-Zionism became international in scope. It first appeared in the universities in the West where the New Left, in cooperation with Arab student associations, attacked Israeli policy.[19]

When the United Nations General Assembly passed Resolution 3379 on November 10, 1975, and declared "Zionism is a form of racism and racial discrimination," it significantly expanded anti-Zionism into the sphere of international nongovernmental organizations (NGOs) and therefore into Third World countries. This was accomplished in a collaboration between the Arabs and the Soviet Union that endowed anti-Zionism with legitimacy and official recognition.[20]

After the First World War, the Arabs expected Greater Syria — which included Palestine and Lebanon — to become a vast, united, and sovereign Arab empire. Instead, the French and the British divided the area into what the Arabs considered "irrationally carved out" entities that became the present-day states of Saudi Arabia, Syria, Trans-Jordan (later Jordan), Iraq, and Israel. The Arabs were outraged that a "non-Arab embryo state in Palestine" had been inserted into an area where it would never be accepted. They claimed that this shattered their dreams of unification and impeded their search for a common identity.[21]

The fight against a Jewish homeland became an integral part of their struggle "for dignity and independence." Israel's existence, they claimed, "implied that not only a part of the Arab patrimony, but also parts of Islam, had been stolen. For a Moslem, there was no greater shame than for that to happen." The only way to eliminate this deeply felt affront — this "symbol of everything that had dominated them in the past" — was to rid the area of "imperialist domination."[22]

Zionism has been branded as the official enemy of the Arab national movement, but Arab governments have long been accused of using the Arab-Israeli confrontation to divert attention from their own critical domestic social and economic problems. When confronted, they respond that if this were not a real concern, it would not resonate so strongly among the Arab masses.[23]

Bernard Lewis, professor emeritus at Princeton University, the dean of Middle Eastern scholars in the West, says Arab fixation with Israel "is the licensed grievance. In countries where people are becoming increasingly angry and frustrated at all the difficulties under which they live — the poverty, unemployment, oppression — having a grievance which they can express freely is an enormous psychological advantage."[24]

The Israeli-Arab conflict is the only local political grievance that can be openly discussed. If the population were permitted freedom of speech, Lewis believes that the obsession with Israel would become far less important. Like most people, Arabs are concerned about their own priorities. For the Palestinian Arabs, who view themselves as the permanent victims, the main issue is their struggle with Israel. If Arabs in other countries were permitted to focus on their own problems, they would do so.[25]

For Arabs, the attempt to blame Western imperialism is nothing more than an excuse to attack Israel, as another historian asserted: "For decades the Arabs have been obsessed by memories of past glories and prophecies of future greatness, mocked by the injury and shame of having an alien and despised race injected into the nerve center of their promised pan-Arab empire, between its Asian and African halves, just at a time when the colonial powers had started their great retreat from their colonial possessions in Asia and Africa."[26]

To lessen their feelings of shame for losing every war against Israel, the Arabs attributed the success of Jewish settlement in Palestine and the Israeli military triumphs of 1948 and 1956 to Western imperialism. As the representative of the Great Powers, Israel became the Arabs' scapegoat whenever they became frustrated in their attempt to transcend "centuries of social, economic, and cultural development, and catch up" with the West. This anti-Israel fixation precipitated a methodical "Manichean metaphysic, the focus of an entire philosophy of history, with the Jew as the devil incarnate from the days of patriarch Abraham himself till his assumption of the role of the linchpin of an American-Imperialist-Zionist world-plot against the Arab world, the Socialist Commonwealth and all colonial peoples."[27]

THE SIX-DAY WAR

The crushing defeat of the Arabs in the 1967 Six-Day War shattered this fantasy and accentuated Arab humiliation, since the Israelis won without the backing of any imperialist nations. Arab rage was exacerbated by the casualty rates in Israel's favor — about 25 to 1 — and by the number of prisoners of war Israel captured. At least 5,000 Egyptian soldiers, including 21 generals, 365 Syrians (30 of whom were officers), and 550 Jordanians were taken. Only 15 Israelis were held as POWs. Arab military hardware losses were in the billions of dollars — most of it coming from Soviet Bloc countries.[28]

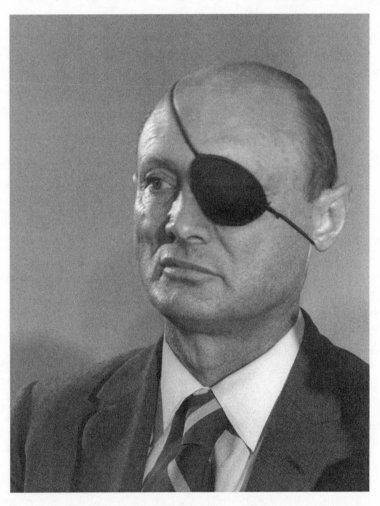

Israel's Minister of Defense during the Six-Day War,
Moshe Dayan, 1967.
(Courtesy of Israeli Government Photo Office)

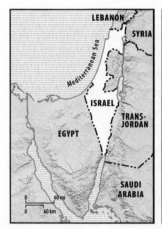

1949
Israel's boundaries after the Israeli War of Independence.

1956
Sinai Campaign; Israel gains control over the Sinai Peninsula territory.

1957
Israel agrees to withdraw its troops from the Sinai Peninsula and the Gaza Strip, handing over these territories to Egypt.

1967
Israel's boundaries following the Six-Day War. Egypt, Jordan, and Syria in a war of aggression lose the territories of the Sinai Peninsula, the West Bank, and the Golan Heights. For the first time, Israel is in control of Jewish Mandated Palestine.

1973
Israel's boundaries following the Yom Kippur War. In a clear act of aggression, Egypt and Syria attacked the State of Israel, but were driven away.

1979–Present
On March 26, 1979, Israel and Egypt signed a peace treaty on the White House lawn. Israel returned the Sinai Peninsula territory to Egypt.

(Courtesy of Eli Hertz.)

Civilian casualties were minimal: Israelis estimate that 175,000 Arab noncombatants fled the West Bank to Jordan; Jordanians claim that number is 250,000. Though the Israelis did not initiate the Arab exodus, they did not attempt to stop it. The refugees were not encouraged to return, but Moshe Dayan, Israel's Minister of Defense, stopped the practice of preventing them from crossing back to the West Bank a week after the war, after observing ambushes and concluding that they were inhumane.[29]

Israelis wanted to resolve the 1948 and 1967 refugee problem — to be determined when a comprehensive peace agreement would be negotiated. The Arabs rejected the offer and insisted that the refugees be allowed to return, unconditionally, and receive compensation. Yet, in the summer of 1967, when Israel agreed to allow Arabs to come back to the West Bank, only a handful returned.[30]

At the same time, the Arabs persecuted and tormented their own Jewish residents. Jews were attacked in Yemen, Lebanon, Tunisia, and Morocco. Synagogues were burned and Jews were arrested and detained. In Damascus and Baghdad, Jewish leaders were fined and imprisoned, and 7,000 Jews were expelled after their property and most of their belongings were confiscated. Eight hundred of Egypt's 4,000 Jews were arrested, including the chief rabbis of Cairo and Alexandria. The UN and the Red Cross did nothing to intervene on their behalf.[31]

Despite this treatment of Jews in Arab lands, the 1.2 million Arabs under Israeli governance did not experience any systematic mistreatment. Looting and vandalism were reported in some areas, but the Israelis repaired whatever damage they found. Though Jordanians had destroyed synagogues in the Old City of Jerusalem and used the tombstones from the Jewish cemeteries on the Mount of Olives to pave roads and use in latrines, Moshe Dayan participated in the Friday prayers at the al-Aqsa Mosque in Jerusalem. Perhaps the greatest trauma for the Arabs was that Israel had conquered 42,000 square miles — and was now three-and-a-half times larger in size than before the war.[32]

Anti-Zionism entered the international scene when Israel and Egypt reached political rapprochement after the Yom Kippur War by signing an interim agreement on September 1, 1975. That agreement emphasized, "The conflict between them and in the Middle East shall not be resolved by military force but by peaceful means."[33]

Concerned that this might lead to peace, the Soviets, Syria, and the PLO tried to exclude Israel from international nongovernmental organizations (NGOs), like UNESCO, "for having transgressed the United Nations Charter, and having failed to adopt its resolutions." When this strategy failed, they began to question Israel's legitimacy and discredit and condemn Zionism in the UN, and to internationalize their propaganda against her.[34]

POLITICAL ANTISEMITISM

Irwin Cotler, Minister of Justice and Attorney General of Canada, wrote:

> Traditional anti-Semitism was the denial of the right of individual Jews to live as equal members in a society. The new anti-Jewishness is the denial

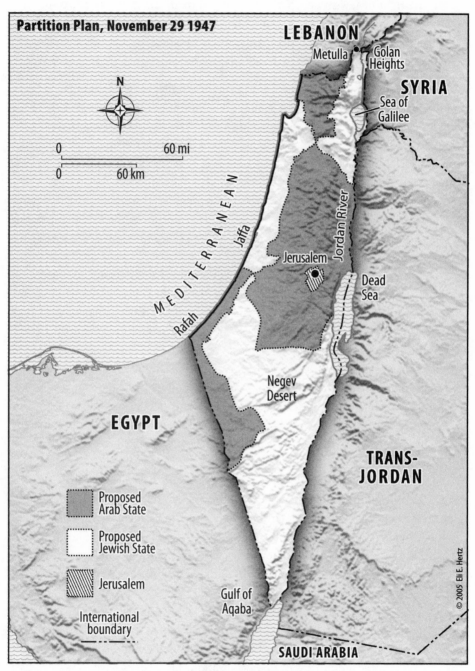

Partition Plan, November 29 1947

N

0 — 60 mi
0 — 60 km

LEBANON
Metulla · Golan Heights
SYRIA
Sea of Galilee

MEDITERRANEAN

Jaffa

Jerusalem

Jordan River

Dead Sea

Rafah

Negev Desert

EGYPT

TRANS-JORDAN

Proposed Arab State
Proposed Jewish State
Jerusalem
International boundary

Gulf of Aqaba

© 2005 Eli E. Hertz

SAUDI ARABIA

Courtesy of Eli Hertz.

of the right of Jewish people to live as equal members in the family of nations. . . . All that has happened is that we've moved from discrimination
against the Jews as individuals to the discrimination against the Jews as a
people.[35]

Demonizing Israel has turned it into a physical target for terrorist organizations,
and into a political target for left wing and reactionary forces. Whether there are
fatwas (legal rulings by Muslim clerics that routinely legitimize suicide terrorism)
or there are organizations demanding divestment from Israeli corporations, destruction of Israel — physical, spiritual, or economic — is one of the mantras of the day.
This is what Cotler calls political antisemitism.[36]

For the majority of the member states in the UN, Israel is a locus of evil, deserving international condemnation — unlike many countries in the UN that practice
ethnic cleansing, offer no rights to women or the poor, starve their own people for
political reasons, and commit genocide.

These same nations, in the halls of an institution that was designed to prevent exactly this from happening, deny Israel her rights even in the courts of international law.
Israel is the target of the majority of UN sanctions, is vilified by the International Court
of Justice at the Hague for defending herself, and is singled out by the Geneva Convention as the utmost violator of human rights.[37]

It has been suggested that this deliberate delegitimization leads to gradual erosion
of Israel's stature and ultimately her right to exist. Those targeted are the last to recognize the transformation until the consequences of ostracism become evident. This
occurs when remarks by the country's spokesman are seen as irrelevant, and when the
leadership is no longer regarded as worthy of engaging in legitimate discourse with
other countries.[38]

Branding Israel as racist portrays her as a country that harms civilian populations, oppresses minorities, and establishes restrictive immigration laws and religious statutes as part of its ideological *raison d'etre*. Thus, Israel's wars — its military
response to terror and laws passed by the Knesset — are racist. A significant danger
to Israel is that if this charge becomes a new stereotype through popular culture, the
media, literature, and daily speech, it will taint the Jewish state and become a part
of the legacy of the West.[39]

How does one respond to such charges? No logical argument ever succeeded in
disputing the blood libels or any other spurious allegation leveled against the Jews.
Yet, limited response to Z=R ensured that anti-Zionist resolutions continued to be
passed. To counter the process of delegitimization, the charges have to be seen as a
"corruption of language and thought," a threat to freedom, and a campaign of disin-
formation orchestrated by the Arab states and the Soviet Union.[40]

This book examines the initial reactions to the Z=R resolution by the United States, Israel, and others, the political and cultural environment at the UN, and the provocative roles played by Arab states, the Former Soviet Union (FSU), African nations, and NGOs in the new war against the Jews.

Endnotes

1. Abraham I. Edelheit, *The History of Zionism: A Handbook and Dictionary* (Boulder, CO: Westview, 2000), p. xv.

2. Ibid.

3. Shlomo Avineri, *The Making of Modern Zionism: The Intellectual Origins of the Jewish State* (New York: Basic Books, Inc. Publishers, 1981), p. 5, 13.

4. George L. Mosse, *Germans and Jews* (New York: Grosset and Dunlop, 1970), p. 42–76. Many Jews, particularly on the left, were influenced by the ideas of the Russian revolution that all oppressed nations should unite in their fight for emancipation against a common enemy. Jacob L. Talmon, *Israel Among the Nations* (London: Weidenfeld and Nicolson, 1970), p. 142.

5. Avineri, *The Making of Modern Zionism: The Intellectual Origins of the Jewish State*, p. 5, 13.

6. S. Ilan Troen, *Imagining Zion: Dreams, Designs, and Realities in a Century of Jewish Settlement* (New Haven, CT: Yale University Press, 2003), p. 7–9, 55, 142.

7. Ibid., p. 151–152, 158.

8. Ibid., p. 70, 90–91, 159.

9. Eli E. Hertz, Reply, *Myths and Facts*, 2005, p. 24. See Yehoshua Porath, *The Palestinian Arab National Movement: From Riots to Rebellion*, Volume 2 (London: Frank Cass and Company, 1977), p. 81–82.)

10. Ibid.

11. Troen, *Imagining Zion: Dreams, Designs, and Realities in a Century of Jewish Settlement*, p. 44; Yosef Gorny, *Zionism and the Arabs:1882–1948* (Oxford: Clarendon Press, 1987), p. 82; Michael J. Cohen, *The Origins and Evolution of the Arab-Israeli Conflict* (Berkeley, California: University of California Press, 1987), p. 64–65.

12. Avineri, *The Making of Modern Zionism: The Intellectual Origins of the Jewish State*, p. 3.

13. Abraham Joshua Heschel, *Israel: An Echo Eternity* (New York: Farrar, Straus, 1967), p. 57.

14. Ibid., p. 55, 61–67.

15. Yaacov Herzog, *A People That Dwells Alone* (New York: Sanhedrin Press), 1975.p. 33; Ibid., p. 57. While Jewish settlement in recent times began in 1881, in the 3rd and 4th centuries, Palestine was probably the largest and most significant Jewish community in the world. Benjamin of Tudela, Saadia Gaon, Maimonides and Judah Halevi were there from the 12th century and Nachmanides from the early 13th century. Rabbi Estori Ha-Parhi, author of *Kaftor va-Ferah*, demonstrates how, since biblical times, Jews have lived on the land continuously.

16. Heschel, *Israel: An Echo Eternity*, p. 59.

17. *The Jewish Case Before the Anglo-American Committee of Inquiry on Palestine* (Jerusalem: The Jewish Agency For Palestine, 1947), p. 63, 65.

18. Ibid., p. 68; David Ben Gurion, "Ben-Gurion and De Gaulle: An Exchange of Letters," *Midstream* (February 1968), p. 12.

19. Yohanan Manor, "Anti-Zionism," (Jerusalem: World Zionist Organization, 1984), p. 8.

20. Ibid.

21. Saul Friedlander and Mahmoud Hussein, *Arabs and Israelis: A Dialogue* (New York: Holmes and Meier, 1975), p. 6, 18, 21.

22. Ibid., p. 9, 34.

23. Ibid.

24. "Islam's Interpreter," *The Atlantic Online* (April 4, 2004), Online.

25. Ibid; Friedlander and Hussein, *Arabs and Israelis: A Dialogue*, p. 32–33, 36.

26. Talmon, *Israel Among the Nations*, p. 169–170.

27. Ibid., p. 170.

28. Michael B. Oren, *Six Days of War: June 1967 and the Making of the Modern Middle East* (New York: Oxford University Press, 2002), p. 305–306.

29. Ibid., p. 306.

30. Ibid.

31. Ibid., p. 306–307.

32. Ibid.

33. Manor, "Anti-Zionism," p. 9–10.

34. Ibid., p. 10.

35. Irwin Cotler, "Why Is Israel Singled Out?" *The Jerusalem Post* (January 16, 2002), Online.

36. Ibid; see also Irwin Cotler, "Human Rights and the New Anti-Jewishness," *The Jerusalem Post* (February 5, 2004), Online; Irwin Cotler, "Durban's Troubling Legacy One Year Later: Twisting the Cause of International Human Rights Against the Jewish People," Jerusalem Center For Public Affairs, Volume 2, Number 5 (August 20, 2002), Online.

37. Ibid.

38. Ehud Sprinzak, "Anti-Zionism: From Delegitimation to Dehumanization," *Forum-53* (Fall 1984), p. 3–5.

39. Ibid., p. 7–8.

40. Ibid., p. 9–10.

CHAPTER ONE

THE FORGOTTEN FRIENDSHIP: ISRAEL AND THE SOVIET BLOC

The Soviet Union played a key role in passing Z=R by establishing the ideological framework to transform Zionism into an evil entity. It vigorously promoted the resolution's enactment by the UN General Assembly and kept the issue alive for a number of years at UN-sponsored conferences — even when there was decreased interest in the subject.

Soon after the resolution passed, the Soviets launched a propaganda campaign against Zionism, exposing it as the enemy of the Soviet Union. From 1975 on, any official Soviet material about Zionism was based on the premise that it was evil. *Zionism as a Form of Racial Discrimination* by Lydia Modzhorian, an expert on international law and a member of the Soviet Academy of Sciences, became the standard work on Zionism.[1]

In the fall of 1984, Soviet representatives on the Committee on Social, Humanitarian and Cultural Affairs (the Third Committee) attempted to include the Z=R formula in a draft resolution by Ethiopia to establish a "Second Decade to Combat Racism and Racial Discrimination." Resistance from the United States, the West, and moderate Third World African countries prevented it. In July 1985, Soviet delegates were thwarted when they tried to insert language into the final conference document equating Zionism with racism and apartheid at the "Decade for Women" UN conference in Nairobi, Kenya.[2]

THE ROOTS OF SOVIET ANTI-ZIONISM

Soviet opposition to Zionism began in November 1917 with the Bolshevik Revolution in Russia and the signing of the Balfour Declaration in Great Britain. After World War II, the establishment of the State of Israel and the post-Six-Day War period were watershed events with severe repercussions.

In the 1920s, Bolshevik leaders essentially ignored the well-organized and determined Zionist organizations developing in Russian and Ukrainian Jewish communities before the revolution, and they rejected Jewish nationalism as reactionary and unscientific.[3] The intense resistance to Zionism came from the Jewish Socialist Bund, giving anti-Zionism the appearance of a clash inside the Jewish community.

During the first decade of the Soviet regime, local Jewish Communist officials from *Yevesktsiia*, a special section of the People's Commissariat for Nationality Affairs, were more vigorous than the Soviet government in harassing and criticizing Zionism as "nationalistic," "counter-revolutionary," and "clerical."[4]

In the post-revolutionary years, however, anti-Zionism was mostly free of antisemitism. In his celebrated 1919 speech against pogroms, Bolshevik leader Vladimir Ilyich Lenin, declared, "Only the most ignorant and downtrodden people can believe the lies and slander that are spread about the Jews. . . . Shame on those who foment hatred towards the Jews, who foment hatred toward other nations."[5] Lenin was disgusted by the persecution and torture perpetrated against Jews under the "accursed Tsarist monarchy," which in its last days sought to "incite ignorant workers and peasants against the Jews."[6] Lenin and other Bolsheviks attacked Zionism for advocating class-collaboration instead of class struggle, but this criticism was in the context of the events from 1917–1920.

The Balfour Declaration worried Soviet leaders after pro-British articles appeared in the Russian Jewish press and pro-British demonstrations were held in Petrograd and Odessa, causing fear that France and Britain could use Zionism against them.

Appeals by the Central Zionist Committee in Russia urged the Jews of Russia to oppose the Soviet regime. Russian leaders feared that a brain drain to Palestine might weaken their ability to recruit Jewish masses into the Red Army during the Civil War as well. Thus, a national separatist movement was seen as a real threat when the Soviet regime was fighting for its existence. They also felt that with the Jews and Zionists supporting nationalistic movements, other nationalities in the country might follow their example and be influenced to secede from Russia.[7]

BLAMING THE ZIONISTS

The Bolsheviks blamed Russian Jewish sympathy for Zionism and the Balfour Declaration for the decline in their own socio-political and economic system. They feared that secular Jewish intelligentsia — doctors, pharmacists, architects, engineers, and experts in banking, commerce, foreign affairs, and the secret police (professionals who were needed to build the Soviet economy) would leave for Palestine. To preclude the further growth of the Zionist movement and keep Jews from emigrating, the Bolsheviks offered them the possibility of civil equality and an agricultural settlement in Russia.[8]

The idea was for Russian Jews to become farmers in the harsh and barren Soviet Far East, in Birobidzhan, a Jewish autonomous region they created in 1934. The Soviets thought that Jews would practice their Jewish national culture instead of Zionism. In addition to Birobidzhan being isolated and harsh, the Jews had no historical, religious, or emotional connection to the area, so the experiment failed. By then, Joseph Stalin had established his totalitarian regime. Those who thought up the Birobidzhan project and the leaders of *Yevesktsiia* were purged, exiled, or imprisoned.[9]

The Soviets were also anxious about the "colonial question" in the Middle East. After the British won Palestine in 1917 and the English and French partitioned the region, Lenin felt they would carve up the globe between them.[10] The Bolsheviks were fundamentally opposed to colonialism, and viewed the British as oppressors and the power most determined to destroy them. Zionist leaders who enthusiastically cooperated with the British government were considered imperialist tools. As a presentiment of their future activities in the area, acting as agent provocateurs, the Soviets sought out Palestinian Arab peasants and workers as a natural source of anti-British sentiment, and told them that part of their problem was the Zionists — even though the Soviets were not yet involved with the Middle East in any significant way.[11]

During the 1929 riots in Palestine and the Arab revolt of 1936–1939, the Soviet press attacked Zionist imperialist oppression. Jewish nationalism until then had marginal importance to the Soviet leadership and criticism of it was left to the officials in *Yevesktsiia*. Although these functionaries were misguided in their zeal to remove Jewish religious institutions, Zionism, and the Hebrew language from Jewish life, they most likely did so to improve the lives of Russian Jews.[12]

When the Nazis invaded the Soviet Union in July 1941, the Soviets reversed themselves and encouraged nationalistic and religious feelings to strengthen the people's resolve against the Nazis, even as antisemitism increased. In April 1942, the Jewish Anti-Fascist Committee was even established to gain material support for the Russian Army in the United States and Britain. Yet Stalin generally discouraged Soviet Jews from identifying with fellow Jews abroad and ridiculed the idea of world Jewry in Soviet anti-Zionist propaganda.

Then in November 1944, Shachna Epstein, secretary of the Jewish Anti-Fascist Committee, wrote that Jews have "a right to political independence in Israel." This, however, had no relevance to Russian Jews who were committed to strengthening communism.

Ironically, Stalin's pro-Israel policy during 1947–1948 occurred while he was attacking Jewish nationalism, Jewish culture, and the Jewish leadership inside his own borders. From 1948 to 1952, the Soviets even murdered their own Jewish intelligentsia.

SOVIET RATIONALE FOR SUPPORTING ZIONISM

The Soviets supported the establishment of Israel for several reasons: the Jews were anti-British, they were on the frontlines of the *armed* "anti-colonial struggle," and Russia wanted to play an active role in the Middle East. Furthermore, her southern flank was becoming more vulnerable to increasing East-West tensions and there was concern that the West would control oil from the Persian Gulf and the Middle East.

Most importantly, this was an opportunity to weaken — and perhaps cause a rift — between the United States and its allies. The Middle East was the most obvious place to provoke this split in order to prevent the British and Americans from strengthening their Cold War alliance,[13] since a split already existed over the future of a Jewish state.

President Harry S. Truman and British Prime Minister Clement Attlee had been at odds over whether the remnants of European Jewry could immigrate to Palestine. The British wanted to stop the flow of Jews, and the Russians believed that after the Holocaust, the British would be criticized in the West for trying to keep them out of Palestine. Thus, the Russians did not interfere with the *Brichah*, the illegal emigration of Jews to Palestine, figuring that they could use sympathy for Jews as a moral cudgel and public relations weapon against the West, instead of playing power politics.[14]

Andrei Gromyko, the Soviet Ambassador to the UN, explained on May 14, 1947, that the "aspirations of an important part of the Jewish people are bound up with the question of Palestine, and with the future structure of that country. . . ." Though Arabs and Jews had historically inhabited Palestine, the "suffering and miseries of the Jewish people are beyond description . . . and it would be difficult to express by mere dry figures the losses and sacrifices of the Jewish people at the hands of the Fascist occupiers." The UN "cannot, and should not, remain indifferent to this situation," he declared, because it would be "incompatible" with the "high principles" of the UN Charter. "This is a time to give help, not in words, but in deeds."

The fact that not one state in Western Europe could protect the Jews from the Nazis and their allies or "compensate them for the violence they have suffered . . . explains the aspiration of the Jews for the creation of a state of their own. . . . And it is impossible to justify a denial of this right of the Jewish people."[15]

At the 125th UN Plenary Meeting on November 26, 1947, Gromyko went further when he reversed his government's long-standing support for a single, federated bi-national state in the Middle East:

> The representatives of the Arab States claim the partition of Palestine would be an historical injustice. But this view of the case is unacceptable,

if only because, after all, the Jewish people have been closely linked with Palestine for a considerable period in history.

Apart from that — and the U.S.S.R. delegation drew attention to this at the Special Session of the General Assembly — they could not overlook the position of the Jews as a result of the recent World War.

> The solution of the Palestine problem into two separate states [added Gromyko] will be of profound historical significance, because this decision will meet the legitimate demands of the Jewish people, hundreds of thousands of whom, as you know, are still without a country, without homes, having found temporary shelter only in special camps in some Western European countries.[16]

To reassure the Arabs, who resented his enthusiastic support for a Jewish homeland, Gromyko prophetically added to his November 26 speech that, "The U.S.S.R. delegation is convinced that Arabs and Arab states will still, on more than one occasion, be looking towards Moscow and expecting the U.S.S.R. to help them in the struggle for their lawful interests, in their efforts to cast off the last vestiges of foreign dependence."

Soviet representatives met privately with members of various UN delegations to reinforce Gromyko's assurances that "the Arabs will soon find out that the Soviet

Andrei Gromyko,
Soviet Ambassador to the UN, 1947
(Courtesy of Marc Schulman)

Union is their friend." The Soviets would be the main provider of weapons to the Arabs and use the Middle East as a testing ground.[17]

The Soviets' apparent willingness to accept a two-state solution prompted Ben-Gurion to intensify efforts to acquire desperately needed arms from Eastern Europe. He sent many Haganah (covert Jewish defense force) agents to buy arms wherever they could, but they ran into a number of obstacles. The Jewish Agency did not represent a recognized government, only an underground army. The United States, the British, and the UN declared an embargo on selling weapons to the Middle East, and the FBI and the British disrupted well-established gun-running operations, heavily funded by American Jews. (Eastern Europe, and especially Czechoslovakia, were the key suppliers of military equipment.)[18]

Without Soviet approval, there would have been no gun and aircraft sales to the Israelis, as since World War II the Czechs needed permission from Moscow for any of their significant economic enterprises. Czechoslovakia had a definite need for an infusion of foreign currency, but exporting of weapons is a political, not simple, trade. Their motivation seems to have been the promise of closer ties to Israel by a "pro-Soviet socialist government." Using Czechoslovakia to funnel weapons and material gave the Russians the ability to blame the Czechs for "ideological errors" if and when the relationship between the Soviet bloc and Israel soured.[19]

Gromyko's use of the Holocaust to tweak the West was a bold and risky move. Russian Jews murdered in the Soviet Union by the Nazis were counted as Soviet citizens and not as Jews. Except for Poland, more Jews were killed in the Soviet Union than anywhere else. Cooperation and, at times, active participation in the process of Jewish destruction by Latvians, Ukrainians, Lithuanians, and White Russians was so pervasive that the Soviets were no better at protecting their Jews than the West was. This argument, had it been raised at the time, might have further justified Jewish immigration to Palestine.[20]

REVERSAL OF SOVIET POLICY

Despite the duplicitous nature of the Soviet posturing, they still realized that the Arabs were not reliable partners with whom they could establish their foothold in the Middle East. The Arabs were tarnished by their connections to fascism and the Nazis, ruled by *effendis*, monarchs, and feudal cliques, and were tied to the British through treaties and alliances. As such, the Soviets condemned the Arab attack on Israel in May 1948 as "reactionary . . . and as having been orchestrated by the British." Typically, once Israel was no longer perceived as a potential source of influence in the area, the Soviets adopted a neutral policy toward the Zionist state between 1948 and 1952.

After 1955, under the regime of Nikita Krushchev — which needed access to oil and the Mediterranean for its growing fleet and industries — an aggressive anti-Israel policy was adopted as part of a pro-Arab approach. Krushchev saw the developing and anti-imperialist Third World countries as natural allies, and granted Egypt military aid.

Anxiously observing the inflow of Soviet military hardware into regional Arab states, Major-General Moshe Dayan, then Chief of Staff of the Israel Defense Forces, noted that the implementation of the Joint Egypt-Syria-Jordan Military Command agreement convinced the Israelis that war was imminent. In 1956, it was clear Egypt was preparing for "an all-out war" against Israel. Acts of terror by groups of trained Arab guerillas "soared to the tens of thousands," and were now being used by Egypt "as a means of warfare." Also, Israeli shipping in the Gulf of Aqaba was blockaded — a clear act of war according to the Geneva Convention. In addition, the massive arms deal concluded between Czechoslovakia and Egypt in September 1955 provided the Arabs with arms greater in numbers and quality than those possessed by Israel.[21]

Realizing that a joint Israeli campaign with Western allies might jeopardize its Arab clients, the Soviets attempted to intimidate Israel. When Israel joined the Anglo-French Sinai campaign against Egypt in 1956, the Soviets sent the Israeli government an ominous note warning that the "very existence of the state" was in question.[22]

After the defeat of its clients in the Sinai Campaign until the Six-Day War in June 1967, Israel became a target of Soviet propaganda. Portrayed in the Soviet press as a puppet of Western imperialists, prepared to initiate unprovoked aggression against its neighbors, Israel became a focal point in Soviet attacks against the West. In this hostile environment, the Soviets assumed the role of guardians of the "national liberation movements in the Third World."[23]

After the resounding defeat in the Six-Day War — a war Israel waged on its own without the assistance of the superpowers, while the Arabs relied on Soviet equipment and advisors — the Soviet ministry of information consistently and constantly began using the term anti-Zionism in its propaganda. Until the 1970s, the phrase was not found in dictionaries. Previously, the Soviets had characterized Judaism as parasitical, seditious, and a disgusting religion at the foundation of Jewish rationalism. In the early 1960s, antisemitism manifested itself in accusations of "economic crimes," and Jews were convicted as economic criminals.[24] Now there was a new locus for the antisemitism so easily stoked to foment international discord.

Zionism became the euphemism for Jews, and Russian Jews were again used to attack Israel. The Soviets wanted to increase military activity in the Middle East and crush the Zionist nationalist stirrings of Soviet Jews, particularly among the young. General Alexander Tsirlin, a military scholar and the grandson of S. Ansky, author of *The Dybbuk*, aggressively criticized Israel by trying to equate Zionism with Nazi racism. Then 51 Ukrainian Jewish professors of medicine, members of the Ukrainian Academy of Science, composers, poets, engineers, actors, journalists, and a Yiddish writer made that same declaration in *Pravda* on March 12, 1970.[25]

By writing letters of protest to Soviet leaders and newspapers, some Russian Jews responded to the defamation of Zionism, the proscriptions on emigration to Israel, and the antisemitic discrimination in universities. The letters were never published, but a number of them were circulated through *samizdat* (self-published, clandestinely copied, and suppressed material). Hundreds of letters were also smuggled to non-Communist countries, bringing Jewish national feelings out into the open.[26]

The vitriolic anti-Zionist campaign gave the Soviets a chance to rationalize the abysmal defeat of their Arab clients in the June 1967 war. Zionism now became number one in the lexicon of "Soviet demonology" with goals to separate Israel from the civilized nations of the world by condemning its alleged aggression — its "genocide" of the Palestinian Arabs — and to force Israel to leave what it labeled the "occupied territories."

Not even during 1952–1953, in Stalin's assault against the Jewish intellectuals, was there such a barrage of hate propaganda against Jews. This anti-Jewish hatred was the subject of thousands of articles, broadcasts, films, and lectures. In academic circles, Jewish religious doctrine was defined as advocating genocide and "the enslavement of non-Jews." Judaism was the foundation for Zionist racism and belligerence in the Middle East. Zionism was a world menace and the Trojan horse for Western imperialism in Africa and Asia.[27]

THE BIRTH OF THE NEW ANTISEMITISM

The antisemitic propaganda campaign conveniently forgot the former Soviet Union's support for the establishment of the State of Israel and Stalin's extensive relationship with Hitler before being attacked by the Nazis. It ignored Soviet involvement with Arab nationalists and fascist governments.

Why did the Soviets replace Nazism and fascism with Zionism as the focus of their animosity? Why did they feed Nazi and Czarist antisemitic propaganda like the caricatures of those in Julius Streicher's *Der Stürmer* and the *Protocols of the Elders of Zion* to the Arabs?

The campaign was most likely a product of the crisis within the Communist system. By blaming Israel for impeding Soviet ambitions in the Middle East, they could deflect attention from the real problems affecting the regime. Because Jews were visible in dissident movements in Eastern Europe and Russia, anti-Zionism was a powerful tool to deter non-Jews from becoming involved in these "instruments of imperialism" or founding their own movements.

If Jewish nationalism was revived and emigration permitted, national separatism would once again become an issue. The nationality policies for the Jews, the Armenians, the Georgians, Ukrainians, the peoples of the Baltic, the Volga Germans, the Crimean Tartars, and the Chechens all failed. An anti-Zionism campaign was supposed to stop the Jews and the others from making their own demands.

The Jews in Russia were certainly the canaries in the coal mine. Intimidation and harassment, threats of imprisonment, exile, and antisemitism were designed to isolate the Jews from elements in Soviet society that might sympathize with them. Having the assimilated Jews join the anti-Zionist campaign gave the operation legitimacy and created an environment for conflict in the Jewish community.[28]

THE ROLE OF SOVIET FOREIGN POLICY

Foreign policy played a role in the anti-Zionist campaign, too, but it was not the decisive factor. Hatred of Israel, according to this view, was because of the ever-changing Middle East landscape. In their quest to influence the Middle East, the Soviets encountered a strong Israel and a U.S. proxy. Since Israel impeded Russian interests in the region, whatever enervated Israel hurt the United States and the West. By identifying Israel as overly aggressive, expansionist, fascist, Nazi-like, colonialists, and racist, the Soviets isolated the Jewish state in order to hasten its ultimate demise.[29]

The anti-Zionists made many of the same accusations against the Jews that the Nazis did. In using these methods they adopted previous methods of antisemitism: "the religious/spiritual and the socio/ethnical/cultural."

Each of these approaches has three distinct steps: creating specific negative character traits for the Jews, isolating them, and then annihilating them. Racism dehumanizes Jews in order to rationalize their removal before being exterminated. The process is then justified as a matter of "public health." Thus, anti-Zionism has more to do with the advocates of antisemitism than it does Zionism.[30]

With a lengthy ideological history of anti-Zionism, it was not difficult for the Soviets to increase the intensity of their campaign in the Middle East to impress the Arabs. The hostility also helped enlist the support of the home front for a policy that would otherwise not be very appealing to those footing the bill.[31]

Endnotes

1. William Korey, "The Kremlin and the 'Zionism Equals Racism Resolution,' " in *Israel Yearbook on Human Rights,* Volume 17 (Dordrecht and Boston: Martinus Nijhoff Publishers, 1987), p. 135, 137, 143–147; William Korey, "Bigotry in the Hall of Brotherhood," *The American Zionist* (January 1972): p. 12–15.

2. Korey, "The Kremlin and the 'Zionism Equals Racism Resolution,' " p. 148–149.

3. Robert S. Wistrich, "Anti-Zionism in the U.S.S.R: From Lenin to the Soviet Black Hundreds," in *The Left Against Zion: Communism, Israel and the Middle East,* Robert S. Wistrich, ed. (London, England: Vallentine, Mitchell, 1979), p. 272–273.

4. Hyman Lumer, ed., *Lenin on the Jewish Question* (New York: International Publishers, 1974), p. 22–24; Wistrich, "Anti-Zionism in the U.S.S.R," p. 273. Their goal was to secure complete control of the Jews and "make the revolution of the Jewish street." Zvi Gitelman, "The Evolution of Soviet Anti-Zionism," in *Anti-Zionism and Antisemitism in the Contemporary World*, Robert S. Wistrich, ed. (New York: New York University Press, 1990), p. 13.

5. Lumer, *Lenin on the Jewish Question*, p. 135–136.

6. Ibid., p. 134–135.

7. Ran Marom, "The Bolsheviks and the Balfour Declaration," in Wistrich, *The Left Against Zion: Communism, Israel and the Middle East*, p. 20–21, 27–28; Wistrich, "Anti-Zionism in the U.S.S.R," p. 274–275.

8. Marom, "The Bolsheviks and the Balfour Declaration," p. 22–25.

9. Wistrich, "Anti-Zionism in the U.S.S.R," p. 276–277; Arnold Krammer, *The Forgotten Friendship: Israel and the Soviet Block 1947–1953* (Urbana, IL: University of Illinois Press, 1974), p. 23.

10. Ibid., p. 275.

11. Marom, "The Bolsheviks and the Balfour Declaration," p. 17–19; Wistrich, "Anti-Zionism in the U.S.S.R," p. 275.

12. Wistrich, "Anti-Zionism in the U.S.S.R," p. 275–276.

13. Ibid., p. 281, 284, 286; Krammer, *The Forgotten Friendship*, p. 2–21, 32–34; Joshua Rubenstein and Vladimir P. Naumov, eds., *Stalin's Secret Pogrom: The Postwar Inquisition of the Jewish Ant-Fascist Committee* (New Haven, CT: Yale University Press, 2001); Walter Z. Laqueur, "Soviet Policy and Jewish Fate," *Commentary* (October 1956): p. 303–312; Jon Kimche, "Middle East Moves and Counter-Moves," *Commentary* (March 1948): p. 214–221; Hal Lehrman, "Partition in Washington: An Inquiry," *Commentary* (March 1948): p. 205–213; Joseph Sherman, "Sevenfold Betrayal: The Murder of Soviet Yiddish," *Midstream* (July/August, 2000), Online.

14. Wistrich, "Anti-Zionism in the U.S.S.R," p. 283.

15. Quoted in Jacob Robinson, *Palestine and the United Nations: Prelude to Solution* (Westport, CT: Greenwood Press, Publishers, 1947), p. 236–239.

16. Krammer, *The Forgotten Friendship*, p. 16, 20–21.

17. Ibid., p. 20–21. For Jewish response to the speeches, see Krammer, *The Forgotten Friendship*, p. 17–18; Clifton Daniel, "Palestine Excited Over Soviet Stand," *NYT* (May 16, 1947), p. 3.

18. Krammer, *The Forgotten Friendship*, p. 56–81; Uri Bialer, "Top Hat, Tuxedo and Cannons: Israeli Foreign Policy From 1948 to 1956 as a Field of Study," *Israel Studies* vol, 7, no. 1 (Spring 2002): p. 41.

19. Krammer, *The Forgotten Friendship*, p. 81–82.

20. Wistrich, "Anti-Zionism in the U.S.S.R," p. 283.

21. Moshe Dayan, *The Sinai Campaign Diary of Moshe Dayan* (New York: Schocken Books, 1967), p. 4–5; Bialer, "Top Hat, Tuxedo and Cannons," p. 7, 48–49; G.F. Hudson, "America, Britain, and the Middle East," *Commentary* (June 1956): p. 516–521; Hal Lehrman, "Three Weeks In Cairo: A Journalist in Quest of Egypt's Terms for Peace," *Commentary* (February 1956): p. 101–111; Hal Lehrman, "Is An Arab-Israeli War Inevitable?": A Challenge to American Leadership," *Commentary* (March 1956): p. 210–221; George Lichtheim, "Nationalism, Revolution, and Fantasy in Egypt: Behind the Arms Deal with Czechoslovakia," *Commentary* (January 1956): p. 33–40; Joel Carmichael, "On Again, Off Again: Egypt's Blockade of the Suez Canal," *Midstream* (Summer 1960): p. 56–64.

22. Wistrich, "Anti-Zionism in the U.S.S.R," p.286; George Lichtheim, "Soviet Expansion into the Middle East," *Commentary* (November 1955): p. 435–439; Krammer, *The Forgotten Friendship,* p. 32–33.

23. Wistrich, "Anti-Zionism in the U.S.S.R," p. 286; Manfred Gerstenfeld, "Language as a Tool against Jews and Israel: An Interview with Georges-Elia Sarfati," Jerusalem Center for Public Affairs, Number 17 (February 1, 2004), Online.

24. Gerstenfeld, "Language as a Tool against Jews and Israel; S.L. Shneiderman, "Russia's Anti-Zionist Campaign: Jews vs. Zionists," *Midstream* (June/July 1970): p. 66; Wistrich, "The Left Against Zion," p. 287.

25. Shneiderman, "Russia's Anti-Zionist Campaign: Jews vs. Zionists," p. 71–72, 75.

26. Ibid., p. 66, 71, 73–75.

27. Wistrich, "Anti-Zionism in the U.S.S.R," p. 288–291.

28. Ibid., p. 294–295. The Zionists pressured the Soviets to let Jews immigrate to Israel. Their constant petitions and appeals were not reported in the Soviet press, but they did reach the outside world. From an ideological perspective, the Zionists demonstrated that the communists had not "solved" the Jewish problem via assimilation, as they claimed they did.

29. Ibid., p. 296.

30. Ibid.

31. Ibid., p. 296, 300; Gerstenfeld, op. cit.

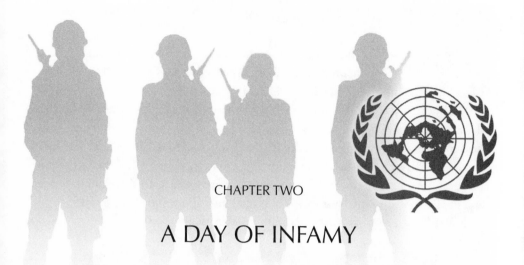

CHAPTER TWO

A DAY OF INFAMY

On November 10, 1975, the 37th anniversary of *Kristallnacht* (Night of the Broken Glass), the United Nations General Assembly declared that "Zionism is Racism" and racial discrimination by passing Resolution 3379 (Z=R). The passage was part of a carefully engineered worldwide campaign to delegitimize Israel, after her enemies had failed to expel her from that body.

On the same day the UN declared Z=R, the General Assembly also adopted Resolution 3376, establishing an Assembly Committee on the Exercise of the Inalienable Rights of the Palestinian People. Ironically, 16 of the original 20 members on the Assembly committee did not have relations with Israel, and some had never acknowledged Israel's right to exist.[1]

In a full-page advertisement in the *New York Times,* the Anti-Defamation League of B'nai B'rith (ADL) warned of drastic changes in the political and diplomatic climate for Jews and Israel with the passage of Z=R. Under a picture of Adolph Hitler speaking to his *sieg-heiling* minions, the ADL said it was disturbing that Nazi ideology still existed. It also said it was more disconcerting to note the number of countries who condoned racist ideology on the floor of the General Assembly. The ad further warned that by introducing the anti-Zionist resolution, the UN had lost its credibility; that passing the resolution would erode the UN's moral standing and jeopardize its financial support. "Kill the resolution, or destroy the UN," the ad declared.[2]

Daniel Patrick Moynihan, the U.S. Ambassador to the UN at the time, recalled that only two people understood its implications. Both were Irish — he and the Israeli Ambassador to the UN, Chaim Herzog, were both born in Belfast, Northern Ireland.[3]

Z=R and other anti-Israeli resolutions were adopted during the two terms Kurt Waldheim served as secretary-general of the UN (1972–1981). His tenure was marked by antagonism toward Israel and Jewish concerns. When he made a visit to Yad Vashem, Israel's national Holocaust museum, he did not cover his head during a memorial service for the six million — the only dignitary to that point who had refused to do so. Waldheim allowed Yasser Arafat, the head of the PLO (Palestine Liberation Organization), to address the UN. When Z=R came up for a vote, Waldheim assumed a passive role. In July 1976, he was the only leader in the free world to declare that Israel's daring rescue of 105 hijacked Jewish and Israeli hostages being held by terrorists at the Entebbe airport was a contravention of Uganda's territorial sovereignty. Throughout his UN tenure, Waldheim successfully hid the fact that he had been a member of the Studentenbund, the Nazi student organization in Austria and the Reitersturm, the Nazi Party's mounted unit of the *Sturmabteilung* (S.A. "Assault Unit"), or brown-shirted paramilitary stormtroopers.[4]

Daniel Patrick Moynihan
U.S. Ambassador to the UN, 1975
(Credit: U.S. Senate Historical Office)

During 1942 and 1943, Waldheim was an intelligence officer on the staff of General Alexander Loehr, the Supreme Commander of Wehrmacht forces in the Balkans, during brutal military campaigns against Yugoslav partisans and the deportations of more than 70,000 Greek Jews to Auschwitz. Many of his superior officers were convicted of war crimes.[5]

In April 1987, when he was president of Austria, the U.S. Justice Department's Office of Special Investigations added Waldheim's name to the list of people prohibited from entering the United States because he was "morally complicit" and "assisted or otherwise participated in the persecution of persons because of race, religion, national origin, or political opinion."[6] They noted that the intelligence reports he prepared were used by the military to identify targets for extermination.[7]

UN Secretary General Kurt Waldheim
(Credit: UN Photo)

Z=R RESOLUTION

The Z=R resolution attracted worldwide attention to Zionism as "a form of racism and racial discrimination," ensuring that Zionism could now be viewed as an international problem. When the UN General Assembly passed the December 14, 1973, resolution condemning the "unholy alliance between South African racism and Zionism," it was the first time that Jewish nationalism (Zionism) was branded racist in such a world forum.[8] Ostensibly, the Arabs were just asking Israel to change her character by uprooting "the Zionist entity." But this was a subterfuge; they knew full well that the "de-Zionization" of the country meant the end of the Jewish character of the state. Israel would cease to exist; she would become an Arab entity.

The Arabs understood that by manipulating history and by denouncing Zionism as racism they could use an acceptable tactic in their war against the Jews in the international arena. Moderate Arabs maintained that they were prepared to accept the legitimacy of Israel's existence *de facto,* but could not recognize the legitimacy *de jure.*

One immediate result of Z=R was that it helped enlist the support of the Third World against Israel, reminded the West of its silence during the Holocaust, and awakened "guilt complexes in Western circles."[9] What it effectively did was question the entire basis of the creation of the Israeli state. How can Israel be absolutely legitimate if she came into being in an illegitimate manner? Recognizing Israel as a legitimate entity means that there is "justice in Zionism." By forcing Jews to reject Zionism as "Jewish nationalism," the Arabs could deprive the Jews of their national status, leaving them only with a religious identity that gave them no rights to a state of their own, according them inferior status as a people. The next step would be to accept antisemitism on an international basis.[10]

IMPLICATIONS OF THE RESOLUTION

"In the UN, words take on a life of their own," noted John R. Bolton, then Assistant U.S. Secretary of State for International Organization Affairs. "To declare as 'racist' the historical and cultural underpinnings of a state is tantamount to branding that state an international criminal, for racism is a crime enumerated in the Genocide Convention and numerous other instruments commonly accepted under international law."[11]

Abba Eban, Israel's first permanent representative to the UN and the man who had negotiated her entry into that body, the man who was later Israel's Minister of Foreign Affairs, believed that this was the first time in history that an international body directed its criticism against ideas and articles of faith venerated by one of its member states — and not against its policies. The UN had never endorsed or denounced an "-ism" before. Even at the height of the Cold War, the United States never sponsored a resolution condemning communism, socialism, or any other "-ism."[12] Now a Jewish "-ism" was branded and shamed on the world stage.

Israeli UN Ambassador Abba Eban
(Courtesy of Israeli Government Photo Office)

A racist state has "no rights at all, not even the right to defend itself," observed Jeanne J. Kirkpatrick, Moynihan's replacement at the UN. After 3379 was passed, Israel became "fair game for armed 'liberation.' " Maliciously, the UN General Assembly had deliberately branded Israel as illegitimate on the same day it recognized the legitimacy of the Palestine Liberation Organization (PLO).[13]

Less than a decade after the passage of the resolution, on July 1, 1982, Kirkpatrick was in Bujumbura, Burundi, celebrating that country's 21st anniversary of independence. Ninety percent of Burundi's population was illiterate; they had no real governance; more than 100,000 people had been killed in tribal warfare during 1972–1973, and the country had limited funds. Yet the Burundi Supreme Revolutionary Council found the resources to erect an enormous banner for the Independence Day parade proclaiming, in French, "Zionism is Racism."[14]

With the passage of Z=R, antisemitic rhetoric in the UN was no longer taboo. Diplomatic representatives were free to use antisemitic stereotypes in their speeches, reflecting classical Christian antisemitism in their political attacks against Israel.[15]

For example, Hazem Zaki Nuseibeh, a lawyer with a Ph.D. in political science from Princeton University, and Jordan's permanent representative to the United Nations, saw the resolution as a perfect opportunity to recall the legendary *Protocols of the Elders of Zion* (the debunked Russian antisemitic screed that postulated Jewish world control) and attack "Jewish dominance" in the world.

> Are the Israelis above the law? Is the world divided into an omnipotent race and subservient Gentiles born into the world to serve the aims of the master race? We, the Gentiles, are several billion souls, and yet how much weight, I wonder, do we carry in the councils of some of the mighty?[16]

In a *Time* magazine article, Nuseibeh claimed that proof of Jewish world dominance is that, every day, Mr. Rothschild "meets with a cabal in London behind closed doors, to fix the price of gold. A telex is sent out to agents around the world to observe the price." This also involved monetary and other financial manipulations. "How," Nuseibeh asked, "can the billions of struggling humanity compete with such awesome power, except by their indomitable spirit and their unshakable faith in justice, equality, goodness, and the inherent worth of the individual?"

Nuseibeh applauded the UN for having the "moral integrity and courage" to say "loudly and clearly" that Zionism was racism. He wondered how anyone who was honest and faithful to humanity's ideals and values could not see that uprooting the Palestinians was the ultimate form of racial discrimination. Zionism had denied the Arabs "their birthright over their soil and the right to determine their own fate." Palestinians everywhere were discriminated against, not because they are good or bad, but "for the sole sin of being a Palestinian" and "not belonging to the Jewish race or faith." Accident of birth, race, and spiritual affiliations had determined their fate. (Nuseibeh served as Jordan Foreign Affairs Minister and political advisor to the late King Hussein before coming to the UN and later becoming a member of the Jordanian senate.)[17]

No attempt was made to pretend there was a difference between Jews and Israelis, or to deal with any facts that would dispute Nuseibeh's inflammatory tirade.

SHARP CHANGE IN RHETORIC

Z=R stood in sharp contrast to the rhetoric heard at the UN in 1947 and 1948, when the future of Palestine was being considered. At the time, the theme of self-determination and the need to resolve the question of the future of the Jewish people and "perhaps even their national survival" was readily discussed by a number of delegations. From Mr. Quo Tai-Chi of China:

The tragedy of the Jewish people, truly a great historic tragedy, cannot but rouse the spontaneous sympathy of the peoples of the entire world. The Jewish people deserves a national home of some sort, deserves a place it can call its own, in which it can live in happiness, free from social and political discrimination, and free from the eternal fear of persecution.[18]

Dr. Jan Papanek, the Czechoslovakian delegate, reminded the council that the British had promised a national home to the Jews 25 years earlier. The Jewish people were now looking to the UN for help in realizing that goal. Sympathy for their plight was not sufficient. Action was needed. "The darkness that has engulfed the Jews for so long can only be dispelled by any ray of light we rekindle here for them."[19]

After Z=R passed, antisemitic rhetoric in the UN assumed an institutional character, first under Waldheim, and then under his successors, Javier de Perez de Cuellar and Boutros Boutros-Ghali. Numerous annual anti-Israel resolutions and antisemitic outbursts made Israel the object of enmity to the UN majority. Israel was chastised for policies of "hegemonism" and "racism"; for being a "non-peace-loving country" and an "affront to humanity."

General Assembly resolutions soon proliferated exponentially, calling for military, economic, and diplomatic sanctions that would have left the country vulnerable militarily, economically, and politically. A review of General Assembly documents, media coverage, and diplomatic activities show how annual and special UN conferences became venues for anti-Israel excess. Today, though the resolution has been rescinded, the antisemitism it unleashed remains rampant.[20]

THE WEAKENING OF THE UN

When the UN was first established in 1945, President Franklin D. Roosevelt expected it to be the catalyst to democratize the nations of the world. This was not to be. From its inception, it could not coerce Communist countries to adopt liberal and democratic values. Furthermore, shortly after World War II ended, the United States and the Soviet Union became involved in the Cold War, with each using the UN as a forum to gain ascendancy for their causes[21] — effectively paralyzing the institution. Typically, the Soviets would complain that the United States held an "automatic majority" with many recommendations of the General Assembly being passed by votes of 50 to 5 — the 5 being cast by members of the Soviet bloc nations.[22]

But UN member states soon recognized that the UN was not the international body that could cure the world's ills, that it could not provide security for them. The Korean conflict, in which millions of people were killed, ended in an armistice that was not a triumph of collective security, but the result of the Soviet Union's absence from the Security Council. The Soviet invasion of Czechoslovakia in August 1968, and the ongoing international tensions in Berlin and in Europe exposed vulnerability in the system as well.

Time and time again, most decisive events in the international arena transpired outside the auspices of the UN. As such, the United States and Western Europe turned to the North Atlantic Treaty Organization (NATO) to ensure security, and later the European nations conducted their own economic and other relations within the European Economic Communities, the forerunner of the European Union. For a brief period, with the admission of Latin American countries into the fraternity, these countries used their 20 votes to play a decisive role in a total membership of 52. When Asian and African countries were admitted to the UN, however, their power was diluted.[23]

As their influence diminished, the Latin American countries turned to the Organization of American States and the Inter-American System to strengthen democracy, advance peace and security, increase trade, and address problems of corruption, drugs, and poverty in the countries of North, Central, and South America, and the Caribbean.

Rapidly, however, despite its relative inability to serve as an international supernumerary agent, new countries continued to join the UN, most of them created as a result of the disintegration of the Western empires and the liberation of nations. But a hundred new countries that were not independent when the UN was established soon changed the nature of the institution. By 1986, there were only 30 democratic member states in the UN out of a total of 158.[24]

Their numerical dominance, however, gravely affected the ideals under which the UN had been established. It especially affected UN operations. Most conflicts in the 1960s — Biafra, Cuba, Vietnam, and Czechoslovakia — of necessity, were not conducted within the UN framework.[25]

As the effectiveness of the UN waned, there were significant changes that affected its makeup and philosophy. According to a skewed voting arrangement, 40 new African nations were entitled to 40 votes; a hundred million Arabs had 20 votes, while the United States and the European community, with 500 million citizens, had just 10 votes. This favored Communist countries and the Third World, enabling them to control the votes in the General Assembly. As such, votes were now determined on the basis of solidarity and self-interest, not objectivity. Once a decision was made, it was falsely justified in terms of its morality and righteousness. "The compassionate and sentimental impulses of 1947–1949 gradually gave way to more concrete considerations."[26]

Another result of this increased membership was anti-Western rhetoric from countries that had recently attained independence and still retained bitter memories of their colonial past. Even though most of the new UN countries were politically and economically insignificant on the world scene, they nevertheless gained a sense of pride by their membership. No matter how insignificant UN resolutions had become, the UN conferred a recognized juridical reality on a nation, as a member of the UN is acknowledged by other nations as having "sovereign equality" with all others. From May 11, 1949, when Israel was admitted as a member of the UN, the question of whether Israel was a state was legally irrelevant. Until 1973, only the Arab states and a few countries with large Moslem populations had denied Israel's legitimacy — and the Soviets and the Africans expressed their concerns with Israel within the confines of the UN.[27] Z=R attempted to change that.

The UN's inability to decide whether to be moral or practical was labeled by Abba Eban as a "malaise," which he ascribed to the UN's failure to decide what it "wants to be" and for not examining "its central purpose or its predominant technique." Is the UN "an instrument for solving conflicts or an arena for waging them"? Eban believed the UN had "fallen between the diplomatic principle and the parliamentary principle," and the two "cannot be reconciled."

> The diplomatic principle tells my adversary that he must seek agreement with me. The parliamentary principle tells him that he does not need agreement at all, he can mobilize votes for my defeat and humiliation. Defeat, victory, majority and minority, have no place within the diplomatic principle, they are quite legitimate within the parliamentary principle.

The parliamentary principle is not useful in the UN "where passions can rage without fear of consequence." Anyone who exhibits irresponsible behavior or votes recklessly in a national parliament is held accountable for his actions since it affects his country's well being. In the UN there is no such restraint or inhibition.[28]

How the Resolution Was Born

The Arabs and Russians cosponsored the anti-Zionist resolution, though each had their own agenda. The PLO wanted to expel Israel from the UN and replace it with a Palestinian state, but President Anwar Sadat of Egypt resisted the move because it would shield Israel from UN sanctions. Since Israel and Egypt, together with the Americans, were in the process of negotiating an interim agreement for Israeli withdrawal from the Sinai, Egypt argued that it couldn't support Israel's expulsion from the institution that would guarantee and supervise Israeli withdrawal.

Most of the African countries backed Egypt, and the Arabs split into pro- and anti-expulsion supporters. But to placate the PLO and its supporters, including Uganda, the resolution denouncing Zionism as a threat to world peace was drafted at the OAU conference in Kampala in July–August 1975.[29]

At the Lima Non-Aligned foreign ministers conference in Peru in August 1975, the PLO again lobbied for expulsion of Israel, and again the Egyptians thwarted the move. This precipitated another attack against Zionism, and the Algerians, allied with the Palestinians, used harsher language against Israel, language taken from the PLO Covenant itself.[30]

The PLO and its supporters continued to look for a way to expel Israel. At the UN Credentials Committee meeting in September 1975, when the UN opened its annual session, the Syrian representative tried to banish "the Zionist regime" from the UN. When no Arab or non-Arab member supported the Syrians, the motion was simply recorded.[31]

On October 1, 1975, Idi Amin, the tyrannical, cannibalistic leader of Uganda, brought his anti-Zionist message to the General Assembly and called upon the American people "to rid their society of the Zionists in order that the true citizens of this nation may control their own destiny." He also called "for the expulsion of Israel from the United Nations and the extinction of Israel as a State."

Moynihan noted that though Amin purportedly spoke for 46 African nations, in truth he spoke for the authoritarian majority in the General Assembly who had given him a standing ovation when he arrived in the hall, applauded him throughout his speech, and gave him another ovation when he left.[32]

The question of Zionism became the subject of debate in the Third Committee as it tried to implement the UN resolution dedicated to fighting racism and racial discrimination beginning in 1973.

The Arab oil-producing nations, having gained considerable economic wealth and political power as a result of their 1973–1974 oil embargo — when they quadrupled oil prices — also attempted to use their new influence, especially at the UN, to advance the Palestinian cause.[33]

Knowing that rejecting the Israeli government's credentials would not work, the Non-Aligned countries and the Soviet Bloc planned a broad offensive against the democratic nations in the UN and targeted Israel by denying the legitimacy of Zionism, the Jewish national liberation movement. Israel would be declared illegitimate and could be censured, expelled, and then subject to extinction. Somalia sponsored the resolution with Cuba and Libya as cosponsors, though everyone knew that these Third World nations were acting on behalf of the Soviet Union.[34]

When the democratic countries of the UN cried foul over the attempt to delegitimize Israel, the official Soviet Tass news agency ridiculed those in the West who cried that the Z=R resolution was unexpected and sensational. They noted (without mentioning their own government's hand in the years-long machinations behind the scenes) that in 1975 alone, Zionism had been denounced by the Organization of African Unity (OAU) at its summit in Kampala, Uganda; by the Conference of Ministers for Foreign Affairs of Non-Aligned Countries held in Lima, Peru; at the UN world conference to commemorate the International Women's Year held in Mexico City; and in other international arenas.[35]

Moynihan discerned a pattern in the Soviet tactics:

A symbolic issue would come along: they might think it up; just as often it would emerge on its own. But they would seize on it, and either directly, or more often, through others, bring it to the General Assembly where it would command general assent as a matter more or less beyond disputing. As the matter progressed, however, more and more specific attacks on the West would be added to or associated with the general issue. In this manner the specific issue of Zionism was gradually associated with the general issue of racism. That an honorable cause was being put to the service of a dishonorable one, few seemed to understand or care.[36]

Speaking before members of the AFL-CIO, Moynihan noted that there were those in the United States "whose pleasure or profit" made them believe that America's assailants are provoked by what is wrong with the country. "They were wrong," Moynihan declared. The United States was assailed for what is right with the country, because it is a democracy. Nothing unites America's enemies more than the belief that "their success depends on the failure of the United States."[37] Free societies throughout the world were under attack "precisely and paradoxically for not being free." They were attacked for "violating human rights" ranging from genocide to unemployment, always following the "Orwellian principle: Hit the democracies in the one area where they have the strongest case to make against the dictatorships."[38]

Resolution 3379 and those adopted by the General Assembly in December 1973, by the OAU, the Non-Aligned countries, and the UN Conference on Women, succeeded in linking Zionism to neo-colonialism, foreign occupation, racial discrimination, apartheid, repression, and to the racist regimes of South Africa and Zimbabwe. All that, Tass concluded, proved that the Zionism problem had desperately needed a solution for a long time. The General Assembly merely provided the forum for the broad consensus to be heard. There were 72 votes in favor of the Z=R resolution, 35 against, with 32 abstentions.[39]

Chaim Herzog, Israel's ambassador to the United Nations from 1975–1978 (and later Israel's sixth president), remarked, ironically, that the vote was the biggest pro-Israel vote in a decade. Moynihan commented that Z=R might be an excusable surprise, since the West, including the United States and Israel, had been working at that time to prevent Israel from being expelled from the UN altogether.[40]

Many Third World delegates later explained that after the drive to expel Israel from the UN failed, a number of governments — especially Syria, Iraq, Kuwait, and the Palestine Liberation Organization — initiated the anti-Israel campaign in order "to save face."[41] But denying Israel her rights in the General Assembly would have violated international law. According to the specific provisions of the UN Charter, the Security Council must recommend the expulsion or suspension of membership, which then needs a two-thirds vote of the General Assembly for approval.[42]

Leonard Garment, Counsel to the U.S. Delegation to the UN, speaking before the Third Committee, the committee that passes amendments to the General Assembly, warned, "To equate Zionism with racism is to distort completely the history of the movement, born of the centuries of oppression suffered by the Jewish people in the western world and designed to liberate an oppressed people by returning them to the lands of their fathers. To ignore and to distort history in this fashion . . ." does a disservice to the UN Commissions, Committees, and Agencies. The conflict in the Middle East is a result of our inability to protect and accommodate the rights of the Jews and Arabs. It is:

> . . . an easy indulgence for individuals to use words which distort and divide, which inflict wounds and draw attention. It is our collective responsibility to use language enlightened by history, to use it precisely, to use it carefully, mindful of our differences but determined to overcome, not enlarge them.[43]

The Third Committee adopted the anti-Zionist draft on October 17 by a vote of 70 to 29, with 27 abstentions and 16 absent.[44] As Abba Eban then noted:

> Zionism is nothing more — but also nothing less — than the Jewish people's sense of origin and destination in the land linked eternally with its name. It is also the instrument whereby the Jewish nation seeks an authentic fulfillment of itself. And the drama is enacted in the region in which the Arab nation has realized its sovereignty in 20 states comprising 100 million people in four and a half million square miles, with vast resources. The issue therefore is not whether the world will come to terms with Arab nationalism. The question is at what point Arab nationalism, with its prodigious glut of advantage, wealth, and opportunity, will come to terms with the modest but equal right of another Middle Eastern nation to pursue its life in security and peace.[45]

Eban viewed the deliberations about the resolution in the Third Committee as "not so much a debate as a doctrinal inquisition, as in the Middle Ages." The purpose of the draft resolution was "to affirm a principle of monolithic exclusiveness for the Middle East, and to iron out all wrinkles of diversity." Arab campaigns to stamp out Kurdish individuality and Christian particularity proved that "in a region where many nations, tongues, and faiths had their birth, the monopoly of independence must be for Moslem pan-Arabism alone." Eban predicted the end result would be that Zionism would be strengthened and the United Nations weakened.[46]

Yasser Arafat as an Instrument of the KGB

If anyone exemplified the extreme nature of racism that the General Assembly tried to ascribe to Israel, it was Yasser Arafat, head of the Palestine Liberation Organization. At the invitation of Waldheim's UN, he spoke to the General Assembly on November 13, 1974. Herzog charged Arafat with calling for a *Judenrein* Middle East. Without having to renounce terrorism or his determination to destroy two member states of the UN (Israel and Jordan), Arafat became the first leader of a non-governmental organization (NGO) to address a plenary session of the General Assembly. He did so while wearing a gun on his hip — the only world leader to do so. He talked about his people's resolve to build a world free of Zionism, colonialism, imperialism, racism, and neocolonialism. He concluded with a challenge to the Israelis to accept peace or war: "Today I have come bearing an olive branch and a freedom fighter's gun. Do not let the olive branch fall from my hand. I repeat: do not let the olive branch fall from my hand."

Who was Arafat? Where did he come from? In the mid-1960s, the KGB (Russian Committee for State Security) groomed Arafat to become the leader of the PLO. They marketed him by creating his image as a fanatical anti-Zionist. His hero was the Grand Mufti Haj Amin al-Husseini — his cousin — who admonished the Germans for not killing enough Jews. The KGB ordered the Romanians to help

UN Secretary-General Kofi Annan
with Yasser Arafat, Chairman of the PLO.
(Credit: UN Photo)

develop Arafat's ability at deception, so that he could perform as one persona on the world stage and hide his murderous intentions behind the scenes.

In March 1978, Arafat was secretly brought to Bucharest to receive his final orders before leaving for Washington, D.C. "How about pretending that you'll break with terrorism? The West would love it. But pretending over and over," Nicolae Ceausescu, the leader of Communist Romania, told him repeatedly. "A snort of a pacifist Arafat day after day [and] the West may even become addicted to you and your PLO — much like a person becomes addicted to cocaine."[47] He was correct, and Arafat became a celebrity in the classic sense. It didn't matter what he did, he was always in the news. A majority of the delegates gave him a standing ovation.[48]

Speaking at a symposium in Tripoli, Libya, Arafat said, "There will be no presence in the region other than the Arab presence." From the Atlantic Ocean to the Persian Gulf only Arabs would be permitted to reside in the Middle East. An early pamphlet from Arafat's national liberation movement organization, Fatah, announced that only violence would abolish the Jewish state. The Israelis would not voluntarily dismantle the country, and he warned that any Israeli opposition would be met by stiff Palestinian resistance: "The hating revengeful masses [would] plunge down the road of revolution, and furiously pour forth to burn everything that stands in their way. We will never stop until we've returned to our home and destroyed Israel,"[49] Arafat assured Oriana Fallaci, an Italian journalist, in March 1972. When she asked what would happen if the Arab states concluded a peace agreement with Israel, Arafat replied:

> We won't accept it. Never! We will continue to make war on Israel by ourselves until we get Palestine back. The end of Israel is the goal of our struggle, and it allows for neither compromise nor mediation. We don't want peace. We want war, victory. Peace for us means the destruction of Israel and nothing else.[50]

In an interview with *al-Anwar*, a Lebanese daily, Arafat said he understood the demise of Israel would take time, but the Arabs would ultimately prevail:

> Our ancestors fought the Crusaders for a hundred years, and later Ottoman imperialism, then British and French imperialism for years and years. It is our duty to take over the banner of struggle from them and hand it on untarnished and flying as proudly as ever to the generations that come after us. We shall never commit a crime against them, the crime of permitting the existence of a racialist state in the heart of the Arab world.[51]

"It is not a picnic. It is a long, hard struggle," is a slogan the Arabs used from the outset to describe the fight that lay ahead, he said. Arafat knew it had taken "the

Vietnamese 35 years of constant war; the Algerians, 150; the Rhodesians, about 100; the Saudis, 500. But from the beginning, we believed that sooner or later, we would achieve our goals, because we are with the tide of history, while Israel is against it."[52]

As early as 1968, Arafat knew he had to relocate his base of resistance to the West Bank and Gaza Strip, territories under Israeli rule since the Six-Day War in 1967. This has to be done in order to turn the "resistance" into "a popular, armed revolution" to weaken Israel by thwarting immigration and promoting emigration, devastating the tourist industry, undermining the Israeli economy, and forcing the country to divert a significant portion of its resources to security.

Arafat believed the way to forge Palestinian identity, unity — and ultimately a nation — was only by fighting.[53] Fatah had long advocated that armed struggle is "not only the most effective means to restore the rights of the people of Palestine, but it is the only way of reaffirming the very existence of the Palestinian's national identity" and awaken the mass consciousness of Palestinians. This was a strategy of attrition based on a long, protracted war.[54] By creating and sustaining a hostile living environment, the Zionists would conclude that it is impossible for them to live in Israel.[55]

That strategy failed because the Palestinians had not as yet developed a sophisticated level of national consciousness, and Israel's counterinsurgency measures were fairly effective.[56] In June 1974, the PLO assumed a "phased strategy," whereby the Palestinians would accept whatever land the Israelis relinquished and use it to acquire additional territory until the "complete liberation of Palestine" was achieved. The same year, the PLO was given official status.[57]

ISRAEL: DISRUPTING NEIGHBORS

To quash dissent over Z=R, Arab spokesmen at the UN countered any criticism by claiming that Zionism and Israel were the source of evil in the Middle East and had to be eliminated. If the Zionist entity could be destroyed and Arab Palestine established, Jews, Muslims, and Christians could once again live as equals with dignity and respect, but this time in a secular democratic state. In discussing European guilt for the destruction of the Jews of Europe, the Jordanian ambassador observed: "There was no situation similar to this in the East, particularly with the civilization where for centuries the Jews lived happily and productively and to which they contributed in every way, namely, the Arab civilization."[58]

Dr. Abdallah Sayegh, a Kuwaiti, stressed Muslim veneration for Judaism and hospitality toward Jews and charged Zionism with having destroyed this harmonious relationship: "It was only when the Zionists came, and instead of the Jews saying, 'I should like to live with you,' the Zionists came saying 'I want to live in your place.' It was only when the Zionists came that our hospitality turned into hostility for the Zionist. . . ."[59]

Jamil al-Baroody, Saudi Arabian ambassador to the UN, added that "our Jews," the Oriental Jews from Arab countries, were not responsible for Zionism. "It was the European Jews who started this movement whose forebears came from the northern tier of Asia" and claimed Palestine as their own country. "If this is not tantamount to racism and discrimination, what is?"[60]

Endnotes

1. Jeane J. Kirkpatrick, "The U.N.'s Day of Infamy," *The Washington Post* (November 11, 1985), p. A23; Harris O. Schoenberg, *A Mandate for Terror: The United Nations and the PLO* (New York: Shapolsky Publishers, Inc., 1989), p. 108–125.

   The voting record was:

   Sponsored by: (25) Afghanistan, Algeria, Bahrain, Cuba, Dahomey, Egypt, Guinea, Iraq, Jordan, Kuwait, Lebanon, Libyan Arab Republic, Mauritania, Morocco, North Yemen, Oman, Qatar, Saudi Arabia, Somalia, South Yemen, Sudan, Syrian Arab Republic, Tunisia, and United Arab Emirates.

   Voted yes: (72) The 25 sponsoring nations above, and additionally 47 nations: Albania, Bangladesh, Brazil, Bulgaria, Burundi, Byelorussian Soviet Socialist Republic, Cambodia, Cameroon, Cape Verde, Chad, People's Republic of China, Congo, Cyprus, Czechoslovakia, Equatorial Guinea, Gambia, German Democratic Republic, Grenada, Guinea-Bissau, Guyana, Hungary, India, Indonesia, Iran, Laos, Madagascar, Malaysia, Maldives, Mali, Malta, Mexico, Mongolia, Mozambique, Niger, Nigeria, Pakistan, Poland, Portugal, Rwanda, São Tomé and Príncipe, Senegal, Sri Lanka, Tanzania, Turkey, Uganda, Ukraine, and the Union of Soviet Socialist Republics.

   Voted no: (35) Australia, Austria, Bahamas, Barbados, Belgium, Canada, Central African Republic, Costa Rica, Denmark, Dominican Republic, El Salvador, Fiji, Finland, France, Federal Republic of Germany, Haiti, Honduras, Iceland, Republic of Ireland, Israel, Italy, Ivory Coast, Liberia, Luxembourg, Malawi, Netherlands, New Zealand, Nicaragua, Norway, Panama, Swaziland, Sweden, United Kingdom of Great Britain and Northern Ireland, United States of America, Uruguay.

   Abstaining: (32) Argentina, Bhutan, Bolivia, Botswana, Burma, Chile, Colombia, Ecuador, Ethiopia, Gabon, Ghana, Greece, Guatemala, Jamaica, Japan, Kenya, Lesotho, Mauritius, Nepal, Papua New Guinea, Paraguay, Peru, Philippines, Sierra Leone, Singapore, Thailand, Togo, Trinidad and Tobago, Upper Volta, Venezuela, Zaire, Zambia. (Source: UN General Assembly Resolution 3379, Wikipedia.com)

2. "Dear Ambassadors," *NYT,* November 10, 1975, p. 27; see also advertisement of the Zionist Organization of America, "Zionist Answer to the Racists in the UN," *NYT,* November 2, 1975, Week in Review, p. 6.

3. Yohanan Manor, *To Right a Wrong: The Revocation of the UN General Assembly Resolution 3379 Defaming Zionism* (New York: Shengold Publishers, Inc., 1996), p. xi.

4. Eli M. Rosenbaum, *Betrayal: The Untold Story of the Kurt Waldheim Investigation and Cover-Up* (New York: St. Martin's Press, 1993), p. 22–23; John Tagliabue, "Files Show Kurt Waldheim Served Under War Criminal," *NYT,* March 4, 1986, p. A1, A6. Waldheim enrolled in the Studentenbund on April 1, 1938, shortly after the Anschluss, the annexation of Austria by Germany on March 12, 1938. He joined the S.A. on November 18, 1938, a little more than a week after Kristallnacht. During that pogrom, the S.A. played a leading role in burning synagogues, breaking windows, and looting Jewish businesses.

5. Tagliabue, "Files Show Kurt Waldheim Served Under War Criminal," p. A6. Shirley Hazzard, a writer who worked for the United Nations Secretariat in New York, believed that anyone who

objectively analyzed Waldheim's leadership at the UN would find it to be "consistent with his revealed past — for obtuseness, self-interest, untruthfulness and for an insensitivity that, in questions of human rights, sank to inhumanity." Shirley Hazzard, "What the Waldheim Case Says About the U.N.," *NYT*, April 16, 1986; see also Shirley Hazzard, "The League of Frightened Men," *The New Republic* (January 19, 1980): p. 17–20; Shirley Hazzard, *Countenance of Truth: The United Nations and the Waldheim Case* (New York: Viking Penguin, 1990).

6. Seymour Maxwell Finger and Arnold A. Saltzman, *Bending With the Winds: Kurt Waldheim and the United Nations* (New York: Prager, 1990), p. 9–10.

7. Douglas Feiden, "His Golden Years," *New York Daily News*, October 14, 2002, Online; see also Robert Rotenberg, "Anti-Semitism and Victimhood in Waldheim's Vienna," Newsletter of the Eastern European Anthropology Group, Autumn, 1989, Online.

8. Thomas Mayer, "The UN Resolution Equating Zionism with Racism: Genesis and Repercussions," London, Institute of Jewish Affairs, April 1985, p. 1; Yohanan Manor, *To Right a Wrong*, p. 4, 8–9.

9. Yehoshafat Harkabi, "Arab Positions on Zionism," in *Zionism and the Arabs*, ed. Shmuel Almog (Jerusalem: The Historical Society of Israel and the Zalman Shazar Center, 1983), p. 189.

10. Ibid., p. 189–191.

11. John R. Bolton, "Zionism Is Not Racism," *NYT*, December 16, 1991.

12. Abba Eban, "Israel, Anti-Semitism and the United Nations," *The Jerusalem Quarterly* (Fall 1976): p. 110, 118.

13. Kirkpatrick, "The U.N.'s Day of Infamy," *The Washington Post*, November 11, 1985, p. A23; Schoenberg, *A Mandate for Terror*, p. 108–125.

14. Daniel Patrick Moynihan, *Loyalties* (New York: Harcourt Brace Jovanovich, 1984), p. 35.

15. Avi Beker, *The United Nations and Israel: From Recognition to Reprehension* (Lexington, MA: Lexington Books, 1988), p. 3, 5, 94.

16. Hazem Zaki Nuseibeh, *Palestine and the United Nations* (New York: Quartet Books, 1981), p. 170–171, 174.

17. Ibid; "UN Protocols," *The New Republic* (December 27, 1980): p. 6–7; Daniel Pipes, "The Politics of Muslim Anti-Semitism," *Commentary* (August 1981): p. 89.

18. Jacob Robinson, *Palestine and the United Nations: Prelude to Solution* (Westport, CT: Greenwood Press, Publishers, 1947), p. 236, 241.

19. Ibid., p. 241.

20. Avi Beker, *The United Nations and Israel*, p. 3, 5, 94.

21. Ibid., p. 8.

22. Eban, "Israel, Anti-Semitism and the United Nations," p. 112–113.

23. Ibid., p. 113.

24. Beker, *The United Nations and Israel*, p. 8.

25. Eban, "Israel, Anti-Semitism and the United Nations," p. 113.

26. Ibid., p. 114, 116.

27. Ibid., p. 114–115.

28. Ibid., p. 116–117.

29. Mayer, "The UN Resolution Equating Zionism with Racism," p. 4–6; Schoenberg, *A Mandate for Terror*, p. 312.

30. Schoenberg, *A Mandate for Terror*, p. 312–313.

31. Mayer, "The UN Resolution Equating Zionism with Racism," p. 5.

32. Daniel Patrick Moynihan, *A Dangerous Place* (New York: Berkley Books, 1980), p. 169.

33. Mayer, "The UN Resolution Equating Zionism with Racism," p. 1; Manor, *To Right a Wrong*, p. 4, 8–9; Y. Harkabi, *The Palestinian Covenant and Its Meaning* (Totowa, NJ: Vallentine, Mitchell and Company, LTD, 1979).

34. Moynihan, *A Dangerous Place*, p. 172–173.

35. Ibid., p. 172.

36. Ibid., p. 173.

37. Ibid., p. 175.

38. Daniel P. Moynihan, "The Politics of Human Rights," *Commentary* (August 1977), p. 21.

39. Regina S. Sharif, ed., *United Nations Resolutions on Palestine and the Arab-Israeli Conflict*, Volume II: 1975–1981 (Washington, DC: Institute for Palestine Studies), p. 7.

40. Moynihan, *Loyalties*, p. 36.

41. Paul Hoffman, "Why and How Anti-Zionism Move Won," *NYT* (November 12, 1975), p. 17.

42. Malvina Halberstam, "Excluding Israel From The General Assembly By Rejection of Its Credentials," *The American Journal International Law*, note 57 (Washington, DC: The American Society of International Law, 1984), Online.

43. Moynihan, *A Dangerous Place*, p. 173–175.

44. "Dear Ambassadors," *NYT*, p. 21.

45. Abba Eban, "Zionism and the U.N.," *NYT*, November 3, 1975, p. 35.

46. Ibid.

47. Lieutenant General Ion Mihai Pacepa, *Red Horizons: The True Story of Nicolae and Elena Ceausescus' Crimes, Lifestyle, and Corruption* (Washington, DC: Regency Gateway, 1987), p. 25, 15–20, 23–29; 32–37, 57–58; Ion Mihai Pacepa, "The KGB's Man," *The Wall Street Journal*, September 27, 2003, Online.

48. Efraim Karsh, *Arafat's War: The Man and His Battle for Israeli Conquest* (New York: Grove Press, 2003), p. 48–49; Pacepa, *Red Horizons*, p. 17; Said K. Aburish, *Arafat from Defender to Dictator* (New York: Bloomsbury, 1998), p. 142–143.

49. Schoenberg, *A Mandate for Terror*, p. 12.

50. Ibid.

51. Yasser Arafat interview with al-Anwar [Beirut], August 2, 1968, quoted in Karsh, *Arafat's War*, p. 4.

52. Yasser Arafat, *Playboy*, "Interview," September 1988, Online.

53. Schoenberg, *A Mandate for Terror*, p. 12–13.

54. Hisham Sharabi, *Palestine and Israel: The Lethal Dilemma* (New York: Pegasus, 1969), p. 198–199, 206.

55. Ibid., p. 55.

56. Karsh, *Arafat's War*, p. 5.

57. Ibid.

58. David S. Landes, "Palestine before the Zionists," *Commentary* (February 1976): p. 48.

59. Ibid.

60. Ibid.

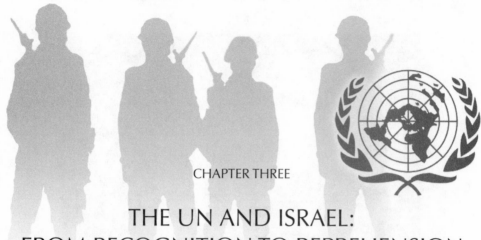

CHAPTER THREE

THE UN AND ISRAEL: FROM RECOGNITION TO REPREHENSION

Israel's formal acceptance as the 59th UN Member State on May 11, 1949, was consistent with the UN's original core beliefs. The UN's Universal Declaration of Human Rights, adopted in December 1948, was issued in response to the "disregard and contempt for human rights" that resulted in the "barbarous acts which have outraged the conscience of mankind," called the Holocaust — the attempt to annihilate the Jews of Europe by the Nazis.[1] Thus, the Jewish state and the human rights revolution "were as one in 1948. . . . There is a clear symbolic — if not symbiotic — relationship between Israel and human rights . . . and Israel was born of that commitment."[2] Israel's Declaration of Independence proclaims that the country will "dedicate itself to the principles of the United Nations Charter." Yet, from the very beginning, Israel's relationship with the UN ranged from ambivalence to hostility.[3]

The UN did not intervene after the armies of Egypt, Syria, Lebanon, Transjordan, Iraq, and a Saudi Arabian contingent attacked on May 14–15, 1948, when Israel was declared independent. Before the invasion, UN Secretary-General Trygve Lie asked the UN's legal department to see if an attack against Israel could be brought to the Security Council under Article 99 as "a threat to international peace and security."

The legal department said it could, and drafted a letter to the president of the Council. The secretary-general then held the letter in abeyance while he waited for the United States to act. He thought it would be "wiser" for the United States to take the lead role in any move by the Council to end the fighting.

When the Arabs attacked Israel on May 15, the Security Council was in session, and the United States "did not say a word." A member of the Soviet delegation was the only one to say anything, and according to Lie "there seemed to be a conspiracy of silence [in the Council] reminiscent of the most disheartening head-in-the-sand moments of the Chamberlain appeasement era."[4]

Trygve Lie
Secretary-General of the United Nations, 1946–1952.
(Credit: UN Photo)

The Secretary General feared that the failure to act would encourage other nations to use force in defiance of their assurances to the UN. Indonesia and Kashmir, already committed to the authority of the Security Council, might be tempted to disregard the Council after Egypt cabled the president of the Security Council on May 15 to inform him of its armed intervention, and its flaunting of the spirit of the Charter. The secretary-general received a similar cable from the Arab League on behalf of the other Arab states on May 16.[5]

As a result, the UN was in danger of becoming an ineffective vehicle to preserve peace unless it took quick action. On May 16, the secretary-general acknowledged in a letter to the permanent members of the Security Council that for the first time, "Member States have openly acknowledged their armed intervention *outside their own territories"* (emphasis added), and in an area of "special concern" of the UN. A Truce Commission was formed and the General Assembly passed a resolution establishing a UN mediator. On May 27, the UN ordered a truce, and threatened sanctions against those who did not comply.[6]

The final armistice agreements between Israel and the Arab countries (who claimed they would drive Israel into the sea) were not signed until July 20, 1949. The defeated Arab states insisted on indirect negotiations with the Israelis, and not face-to-face mediation favored by the Israelis. The UN's Conciliation Commission (the PCC), established by the UN on December 11, 1948, sided with the Arabs.[7]

PEACE NEGOTIATIONS

The Commission was composed of representatives from France, the United States, and Turkey. When the Israeli delegation arrived in Lausanne, Switzerland, to meet with their counterparts, the Arabs refused to be in the same room with them. For five months, the delegations did not officially convene. Israelis met each of the Arab delegations separately and in secret so their counterparts would not know they were talking to Israelis. No concessions to publicly stated Arab policy were possible.[8]

The Arab states said there was nothing to discuss unless Israel repatriated the refugees and returned to the 1947 partition boundaries. When the Israeli delegation arrived in Lausanne, Mark Ethridge, the U.S. representative on the UN's PCC and the chairman of the Commission for that month, asked Walter Eytan, director-general of Israel's foreign ministry, to make concessions to ease the hardships of the refugees without asking anything in return. Allowing parents and children and husbands and wives who had been separated during the war to be reunited would be an Israeli goodwill gesture, Ethridge believed, and would be seen by the Arabs as a "great humanitarian act," and, perhaps, get the talks moving. The "reunion of families" arrangement was made and the Israelis admitted 6,000 refugees.[9]

But the Arabs persisted in being uncooperative and created an intolerable environment for the talks, responding to the Israeli act of goodwill with disdain and indifference and seeing the concessions as a sign of weakness. The PCC then asked Israel to reimburse the Arabs for land that had been abandoned and previously developed. Israel paid $10,000,000 to Arabs in Arab countries and released their assets from safe deposit boxes. No legitimate claim was denied.[10]

Then the United States asked Israel to allow between 200,000 to 300,000 Arabs back into the land, out of approximately half a million refugees. The Israelis estimated the number at 520,000; the British, 726,000; and the UN, 810,000.[11] Israel finally said it might allow 100,000 refugees to return. The Arabs rejected this proposal, insisting all refugees "outside" Israel return to their homes immediately.[12]

Eytan told them on May 25, 1949, "There could be no return to the status quo ante. The clock could not be turned back." If an Arab refugee assumes he will live in "the house he abandoned, or plying his trade in the workshop he formerly rented, or tilling in the fields in the vicinity of the village he once knew, he is living under an illusion which it seems to me is essential to dispel. His house, his workshop, his village, possibly no longer exist." Any effort to recreate the circumstances before the war would thwart progress of the talks and "ultimately lead to their collapse."[13]

There was also a fear that fifth columnists among the returning refugees would become terrorists against the state. Allowing 100,000 to return might encourage intense international pressure to admit even more. Among Jews from Arab states who were forced to leave their homelands because of Arab pressure, violent attacks, and fear for their own safety, this was not a popular policy and it created enmity toward the United States. Israelis then discovered that among the books translated and distributed extensively in Arab countries was the *Protocols of the Elders of Zion*, which reinforced their concerns.[14]

As of January 1949, Israel held the 5,600 square miles allocated to it by the UN, with an additional 2,500 square miles it won during the war. Transjordan controlled the eastern sector of Jerusalem and the West Bank. The Gaza Strip was under Egypt's rule. Approximately one percent of the Israeli population — more than 6,000 souls — had been killed.[15]

LESSON LEARNED FROM THE UN RESPONSE

The anemic response to the attack on Israel demonstrated the UN's inability to enforce its own decisions and highlighted its limitations. All the concessions forced upon Israel did not change Arab behavior. As Walter Eytan observed,

> The Arabs saw that, under the PCC's pressure, they could apparently rely on Israel's making concession after concession without their having to give up anything in return. The only effect of these one-sided concessions by Israel was to convince the Arabs of the rightness of their policy and tactics. As time went on, Israel became more and more reluctant to make such concessions, and even the Commission came to see that they only stiffened the Arab attitude and made prospects of any real success increasingly dim.[16]

The Arabs learned that there was no compelling reason for them to temper their positions.[17]

This frustration with the UN's deference to the Arabs was expressed by a senior Israeli officer, who explained that in the pre-state whenever the Arabs would kill Jews, the British intervened to stop the bloodletting or did nothing. If the British did not come to the aid of the Jews, the Arabs

> . . . paraded in the streets and shouted "The government is with us!" and killed more Jews. Today [1954] the Arabs are killing people again. This

time the UN does not interfere. It gives the Arabs microphones. It lets the killers make speeches. And over there [pointing to Jordan] the Arabs now are shouting "The world is with us!" With such incentive to murder, why should they ever make peace?[18]

The Arabs had long enjoyed a rich history of manipulating authorities. After the 1921 Arab riots broke out in Jaffa, Rehovoth, and Petach-Tikva, Sir Herbert Samuels, the British High Commissioner and his staff "seemed to have been hypnotized by the danger and everything was done to placate the Arab," wrote Colonel Richard Meinertzhagen, a non-Jewish Englishman who served as Chief Political Officer in Palestine, Syria, and Transjordan, and later as Military Adviser to the British Colonial Office.

The British then temporarily halted immigration, and discussed the establishment of elective assemblies, whereas Meinertzhagen believed that Arabs deserved "a good sound punishment for breaking the peace and killing Jews. The Arab is fast learning that he can intimidate a British Administration."[19]

Samuels said that Jews were expected to immigrate to Palestine within certain fixed limits "to help with their resources and efforts to develop the country, to the advantage of all its inhabitants."[20] Jewish immigration, Winston Churchill assured the Arabs, was being monitored with regard to the numbers and character of the people. The country was "greatly under-populated," which allowed for more people to build a life there. The work already accomplished by the Jews during the last 20 to 30 years could not be "brutally and rudely overturned by fanatical attacks of the Arab population."[21]

The British appointed Sir Thomas Haycraft, Chief Justice of Palestine, to investigate the riots, resulting in the Haycraft Commission of Inquiry Report. This established the model for dealing with the Arabs: Arabs riot causing Jewish deaths and casualties, the British follow-up with an official inquiry, and then appease the Arabs.[22]

Trygve Lie resigned in November 1952, while the Armistice Agreements of 1949 were still in effect, but there was no real peace. In his fourth annual report to the General Assembly, he wrote that the establishment of Israel was "one of the epic events in history . . . coming at the end of two thousand years of accumulated sorrows, bitterness, and conflict. . . ." Whether a more enduring resolution to the Arab-Israeli conflict would be possible, he concluded, would depend on the willingness of Arab leaders and statesmen to accept "a more realistic approach." The State of Israel "now exists as a sovereign state: a member of the United Nations, maintaining diplomatic relations with a majority of the countries of the world. Without the recognition of the Arab states, Palestine will remain a source of conflict."[23]

For a number of years after its establishment, the UN seemed capable of becoming the central forum for discussing and resolving international conflicts. In many areas, the UN is the primary authority that provides legitimacy in the international arena. There is no other forum where the nations of the world can voice their policy views. On significant issues, the UN appears to define world opinion and often speaks as the collective voice of humankind. UN resolutions and declarations are amplified by the world's largest international public relations machines. In other words, the UN is important because it decides what matters.[24]

FOCUS ON ISRAEL

Something changed dramatically to convince the Arabs and the Russians to use the UN even more vigorously than before to advance their own agenda against the Jewish State. As two Egyptian activists and writers explained, the Six-Day War forced the Arabs to acknowledge their "own weakness and accept not only the existence of Israel but also its hegemony. . . ." Arabs throughout the Middle East responded with a sense of "crushing humiliation" after realizing that the combined strength of all their countries was no match against this small state, whose power they had thought until 1967 was insignificant. The defeat also meant an attempt to "resurrect their dignity, which Israel was trampling underfoot."[25]

The Soviets also suffered an enormous loss in the war. Many of their weapons were lost or were in the hands of the West. At Arab insistence, the Soviets replenished the military hardware lost, allowing the Egyptians to launch another war, a three-year war of attrition against the Israelis in the Sinai. While at the UN the attempt to find a solution to the Arab-Israeli conflict continued,[26] the Arabs and the Soviets used the forum to try to delegitimize and dehumanize Israel.

Throughout its history, the UN General Assembly has held only ten emergency sessions. Six of them have been about Israel. Since June 1967, approximately 30 percent of all the resolutions issued by the UN Commission on Human Rights have been about Israel. It is the only country that became the subject of an entire agenda of the Commission for this period.[27]

During those same years there were murderous coups in Africa, genocide in Rwanda, a decade-long campaign of ethnic cleansing in the former Yugoslavia, the occupation of Tibet by the People's Republic of China, genocide in Timor and Darfur, a region in the Sudan. In April 2004, after 30,000 were killed and 900,000 were left in appalling conditions, the United States proposed a resolution to censure "the grave violations of human rights and international humanitarian law in Darfur," and insist that the government of Sudan stop attacking civilians.[28]

Instead of condemning the ethnic cleansing, the UN Human Rights Commission declared: "The Commission expresses its solidarity with the Sudan in overcoming the current situation." None of the UN member states responsible for these atrocities were censured by the General Assembly's emergency special sessions. There has never been a single resolution against human rights violations in Saudi Arabia or Syria. But Israel is repeatedly condemned for refusing to capitulate to a policy of terrorism that has killed hundreds and injured and maimed thousands of her citizens. Attempts to condemn human rights abuses in China and Zimbabwe in 2004 were blocked by procedural motions. A resolution against Iran could not be brought up at all.[29]

THE UN COMMISSION ON HUMAN RIGHTS

Established on December 19, 1968, the UN Commission on Human Rights, an investigative body, is composed of member states, not human rights experts.[30] The Committee annually submits two or three comprehensive reports to the

Richard Meinertzhagen, a non-Jewish Englishman who served as Chief Political Officer in Palestine, Syria, and Transjordan, and later Military Advisor to the British Colonial Office.
(Photo courtesy of Randle Meinertzhagen)

secretary-general. Among the areas they examine are: Israeli settlement policy and annexation; Israeli settler activities; collective punishment; confiscation of land; harassment and physical abuse; expulsions; treatment of prisoners and detainees; demolition of houses; closures and curfews; health, economic, and social conditions; actions that affect education, freedom of movement and expression, and religion and conditions in the Golan. The reports are then circulated to the members throughout the session.[31]

Another UN body is the Committee on the Exercise of the Inalienable Rights of the Palestinian People. Established on November 10, 1975, the same day as Z=R was passed, the Committee promotes financial and political support for Palestinian people. Through international conferences and meetings attended by politicians, government and intergovernmental representatives, academics, UN officials, and the media, the Committee increases awareness about the question of Palestine. The Committee also monitors conditions on the West Bank and Jerusalem, and supports all international activities to resolve the conflict.[32]

On April 7, 2005, Secretary-General Kofi Annan accused the UN Human Rights Commission of failing to uphold human rights and said a new permanent body is needed. In his address before the annual session of this Commission in Geneva he said, "We have reached a point at which the Commission's declining credibility has cast a shadow on the reputation of the UN system." Despite his warning that there were similarities in Darfur to the Rwanda genocide, and in spite of evidence of Sudan's involvement, no resolution passed condemning Sudan, and this country was even re-elected to the Commission.[33]

As part of his program of UN reforms, Annan sought to create a scaled-down Human Rights Council whose members uphold the highest human rights standards. Today, current members include Sudan, Zimbabwe, China, Russia, and Saudi Arabia — all accused of rights abuses.

Each year, the Committee observes the International Day of Solidarity with the Palestinian People at UN offices around the world and in New York to commemorate the General Assembly resolution partitioning of Palestine on November 29, 1947, which Arabs commemorate as *Al Naqba* — The Day of Disaster.[34] It was not until January 2005, for the 60th anniversary of the liberation of Auschwitz, that the UN held its very first Holocaust commemoration at UN headquarters in New York. Then in March 2005, Secretary-General Kofi Annan went to Israel for the opening of the new Holocaust History Museum at Yad Vashem.

There he said:

> A United Nations that fails to be at the forefront of the fight against antisemitism and other forms of racism denies its history and undermines its future. That obligation binds us to the Jewish people, and to the State of

UN Secretary-General Kofi Annan
(Credit: UN Photo)

Israel, which rose, like the United Nations itself, from the ashes of the Holocaust. And it binds us to all people who have been, or may be, threatened with a similar fate. The United Nations must remain eternally vigilant.[35]

The day before he made that statement at Israel's official Holocaust memorial, Kofi Annan went to Ramallah and laid a wreath on Yasser Arafat's grave. The *New York Post* wondered why Annan bothered to go to Yad Vashem at all. Perhaps, to seem evenhanded, he paid his respects at the grave of a mass murderer of Jews. The paper noted that when Arafat was alive, most diplomats visiting the Middle East came to see him, but "now that he's dead and buried and everyone else has moved on — the Palestinians not the least — Annan has to pay his respects. Kofi clearly doesn't forget his friends. And no one who wants an impartial chief at the UN should forget this affair."[36]

ISRAEL IN THE MIDDLE EAST

The long-held view that Zionism "serves as a tool" of the West further exacerbated the relationship between the Arabs and the Jews. Abd al-Hamid II, the Ottoman Sultan between 1876 and 1909, thought it natural for the French to protect the interests of the Maronites living under his rule, for the Russians to look after the Armenians, for the Druse to be allied with the British, and for the Zionists to have their own guardians. The Zionists did not have a sponsor, but the perception that they had one endured.[37]

The Muslims viewed the British support for a Jewish national home during the period of the British Mandate (1918–1947) as a means for British government to safeguard the Suez Canal and its trade route to India. After India gained independence in 1947, the British remained in the Middle East to protect their business interests in the region. The Egyptian Muslim Brethren claimed the British had organized "thousands of vagabonds and aliens, bloodsuckers and pimps, and said to them, 'Take for yourselves a national home called Israel.' "[38]

Yasser Arafat proclaimed in 1990 that "the Zionist Entity represents the head of the body of hostile world forces inside the Arab nation; its role is to protect the interests of those forces."

Ash-Sha'b, a leftist Egyptian newspaper, saw Israel as an official extension of the Central Intelligence Agency, needing the CIA's approval and support before embarking on any mission.

Ahmad Jibril, leader of the Popular Front for the Liberation of Palestine-General Command, called Israel "America's aircraft carrier." PLO leader Khalid al-Hasan viewed the Jewish state as "something like a conglomerate — General Motors for example."[39]

For Gamal Abdul-Nasser of Egypt, the Pan-Arab leader, Israel was created to prevent Pan-Arab nationalism. For others, it was a means to appropriate Arab oil or to restrain Muslim fundamentalists who practiced true Islam. Hezbollah, the pro-Iranian group, and Hamas, the Palestinian fundamentalist group, accuse Israel of trying to annihilate Islam. Still others fault Israel for weakening the Arabs by compelling them to divert funds for war, rather than focusing on economic expansion, thus enabling Arab dictators to remain in office.[40]

The potential danger of Zionism, apprehensive Arabs proffer, might also be genocide. After the Israelis assassinated Hamas leader Sheikh Ahmed Yassin on March 22, 2004, an editorial in *Al-Jazeerah* claimed, "The actual killers are the government of President George Bush who still insists that the Zionist terror and the war of genocide waged by Sharon is an act of legitimate self-defense while the Palestinian resistance to the occupation is terrorism. It is the American administration that gives the Zionists international protection and supplies them with money and weapons."[41]

Blaming America and Britain via their proxy Israel makes Arab defeats and failures easier for Arabs to understand and live with. How, after all, could they possibly win against an Israel assisted by the British and Americans? Living under authoritarian rule that exploits the situation to deflect attention from real problems, the general Palestinian population's ability to understand the significance of personal, political, and cultural ties between free peoples is clouded.[42]

Confused and bewildered by an alliance that makes no sense to them, the Arabs assume that Israel is either controlling the Americans or being manipulated by them. They believe that Israel is nothing more than an imperialist outpost or the center of a conspiracy.[43]

MUSLIM SUPPORT FOR THE BRITISH AND THE NAZIS

When accusing the Jews of being tools of the British and the West, the Arabs fail to mention their own involvement with the British and German imperialism. During the First World War, in 1916, the Sharif, Hussein of Mecca — supported by Britain and France — initiated an uprising against the Ottoman Empire.[44]

At the end of the Second World War, Colonel Richard Meinertzhagen, the chief political officer for Palestine, observed that all the countries in Asia and Europe had sacrificed considerably, including Britain, which was now exhausted. Only the Arabs had not had to give up anything.

During both world wars, the Arabs had

. . . gained everything and contributed nothing. . . . Why should not the Arabs give up something to suffering humanity? Palestine is but a small part of the Arab countries. On the other hand, the Jews have contributed a great deal during both wars and have suffered more than any other nation. It is gross injustice that they should be refused a home which once was theirs. This simple act of justice is held up for fear of the Arabs and hatred of the Jews. A policy of fear leads nowhere; it is no policy.[45]

To those who suggested that Jews immigrate to countries other than Palestine, he responded: "Zionism without Zion is nothing at all. The Jews want a Home, not an Apartment."[46]

During World War II, Jews in Palestine volunteered to protect the British position in the Mediterranean. About 1,200 Jews were recruited during the war, while only 150 Arabs enlisted out of a population ten times the number of Jews.[47] The British used the Haganah, the *Yishuv's* underground military organization, behind enemy lines and considered it the "one reliable force and Palestine the one base whose loyalty was never in doubt for a moment."[48]

THE MUFTI OF JERUSALEM

While the Jews rallied to help the British, Haj Amin el-Husseini, the mufti of Jerusalem and the leader of the Muslim community in Palestine, undermined their position. In 1936, Admiral Wilhelm Canaris, head of the *Abwehr,* German military intelligence, provided funding so that the Arabs could riot against the Jews. The Germans also encouraged Jewish immigration to Palestine to rally the Arabs against the British and to divert British attention from the battlefields of Europe. The German Propaganda Ministry financed Arab newspapers, especially the *Difa* in Jaffa, whose editor was an informer for the Gestapo.

In a letter he wrote while on a tour of the country in 1937, Schwarz van Berk, the editor of the Berlin newspaper *Der Angriff* (The Attack), founded by Joseph Goebbels in 1927, explained why Jews should be allowed to immigrate to Palestine: ". . . It is good that the Jews from Germany come to Palestine. . . . [T]hey will not take root here, their fortunes will be spent and the Arabs will liquidate them. . . . [T]he Jews in Palestine are doomed, their end will be to leap from the frying pan into the fire."[49]

On May 9, 1941, the now ex-mufti broadcast "a *fatwa* announcing a *jihad* against Britain" over Iraqi and Axis radio, and appealed to all Muslims to defend Islam and "her lands" against its "greatest foe. . . ."[50] He had gone to Baghdad to start a pro-Nazi rebellion that failed. The mufti fled to Germany in November 1941,[51] where Adolf Hitler told him:

> The foundations of the difficult struggle [I am] waging are clear. [I am] waging an uncompromising struggle against the Jews. It pertains to the struggle against the Jewish home in Palestine, since the Jews wish to use it to create a national centre for their pernicious actions in other

Haj Amin el-Husseini, the mufti of Jerusalem and the leader of the Muslim community in Palestine, with Adolf Hitler.

countries. . . . A decision has been made to solve the Jewish problem step by step and to demand that other peoples, including non-European peoples, do the same. . . . [Once Germany entered the Middle East, the] objective would then be solely the destruction of the Jewish element residing in the Arab sphere under the protection of the British power.[52]

At that point, Hitler would publicly assure the Arab world of his intentions, and the mufti, who "would be the most authoritative spokesman for the Arab world," would then "set off the Arab operations which he had secretly prepared" in the Middle East to help the Germans defeat the British.[53]

The Nazis provided the mufti with offices in Berlin, with branches in other parts of Germany and in Italy, where he could broadcast his radio program and encourage Arabs around the world to become a fifth column to carry out acts of sabotage against the Allies and kill Jews. He helped establish espionage and saboteur networks. He also recruited tens of thousands of Muslims in the Balkans into the Wehrmacht.[54]

In a speech on January 21, 1944, he observed, "National-Socialist Germany is fighting against world Jewry. The Koran says: 'You will find that the Jews are the worst enemies of the Moslems.' " He added, "There are also considerable similarities between Islamic principles and those of National-Socialism. . . . All this brings our ideologies close together and facilitates cooperation."[55]

(The mufti was "one of the initiators" of the systematic destruction of the Jews of Europe and was an advisor to Adolf Eichmann and Heinrich Himmler. As one of Eichmann's best friends, the mufti continually goaded him to accelerate the extermination process. He even visited Auschwitz and Majdanek.[56])

The mufti of Jerusalem reviewing Bosnian SS troops.

Throughout the years of the Third Reich and for a number of years thereafter, the word "Nazi" was not generally viewed as an offensive term among Arabs. A connection with Adolf Hitler and the Third Reich was a matter of pride instead of embarrassment. Many Arab nationalist leaders, including a number in power during the late 1970s, were personally associated with the Nazis.[57]

During the early years of Gamal Abdul-Nasser's administration in Egypt, for example, some Latin American countries and Egypt harbored Nazis and other Axis war criminals. Their influence was clearly visible in the repression and propaganda techniques the Arabs adopted.

Some Arab writers, including many on the left, could not bring themselves to criticize the murder of the six million Jews during the Holocaust. Instead they tried to defend, diminish, mitigate, and even deny that the Holocaust occurred.[58]

Among those involved with the Nazis during World War II were Anwar Sadat and Gamal Abdul Nasser, who belonged to Young Egypt, the most important Arab Nazi organization in the region, which spied on the British for General Erwin Rommel's Afrika Korps. Sadat was even incarcerated for his involvement.[59]

NGOs AS PROPAGANDISTS FOR ANTISEMITISM

In 1993, in response to accusations by the Palestinians, the UN Commission on Human Rights created the position of Special Rapporteur to investigate human rights violations by the Israeli military in the Palestine Occupied Territories. The commission never established a mandate to examine acts of terror by the Palestinians against the Israeli civilian population and military.[60]

A declaration made at the World Conference on Human Rights in Vienna in June 1993 called for a commitment to eliminate "all forms of racism and racial discrimination, xenophobia and related intolerance." No mention was made of antisemitism because it was "too controversial."[61]

The Security Council is the only UN body that can adopt binding resolutions, but different organizations under the UN umbrella influence public opinion and are far more dangerous than resolutions passed by the Security Council. These nongovernmental organizations (NGOs) wield considerable power. As "grassroots" organizations, they represent those overlooked by political parties and are not bound by parochial interests. They are global in outlook and are vital to international civil society. The UN Commission on Human Rights in Geneva works with a wide range of institutions, including NGOs, academic institutions, and the private sector, to encourage a commitment to human rights.[62]

Officially, NGOs are supposed to concentrate on legal, environmental, and media issues, yet they also have clear political agendas, and legal groups have the most profound influence. The NGOs are in the vanguard of those demonizing Israel and promoting antisemitism. In their reports, public statements, and through their influence in the UN, the media, and the academic and diplomatic world, many NGOs misrepresent facts to advance their goals and objectives without any external accountability.[63]

In 1948, there were 69 NGOs; in 2000 there were more than 2,000, most focusing on universal human rights. Many radical political leaders from the 1970s, who were involved in anti-Israel activities then, now run some of them.

Some NGOs have thousands of members and multimillion-dollar budgets. The Ford Foundation, the New Israel Fund, USAID, Christian Aid, and the Advocacy Project are among institutions providing significant funds and technical support to NGOs.[64] But local and regional NGOs like Al Mazen, the Palestinian Center for Human Rights, Physicians for Human Rights-Israel, and LAW, are mostly led by supporters of the PLO and share their objectives.

The European Union funds some of the most politicized NGOs, including B'tselem and Adaalah I'lam. The EU Commission office in Israel, and a number of embassies in the country, support politicized groups like Physicians for Human Rights-Israel and the Israeli Committee against Housing Demolitions (ICHAD).[65]

Legal groups have the most profound influence. Key NGOs in Israel and the disturbed territories involved with rule of law are LAW, Al-Haq, and Al Mazen, which are Palestinian, and B'tselem and Adaalah in Israel. These NGOs generate, disseminate, and use negative reports about Israel to lobby government agencies around the world and make Israel look like it is the major abuser of human rights. These NGOs file appeals on alleged human rights abuses in the Israeli Supreme Court and create negative publicity for Israel.[66]

The Palestinian NGOs publish accounts to prove the Israelis are responsible for all of Palestinian misery and hardship. These claims are seldom sustained by independent or outside investigators, yet are still used by local and international NGOs "to invoke the pseudo-rhetoric of international law, using terms such as war crimes, crimes against humanity, disproportionate use of force, excessive response, indiscriminate killing, arbitrary use of force."

By misusing and distorting international legal terms, the NGOs perpetuate wrong and naïve notions that blame Israeli military activities for the suffering of the Palestinians in the West Bank and Gaza.[67]

As one law professor observed, "To judge by international authorities . . . Israel . . . is the world's most odious regime. Driven in large part by the NGO agenda, the UN Human Rights Commission issued six condemnations of Israel in 2001 and eight condemnations in 2002, while no other state has ever received more than one condemnation in the same year."[68]

The success of these NGOs was visible in 2001 at the UN World Conference against Racism in Durban, South Africa. Accusations that Israelis massacred Arabs in Jenin, protests against the security fence, and pro-Arab manipulation of the International Court of Justice consumed the agenda. The public relations operations of Amnesty International, Oxfam (which fights poverty), Christian Aid, and Human Rights Watch were combined to become an effective and powerful tool that "captured and severely distorted the core human rights agenda and [took] the lead in demonizing Israel."[69]

THE UN OBSESSION AGAINST ISRAEL

For more than 30 years, 15 percent of the UN Commission on Human Rights' time was spent on excoriating Israel and passing 30 percent of country-specific resolutions against her. Israel is barred from Commission membership, while Libya chaired the Commission, whose members included Algeria, Bahrain, China, Cuba, Saudi Arabia, Sudan, Syria, and Zimbabwe — all of them abusive regimes.[70]

Yet according to the UN's own rules, none of these resolutions against Israel are legally binding or enforceable.[71] Significantly, in more than 50 years, the UN voted in favor of Israel only three times: in November 1947 when it voted for the partition of Palestine, in May 1949, when Israel was admitted to the UN, and when the UN revoked Z=R in 1991.[72]

This UN fixation against Israel comes at a price. By allowing the Arab countries "to internationalize their war against the Jewish State," the UN lends its "presumed legitimacy and prestige to antisemitism."

Supporters of earlier manifestations of antisemitism could be opposed morally, if not militarily. But on American university campuses today, students cite the UN as the reason for their hostility toward Israel. They accept the UN and NGO condemnations of the Jewish state as a sign that Israel is corrupt.

The international community has not yet learned that antisemitism is a tool of anti-democratic politics and leads to political demonization. The more antisemitism is used to incite hatred against the Jews and Israel, the greater the possibility of war becoming the only means to release that loathing and rage. The increase of antisemitism at the UN corresponds to the escalation of "the politics of resentment against what Jews represent — an open and democratic society, the ethic of competition and individual freedom."[73]

Endnotes

1. Universal Declaration of Human Rights (December 10, 1948), Online.
2. Irwin Cotler, "Human Rights at 50," *The Jerusalem Post* (December 29, 1998), Online.
3. Michael B. Oren, "Ambivalent Adversaries: David Ben Gurion and Israel vs. the United Nations and Dag Hammarskjold, 1956–57," *Journal of Contemporary History* vol. 27 (1992): p. 89–127.
4. Trygve Lie, *In the Cause of Peace: Seven Years with the United Nations* (New York: The Macmillan Company, 1954), p. 174–175.
5. Ibid., p. 176–177.

6. Ibid., p. 178–179; see also Ruth R. Wisse, "The U.N.'s Jewish Problem; Anti-Semitism Has Found a Comfortable Home on the East River," *The Weekly Standard* vol. 007, issue 29 (April 8, 2002), Online; Efraim Karsh, *The Arab-Israeli Conflict: The Palestine War 1948* (Botley, Oxford: Osprey Publishing Limited, 2002), p. 8.

7. Oren, "Ambivalent Adversaries," p. 90.

8. Walter Eytan, *The First Ten Years: A Diplomatic History of Israel* (New York: Simon and Schuster, 1958), p. 50, 52–53. See also Itamar Rabinovich, *The Road Not Taken: Early Arab Negotiations* (New York: Oxford University Press, 1991), p. 29–64.

9. Ibid., p. 55.

10. Ibid., p. 56.

11. Martin Gilbert, *Israel: A History* (New York: William Morrow and Company, Inc.), p. 255.

12. Eytan, *The First Ten Years,* p. 56.

13. Neil Caplan, *The Lausanne Conference, 1949: A Case Study in Middle East Peacemaking* (Tel-Aviv: The Moshe Dayan Center for Middle Eastern and African Studies, Tel-Aviv University, 1993), p. 56.

14. Gilbert, *Israel: A History* p. 255.

15. Ibid., p. 122, 124; Benjamin Shwadran, "The Palestine Conciliation Commission," *Middle Eastern Affairs* vol. 1, no. 10 (October 1950): p. 277; see also Saadia Touval, *The Peace Brokers: Mediators in the Arab-Israeli Conflict, 1948–1979* (Princeton, NJ: Princeton University Press, 1982), p. 76–105.

16. Eytan, *The First Ten Years,* p. 56.

17. Ibid; Shwadran, "The Palestine Conciliation Commission," p. 272–274; Uri Baler, "Top Hat, Tuxedo and Cannons: Israeli Foreign Policy From 1948 to 1956 as Field Study," *Israel Studies* vol. 7, no. 1 (Spring 2002).

18. Hal Lehrman, "American Policy and Arab-Israeli Peace," *Commentary* (June 1954): p. 546.

19. Colonel Richard Meinertzhagen, *Middle East Diary 1917–1956* (New York: Thomas Yoseloff, 1959), p. 101–102; M. Mossek, *Palestine Immigration Policy Under Sir Herbert Samuel British, Zionist, and Arab Attitudes* (Frank Cass and Company Ltd., 1978), p. 17–31.

20. "Extracts From Speech Delivered By H.E. The High Commissioner For Palestine on 3 June, 1921," T.N.A. CO 733/7, p. 255–256.

21. "Extract From Speech On The Middle East By Mr. W. Churchill on the 14th June, 1921," T.N.A. CO 73 3/7, p. 256–258.

22. "What Happened During the Arab Riots of 1920–1921?" Palestine Facts, Online.

23. Lie, *In the Cause of Peace,* p. 194, 198.

24. Schoenfeld, *A Mandate For Terror: The United Nations and the PLO,* p. 3.

25. Eban, "Israel, Anti-Semitism and the United Nations," p. 110–111. Eban pointed out that during 1947–1949, the Security Council arranged for Soviet troops in Azerbaijan, Iran, and the Council played a role in securing a resolution that resulted in Indonesia's declaration of independence from Dutch. From 1950–1953, the UN force in Korea fought with South Korea against attacks from North Korea. UN activities in non-political areas also seemed promising. The Covenant on Human Rights expressed the fundamental elements of a free society and a compassionate and humane international community. The specialized agencies — The Food and Agricultural Organization; the United Nations Education, Scientific and Cultural Organization (U.N.E.S.C.O.); the International Labor Organization (I.L.O.); and the World Health Organization seemed to transcend ideology and politics.

President Woodrow Wilson's spirit, as defined by the League of Nations, was definitely in vogue. "Open covenants of peace, openly arrived at, after which there shall be no private international understandings of any kind but diplomacy shall proceed always frankly and in the public view." This sentence, from Wilson's Fourteen Points, is the guiding principle of the United Nations. The more participants engaged in an international issue, the greater the possibility reason would prevail. Moreover, no conflict would be confined to only those directly involved in the dispute. During the first decade of the UN's existence, these two principles — maximum exposure and universal involvement — guided the institution. In this environment, it is no wonder that Israel's fate was discussed in a chivalrous and almost disinterested manner.

That worked as long as the Western states that practiced parliamentary democracy were in the majority. Self-determination for all peoples was the principle around which the international community was organized, and in that atmosphere one could not countenance the absence of the single nation that suffered more under the Nazis than had any other. Their anonymity and "the lack of an independent state, had had such calamitous consequences. . . ."

26. Oren, *Six Days of War,* p. 318–327.

27. Anne Bayefsky, "The U.N. and the Assault on Israel's Legitimacy: Implications for the Roadmap," *Jerusalem Viewpoints,* Jerusalem Center for Public Affairs (15 July–1 August 2003), Online; Anne Bayefsky, "General Emergency Special Sessions" (December 11, 2003), Online; "One Sided: The Relentless Campaign Against Israel in the United Nations," The American Jewish Committee (September, 2000), Online; Shlomo Shamir, "EU Thwarts PLO's Anti-Israel Move in UN," Haaretz (December 19, 2003), Online; Shlomo Shamir, "NGOs Meeting at UN Call for Embargo of Israel," Haaretz (September 9, 2004), Online.

28. David Tell, "The U.N. Israel's Obsession," *The Weekly Standard* (May 6, 2002), Online; Anne Bayefsky, "Business as Usual: No love for Israel in Geneva," *National Review* (April 26, 2004), Online.

29. Bayefsky, "Business as Usual."

30. The Special Committee to Investigate Israeli Practices Affecting Human Rights of the Palestinian People and Other Arabs of the Occupied Territories, Online; Bayefsky, "Business as Usual."

31. Ibid.

32. "The Committee on the Exercise of the Inalienable Rights of the Palestinian People and the Division for Palestinian Rights," New York: United Nations (September 3, 2002), Online; Bayefsky, "Business as Usual." The Committee publishes monthly and periodic bulletins, studies, and other documents including an annual collection of General Assembly and Security Council resolutions and decisions relating to Palestine. In cooperation with the Permanent Observer Mission of Palestine at the U.N., usually two staff members of the Palestinian Authority are brought to UN headquarters each year to learn about the organization's activities. Trainees attend meetings of UN committees and commissions, and are briefed by secretariat officials, interact with delegates to the General Assembly and with members of permanent missions to the UN, and conduct research and write papers.

Yohanan Manor observed that "rather than focus on real threats such as terrorism and genocide, the UN devotes lots of its time to issues whose sole importance is that one can muster a majority around them — such as blaming Israel — instead of addressing real dramatic and tough problems, like Darfur or taking preemptive steps to neutralize unconventional forms of terrorism." Yohanan Manor, Communication, "Daily Highlights-World Conference against Racism," (August 31–September 7, 2001), Online.

33. "Geneva, April 7, 2005, Secretary-General's Address to the Commission on Human Rights," Online.

34. Ibid.

35. "UN Foundation Supports UN Secretary-General's Commitment to Lead a UN that Fights Anti-Semitism," (March 15, 2005), unfoundation.org.

36. "True Colors," *New York Post* (March 16, 2005), Online; Meghan Clyne, "Annan's Bow at Arafat's Grave Sparks Outrage in City," *The New York Sun* (March 17, 2005), Online.

37. Daniel Pipes, "Israel, America and Arab Delusions," *Commentary* (March 1991): p. 27–28.

38. Ibid.

39. Ibid. See also Said K. Aburish, *A Brutal Friendship: The West and the Arab Elite* (London: Indigo, 1998), p. 30, 13–14.

40. Ibid.

41. Aljazeerah 3.24.04 www.aljazerrah.info/25o/Assissination; Edward Said, "What Israel Has Done," *The Nation* (May 6, 2002), Online. See also, "Israel Boosts Security After Yassin Assassination" (March 28, 2004), http://www.foxnews.com/printer_friendly_story/0, 3566, 115432, 00.html); For an analysis of Hamas see Matthew Levitt, "Hamas from Cradle to Grave," *Middle East Quarterly* (Winter 2004), Online.

42. Pipes, "Israel, America and Arab Delusions," p. 27–28; "On the Democracy and Human Rights Conference Convened in Yemen," MEMRI Special Dispatch Series Number 659 (February 9, 2004), Online.

43. Pipes, "Israel, America and Arab Delusions," p. 27–28; see also Said K. Aburish, *A Brutal Friendship*, and Samuel W. Lewis, "The United States and Israel: Evolution of an Unwritten Alliance," *Middle East Journal* vol. 53, no. 3 (Summer 1999): p. 364–378; Anthony Hartley, "The U.S. the Arabs & Israel," *Commentary* (March 1970): p. 47.

44. Efraim Karsh and Inari Karsh, *Empires of the Sand* (Cambridge, MA: Harvard University Press, 1999), p. 184–190.

45. Colonel Richard Meinertzhagen, *Middle East Diary 1917–1956* (New York: Thomas Yoseloff, 1959), p.197.

46. Ibid., p. 171.

47. *Palestine: A Study of Jewish, Arab, and British Policies*, Esco Foundation for Palestine, Inc., Volume One (New Haven, CT: Yale University Press, 1947), p. 206.

48. Ibid., p.209; 227–228; see also Joseph Schechtman, *The Mufti and the Fuehrer: The Rise and Fall of Haj Amin el-Husseini* (New York: Thomas Yoseloff, 1965), p. 108–115.

49. David Yisraeli, "The Third Reich and Palestine," in *Palestine and Israel in the 19th and 20th Centuries*, Elie Kedourie and Sylvia G. Haim, eds. (Totowa, NJ: Frank Cass, 1982), p. 104, 106–109.

50. Schechtman, *The Mufti and the Fuehrer*, p. 110–114; Jorge Garcia-Granados, *The Birth of Israel: The Drama As I Saw It* (New York: Alfred A. Knopf, 1948), p. 204–205.

51. Zvi Elpeleg, *The Grand Mufti: Haj Amin Al-Hussaini* (Portland, OR: Frank Cass and Company, Ltd. 1993), p. 66.

52. Dan Michman, *Holocaust Historiography: A Jewish Perspective* (Portland, OR: Vallentine Mitchell, 2003), p. 112; Christopher R. Browning, *The Origins of The Final Solution: The Evolution of Nazi Jewish Policy, September 1939–March 1942* (Lincoln, NE: University of Nebraska Press 2004), p. 406.

53. "German Chancellor Adolf Hitler and Grand Mufti Haj Amin al-Husseini: Zionism and the Arab Cause," (November 28, 1941) in *The Israeli-Arab Reader*, Walter Laqueur and Barry Rubin, eds. (New York: Penguin Books, 2001), p. 54–55.

54. Ibid., p. 127–147.

55. Ibid., p. 140.

56. Ibid., p. 160; Schechtman, *The Mufti and the Fuehrer*, p. 17–18; Benny Morris, *The Road To Jerusalem: Glubb Pasha, Palestine and the Jews* (London and New York: I.B. Tauris Publishers), p. 33–34; Arieh Stav, "Arabs and Nazism," *The Outpost* (January 1996), p. 7.

57. Bernard Lewis, *From Babel to Dragomans: Interpreting the Middle East* (New York: Oxford University Press, 2004), p. 278.

58. Ibid.

59. Stav, "Arabs and Nazism," p. 6; Alan Lazerte, " 'Mein Kampf' and the 'Palestinian Covenant,' " *Anti-Semitism and Holocaust*, Online.

60. The U.N. Commission on Human Rights (June 14–25 1993), Online; Bayefsky, "Business as Usual: No love for Israel in Geneva."

61. Anne Bayefsky, "World Conference on Human Rights in Vienna," (June 1993), Online.

62. "President's Message," The International Association of Jewish Layers and Jurists," (n.d. 2003), http://www.intjewishlawyers.org/html/president.html; Gerald M. Steinberg, "Abusing the Legacy of the Holocaust: The Role of NGOs in Exploiting Human Rights to Demonize Israel," *Jewish Political Studies Review* 16:3-4 JCPA (Fall 2004), Online.

63. Steinberg, "Abusing the Legacy of the Holocaust."

64. Ibid.

65. Ibid; "ICHAD-EU Funding For One-Man NGO Promoting Extremist Anti-Israel Agenda," *JCPA* (March 7, 2005), www.ngo-monitor.org.

66. Steinberg, "Abusing the Legacy of the Holocaust."

67. Ibid.

68. Ibid.

69. Ibid.

70. Anne Bayefsky, "The U.N. Human Rights Agenda: A Strategy of Diversion," *Capitalism Magazine* (December 26, 2002), Online.

71. Julian Schvindlerman, "Israel Faces Rampant Discrimination at the United Nations," *The Miami Herald* (November 1, 2002), Online. Security Council resolutions are legally binding, but the way in which they are implemented varies according to the chapter of the UN Charter under which they were approved. Resolutions adopted under Chapter VI, entitled "Pacific Settlements of Disputes," have to be negotiated. UN Security Council resolutions 242 and 348, for example, adopted in 1967 and 1973, respectively, require Israel to withdraw from disputed territories once a comprehensive peace agreement has been reached.

    Resolutions approved under Chapter VII of the UN Charter, entitled "Action With Respect to Threats to Peace, Breaches of the Peace, and Acts of Aggression," can be enforced by a third party. Under Article 42 of the Charter, if the resolution is violated, the UN is permitted to use military force. All UN Security Council resolutions concerning Israel were issued under Chapter VI of the UN Charter. Except for two UN Security Council resolutions involving Iraq's invasion and ensuing occupation of Kuwait, the rest were approved under Chapter VII of the UN Charter. This means that there is no legally valid justification to compare the compliance of Israel to that of Iraq.

72. Ibid.

73. Wisse, "The U.N.'s Jewish Problem."

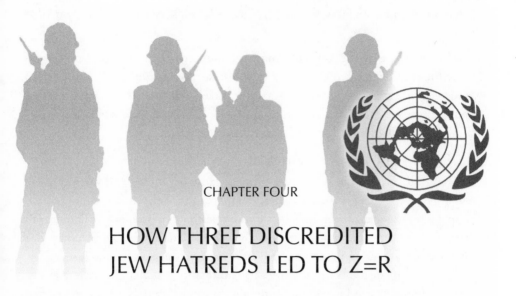

CHAPTER FOUR

HOW THREE DISCREDITED JEW HATREDS LED TO Z=R

What were all those nations at the UN voting for when they passed the Z=R resolution? According to the Palestinian National Covenant of 1968, Zionism is a racist ideology that uses fascist and Nazi methods to achieve its objectives. Article 22 of the Covenant describes it like this:

> Zionism is a political movement that is organically linked with world imperialism and is opposed to all liberation movements or movements for progress in the world. The Zionist movement is essentially fanatical and racialist; its objectives involve aggression, expansion and the establishment of colonial settlements and its methods are those of the Fascists and the Nazis. Israel acts as cat's paw for the Zionist movement, a geographic and man-power base for world imperialism and a springboard for its thrust into the Arab homeland to frustrate the aspirations of the Arab nation to liberation, unity and progress. Israel is a constant threat to peace in the Middle East and the whole world. Inasmuch as the liberation of Palestine will eliminate the Zionist and imperialist presence in that country and bring peace to the Middle East, the Palestinian people look for support to all liberals and to all forces of good, peace and progress in the world, and call on them, whatever their political convictions, for all possible aid and support in their just and legitimate struggle to liberate their homeland.[1]

This essentially Communist view, married to Nazism — both discredited "-isms" in the West — depicts Jews as the personification of colonialism and racism. It was calculated to provoke hostility toward Israel from Afro-Asian countries, who relied on Israel for nascent technologies.

The influence on the Arabs was more pronounced. They declared Zionism was created to humiliate them and, reacting with resentment, rioted. They were given an ideological excuse to commit politicide on Israel, a slow, methodical process that would ensure her extinction as an autonomous political and social body. This image of the Jew inflamed hatred and nurtured a need for retribution.[2]

ZIONISM AS THE ROOT OF ALL EVIL

The Arabs define Zionism as the primary cause of conflict and the root of all evil. The Covenant is not a reflection of the more radical elements within the Arab camp, but of the mainstream members of the Palestinian movement. It signifies "an egotistic stand that does not show the slightest consideration for the adversary, nor any trace of recognition that he too may have a grievance, a claim, and justice."[3]

The movement professes "absoluteness and totality" — there is absolute justice in the "Palestinian stand in contrast to the absolute injustice of Israel; an unqualified Manichaean division of good and evil; right is on the Palestinian side only — only they are worthy of self-determination. [Accordingly,] Israelis are barely human creatures who at most must be tolerated in the Palestinian State as individuals or as a religious community, with their numbers reduced to five percent (Article 6 in the 1968 version) and then assimilated in an Arab environment; the historical link of the Jews with the land of Israel is deceit; the spiritual link as expressed in the centrality of the land of Israel in Judaism is a fraud; international decisions such as the Mandate granted by the League of Nations and the United Nations Partitions Resolution are all consigned to nothingness in a cavalier manner."[4]

Zionism is described as a "spiritual sister" and "spiritual heir" of Nazi ideology — though Nazi ideology post-dated Zionism. Zionism's original sin was its supposed calculated scheme to steal another people's land:

> The concept of a "chosen race" in Zionism differs from the concept of a "chosen race" in Nazism, only in the identity of that race — the Zionists speaking of a "Jewish race" and the Nazis of an "Aryan race." But anti-Semitism, Nazism, and Zionism are different manifestations of a racism and nationalism which grew up in the same area and in the same intellectual climate.[5]

An Arab foreign affairs expert added, "the Zionist concept of the 'final solution' to the 'Arab problem' in Palestine and the Nazi concept of the 'final solution to the Jewish Problem' in Germany consisted essentially of the same basic ingredient: the elimination of the unwanted human element in question. The creation of a 'Jew-free Germany' was indeed sought by Nazism through more ruthless and more inhuman method than was the creation of an 'Arab-free Palestine' accomplished by the Zionists: but behind the difference in techniques lay an identity of goals."[6]

The current President of the Palestinian Authority Mahmoud Abbas (Abu Mazen), claimed that the Nazis and the leadership of the Zionist movement conspired together during the war. In 1984, his doctoral dissertation for Moscow's Oriental College was published. In it he wrote:

> When discussing declared Zionist ideas, which have been espoused with profound conviction and faith by the movement's followers, one finds that they believe in the purity of the Jewish race — as Hitler believed in the purity of the Aryan race — and the movement calls for finding a deeply rooted and decisive solution to the "Jewish problem" in Europe via immigration to Palestine. Hitler also called for this, and carried it out. The Zionist movement maintains that antisemitism is an eternal problem that throbs in the Gentiles' blood; that it is not possible to put an end to it or get away from it; and thus it is the basic motive for Zionist immigration. It follows that if anti-Semitism did not exist it would be necessary to invent it, and that if its flame dies away it must be fanned. David Ben-Gurion defined the Zionist movement as immigration [to Israel] and nothing else; whoever does not immigrate [to Israel] denies the Torah and the Talmud and therefore is not a Jew. . . . These ideas provide a general dispensation to every racist in the world, most prominently Hitler and the Nazis, to treat the Jews as they wish, as long as this includes immigration to Palestine.[7]

In speaking of the Holocaust, Abu Mazen acknowledged the gravity of the catastrophe, but expressed skepticism about the concept of six million Jewish dead:

> The truth of the matter is that no one can verify this number, or completely deny it. In other words, the number of Jewish victims might be six million and might be much smaller — even less than one million. [Nevertheless], raising a discussion regarding the number of Jews [murdered] does not in any way diminish the severity of the crime committed against them, as murder — even of one man — is a crime that the civilized world cannot accept and humanity cannot accept.[8]

ARAB ANTISEMITISM: THE MOST DANGEROUS HATRED SINCE THE 1930s

Antisemitic imagery is ubiquitous in the Arab press, in countries where nearly half of the population is illiterate, and illustrates the intensity of the hatred toward Israel and the Jews by the ruling elites. Arab caricatures are direct, authentic, and a very clear example of how Arabs view the world. Caricatures regularly portray Jews as having satanic power. Israel's army is depicted as German soldiers goose-stepping on their way to further conquests.[9]

Constant use of the swastika and the idea of "Na-Zionism," a left-wing construct defining Zionism as a Judeo-Nazi fascist monster, are accepted themes in Arab propaganda. The Syrians and Egyptians adopted them after they were used in the Soviet press, and were also influenced by Nazi émigrés who found refuge in Nasser's Egypt, Syria, Lebanon, and elsewhere. *"Israel Uber Alles,"* read a caption in an Egyptian newspaper.[10]

Even today, the delegitimization of Israel as a recognized sovereign state is most Arabs' final objective, since they say they believe Israel's continued existence poses a threat to world peace. Caricatures of Jews in Arab propaganda portray all Jewish people as objects worthy of annihilation.[11]

Arab antisemitism is the most perilous expression of hatred toward Jews since the late 1930s. Arab antisemites refer to Jews as descendants of apes and pigs because the Qur'an says Jews who violated the Sabbath were turned into apes and pigs — an effective means of dehumanizing Jews and validating their need for elimination.

This message is often transmitted in political writings and in Friday sermons to Arab worshipers. At the Al-Haram mosque in Mecca, the most important Muslim holy site, they preach:

> Read history and you will understand that the Jews of yesterday are the evil fathers of the Jews of today, who are evil offspring, infidels, distorters of [God's] words, calf-worshippers, prophet-murderers, prophecy-deniers . . . the scum of the human race whom Allah cursed and turned into apes and pigs. . . . These are the Jews, an ongoing continuum of deceit, obstinacy, licentiousness, evil, and corruption.[12]

The idea that Jews have been transmogrified into pigs, apes, and other animals has become so ingrained in the mind of the Arab public that children are deeply influenced by the images. In May 2002, Iqraa, the Saudi satellite television station that strives "to highlight aspects of Arab Islamic culture that inspire admiration . . . to highlight the true, tolerant image of Islam and refute the accusations directed against it," interviewed a three-and-a-half-year-old "real Muslim girl" about Jews, on *The Muslim Women's Magazine* program.

When the little girl was asked if she liked Jews she said, "No." When asked why not, she replied that Jews were "apes and pigs" . . . [and that] "Our God" had said this "in the Qur'an." At the end of the segment, the interviewer noted with approval: "No [parents] could wish for Allah to give them a more believing girl than she. . . . May Allah bless her and both her father and mother."[13]

A common antisemitic theme is "The Promise of the Stone and the Tree," an extensively quoted *hadith* (a narration of Islamic history and biography). It asserts that prior to the Day of Judgment, the Muslims will fight and kill the Jews. Seeking sanctuary, the Jews will hide behind stones and trees, and the stones and trees will exclaim, "Oh Muslim, Oh Servant of Allah, a Jew is hiding behind me. Come and kill him."[14]

And Jews, they teach, are responsible for their own suffering:

> One might ask why so many disasters and calamities befell those people in particular. The answer to this question is not difficult. Their wicked nature, which has always alienated them from mankind, lies at the bottom of this fact. This is borne out by their history.[15]

Palestinian children have assimilated the attitudes of their parents as evidenced by the trading cards they collect. Instead of baseball cards, they save cards of terrorist "martyrs." During the first two years of the second Intifada, six million cards were sold. Children who fill albums with 129 pictures on cardboard shaped like Israeli tanks can win bicycles, computers, or other items. Their role models and heroes are guerillas and suicide bombers.

The head of the Balata teachers association says Palestinian children "are convinced that martyrdom is a holy thing, something worthy of the ultimate respect. They worship these pictures. I think it will lead them in the future to go out and do the same thing."[16]

Palestinian Text Books

In the *History of Modern and Contemporary World*, Grade 10, published in 2004 by the Palestinian Authority, are represented documents adopted at the First Zionist Congress. According to reports from the Center for the Monitoring the Impact of Peace (CMIP), an organization that monitors xenophobia in classrooms, the PA never mentions Israel as a sovereign state in the 160 schoolbooks it publishes, and the State of Israel does not appear on maps in these works.[17]

On April 11, 2005, Natan Sharansky, then Minister of Diaspora, Society and Jerusalem, wrote to Prime Minister Ariel Sharon:

> There is no doubt that this information is demonstrative of the fact that the Palestinian leadership is not demonstrating the necessary willingness to end incitement and change the threatening tone between our nations. More than that, there is an intensifying of the incitement that seeks to raise the level of anti-Semitism past that which has been present for years.[18]

"Real progress in the peace process," he continued "is not possible while incitement continues to be spread through textbooks, especially when it is intensified in the new books just introduced into the system."[19]

In May 2006, after three years of Saudi promises to reform their textbooks to stop teaching hate, and a public relations campaign that simply lied to Americans, a review of a sample of official Saudi textbooks for Islamic studies used during the current academic year reveals that, despite the Saudi government's statements to the contrary, an ideology of hatred toward Christians and Jews and Muslims who do not follow Wahhabi doctrine remains in this area of the public school system. The texts teach a dualistic vision, dividing the world into true believers of Islam (the "monotheists") and unbelievers (the "polytheists" and "infidels").[20]

This indoctrination begins in a first-grade text and is reinforced and expanded each year, culminating in a 12th-grade text instructing students that their religious obligation includes waging jihad against the infidel to "spread the faith."[21]

RELIGIOUS DIMENSION

There is a religious dimension to Muslim hostility toward Zionism. Israel is the infidel that took control of *dar el-Islam,* hallowed Muslim land. Many Muslims are angry about Jewish control over Islamic holy sites and the "potential danger" this poses to their sacredness. Jews are targets in Islam's conflict against heretics, especially those involved in trying to occupy Jerusalem and the land of Israel. The Crusades were a religious struggle, and many Muslims see the Intifada in that same light.[22]

Though Jews fared better in Muslim countries than they did in Christian lands, the belief that Jews are flawed morally and spiritually influenced the way they were treated by Muslims in the past and in the present.

A theological assertion widely accepted among Arab intellectuals is that Jews are a religious group, not a nation, and therefore are not entitled to political sovereignty. The nation of Jews is not entitled to equal rights, as are other nations. Thus, the notion of a Jewish state is inconsistent with Islamic teaching regarding the rights of religious minorities. Jews are heretics who have to be endured because of their belief in monotheism, but they are inferior and not entitled to enjoy the rights of other human beings. These ideas about Jews intensified the deeply rooted feeling of injustice in the Muslims, because they were told their land was stolen from them to establish the Jewish state. But they were not the key factor of Muslim hostility against Israel.

From a religious perspective, Israel is seen as the West's representative in the Middle East, bent on undermining the social, religious, and moral values of Islam. Familiarity with the Jewish State does not lessen the animosity. In Israel, observant Muslims see the decadence and depravity of the West as a direct threat to the mores of Muslim society.[23]

WESTERN INFLUENCE

Western antisemitic myths found fertile ground in the Middle East — even those regarded as so excessively primitive that have been discredited by antisemites in the West. Among them are *The Protocols of the Elders of Zion,* blood libels, and the accusation that the Jews killed Jesus.[24] The other topic that took hold is Holocaust denial.

The Protocols originated in Russia during the 19th century and claimed that Jewish elders conspired to gain control of the world by manipulating the financial markets and by directing the media and political arena.[25]

Significantly, a number of educated Arabs attribute the *Protocols* to Zionism and not to the Jews. They maintain the *Protocols* are authentic, but are of Zionist origin. The problem is that the *Protocols* assume a Jewish plot, not a Zionist one. When asked if Zionism is the source of the Zionists' aspiration to rule the world, they counter that this repugnant ambition comes from the notion of being the "chosen people." This concept is Jewish because it comes from the Bible, not Zionism. The claim that Zionism uses Eretz Israel (the Land of Israel) to launch its program for world domination demonizes Zionism and the Jewish people.[26]

The authenticity of the *Protocols* is, for the most part, accepted as "axiomatic" in the Arab world. Some Arab writers dealing with Jewish matters rank the *Protocols* behind the Bible and the Talmud in terms of importance to Judaism.[27]

At various times, the *Protocols* were cited or publicly recommended by Presidents Gamal Abdul-Nasser and Anwar Sadat of Egypt, President Arif of Iraq, Colonel Qaddafi of Libya, King Faysal of Saudi Arabia, and other kings, prime ministers, intellectual, political, and religious leaders in Arab lands.

To this day, major publishing houses, including those owned by Arab governments, publish the *Protocols*. The lies in the book are often quoted in the media by respected magazines and newspapers and on national radio and television stations. They are used in some textbooks on every level — from kindergarten to graduate school — as a basis of discussion about the Jewish people and Judaism. Agencies in several Arab countries, including Iran, have disseminated the *Protocols* and other antisemitic literature, saturating Africa and Southeast Asia with hate literature.[28]

As a result, no one was shocked when the Egyptians produced 41 episodes of a TV series called "A Knight without a Horse." On November 6, 2002, a number of Arab television stations broadcast the first episode, recalling the defeat of the Arabs in 1948 by the "Children of Zion, who "took it [the land] with treachery.""[29]

Most of the Arab press disagreed with some Arabs and those in the West who condemned the series or had reservations about it. The U.S. State Department went so far as to ask the Egyptian government to stop showing the program. A few Arab writers took issue with what they viewed as Egypt's fixation with antisemitic writings.[30]

In response to the severe condemnation, Osama el-Baz, Egyptian president Mubarak's chief political advisor, responded in a series of three articles published in *Al-Ahram*. Arguing that antisemitism is a European phenomenon and alien to Islam and the Arab world, he wrote, "There is a large body of evidence suggesting the *Protocols* were a forgery. It is hardly credible that a handful of individuals from a small minority should meet and set down their scheme to rule the world in a 110-page pamphlet that would be exposed sooner or later."[31]

Osama el-Baz
(Credit: UN Photo)

At an exhibit at the newly renovated Alexandria Library in Egypt in November 2003, Dr. Yousef Ziedan, director of manuscript museum at the library and an avowed Holocaust denier, placed the *Protocols* next to the Torah until pressured to remove it. In an interview explaining why he did that, he said:

> Although it is not a monotheistic holy book, it has become one of the sacred [tenets] of the Jews, next to their first constitution, their religious law, [and] their way of life. In other words, it is not merely an ideological or theoretical book. Perhaps . . . [it] is more important to the Zionist Jews of the world than the Torah, because they conduct Zionist life according to it. . . . It is only natural to place the book in the framework of an exhibit of Torah [scrolls].[32]

In response to attacks against the library for displaying the *Protocols* (and then removing it), Dr. Ismail Serageldin, the library's director, said the *Protocols* was never displayed next to the Torah, but in a showcase with other unusual items. He explained that the book was an example of hate literature and called those promoting the book "stupid." Those who attacked the library were harming the cause of Arab and Muslim rights.[33]

Dr. Riad Al-Astal, a history lecturer at Al-Azhar University in Gaza, explained on Palestinian Authority television in December 2003, how the *Protocols* were presented at the first Zionist Congress in Basel, Switzerland, in 1897:

... to plan the exploitation of the powers' struggle and the struggle of Europe over the Middle East. . . . The European states of course welcomed this idea and were striving to plant Israel as a functional state, which will serve Imperialism, and as a bridgehead for ruling over the world, the Near East and from there the Middle East and the Far East. . . . [T]he international conspiracy was bigger than us [the Palestinian People].[34]

Other writers and intellectuals recognize that the *Protocols* are forged, but continue to use them, arguing that it does not matter whether they are fact or fiction: Their predictions have largely come true.

Lebanese Christian journalist Ghassan Tueni provides an excellent example of this thinking:

Had we not known that *The Protocols of the Elders of Zion* were forged by Russian intelligentsia in the 19th century . . . we would say that what is happening in the world today is exactly what world Jewry planned, due to the great similarity [between what is actually happening and] what is falsely attributed [in the *Protocols*] to [world Jewry]. [I refer] to the conspiracy to take over the world and to plunder it; to the deeds [of world Jewry] everywhere, and to the financial, political, and military status [world Jewry] has attained. This is in addition to their attempt to destroy everything that others hold sacred.[35]

A few individuals, including Dr. Sadeq Jala al-Azm, Osama el-Baz, and Dr. Abd al-Wahhab al-Masiri, author of an Arabic-language encyclopedia of Judaism, are exceptions to this rule and reject the authenticity of the *Protocols*.[36]

On Al-Nas television in Egypt on June 21, 2006, "Today's Lesson for Egyptian Children": "The Jews are the people of treachery, betrayal, and vileness" was a story from Islamic tradition in which a Jewish woman tried to poison Muhammad. After telling the story, the sheikh took a call from a child viewer. "Ruqaya, what did you learn from today's show?" the sheikh asked. "I learned that the Jews are the people of treachery and betrayal. . . ."[37]

Sheikh Al-Din interrupted the caller, shouting, "Allah Akbar!" Turning to the children in the studio, he instructed:

Say Allah Akbar! What did Ruqiya say? The Jews are the people of treachery and betrayal. May Allah give you success. We want mothers who teach their sons Jihad, the love of Allah and His messenger, sacrifice for the sake of Islam, and love for the countries of the Muslims. Loving the country of the Muslims. May Allah bless you, Ruqaya. That is the most beautiful thing I have heard — that the Jews are the people of treachery, betrayal, and vileness.

On June 15, 2006, the program for children promoted Jihad against "infidels." The host of the program, Sheikh Muhammad Nassar of the Egyptian ministry of religious endowment, told the children about the courage of a child, and how, when a child is brought up in a good home, and receives proper education, he loves martyrdom.[38]

BLOOD LIBEL: REBIRTH

To offer credence to the concept of Zionist attempts to destroy other peoples, Israelis were blamed for poisoning Arab middle school girls in the village of Arrabeh, near Jenin. On March 21, 1983, a number of schoolgirls complained of nausea, headaches, problems with vision, and drowsiness. Some vomited and fainted. A number were sent to the hospital in Jenin, where no physiological reason was found for this "mass phenomenon." Five days later, 56 girls at the Zahra Middle School in Jenin complained of similar symptoms and were sent to a private clinic in the town, the local hospital, and as more students from nearby villages came in for treatment, they were sent to hospitals throughout the West Bank.

Three hundred and ten girls from five different schools were hospitalized by the beginning of April, all suffering from the "Jenin Syndrome." Serious cases were sent to Rambam Hospital in Haifa for analysis and treatment. Cases were also reported in Hebron, Anabta, and in the village of Matlul. Israelis were accused of attempting to interfere with the ability of these young Palestinian girls to procreate.

To forestall the possibility of negative international repercussions, the Centers for Disease Control in Atlanta launched an independent investigation, the World Health Organization sent a team, and so did the Red Cross. They found no physiological evidence to explain the phenomenon; it was diagnosed as mass hysteria among Arab girls.[39]

From December 13, 2004, Iran's Sahar 1 TV station ran a weekly series called *For You, Palestine*, or *Zahra's Blue Eyes*, showing "mad" Israeli doctors stealing eyes and organs from Palestinian children.[40]

In Arab lands, there is a new blood libel accusing Jews of using blood in the traditional *hamantaschen*, a fruit-filled pastry that is eaten on the holiday of Purim. The original blood libel, which accused Jews of putting blood in Passover matzoth, was linked to the Christian notion of transubstantiation — the *matzoh* of the Last Supper as the flesh of Jesus and the wine as His blood.

The blood in the *matzoh* fiction has been around for a long time. Originally, Jews were charged with killing a Christian, preferably a child, on Easter to denigrate Jesus on the day commemorating His crucifixion. Since Easter and Passover occur at the same time each year, the story grew to include the accusation that Jews used "the blood of their victims in religious rituals. . . . It was also said that Jews used blood in the manufacture of medicines."[41]

Syrian Defense Minister Field Marshal Mustafa Tlass played a key role in bringing the blood libel to "canonical" importance through his book *The Matzoth of Zion*. The book was published by the Syrian government, became required reading by the Syrian military, and it is still a best seller in the Arab world. The book was used to mobilize Syrian troops and citizens against the Jewish state.[42]

The Supreme Court of Paris subpoenaed Ibrahim Naafi, editor of the Egyptian daily *Al-Ahram*, in August 2002, for inciting antisemitism and racist violence by publishing "Jewish *matza* is made from Arab blood" in the October 28, 2000, edition of his paper. The article linked the 1840 Damascus blood libel with Israel's military actions in the West Bank, where they are accused of using Arab blood in making *matzoh* for Passover.[43]

Accusations against Naafi, chair of the Arab Journalists' Union and its senior representative, created resentment, indignation, and anger throughout the Arab world. The Arab media called the charges "intellectual terrorism," "a Zionist attack on the Egyptian press," "extortion by the Zionist lobby in France," "a blow to freedom of expression," and "an insult to the entire Arab press."[44]

Osama el-Baz, an advisor to Mubarak, objected to antisemitic canards because "the Arab cause is just and there is no excuse for borrowing from a legacy inconsistent with the tenets of our beliefs and the realities of our history, no excuse for not presenting our cause in its proper logical and moral framework."[45] He asked the Arabs to stop exploiting the *Protocols* and the myth of Jews using Christian blood in their rituals in their attacks against the Jewish State. "We should not sympathize in any way with Hitler or Nazism. The crimes they committed were abominable, abhorrent to our religion and beliefs."[46]

DEICIDE, KILLING JESUS

Blaming Jews for killing Jesus is a cliché in Arab circles. When the Palestinian militants took refuge in the Church of the Nativity and the statue of the Virgin Mary was damaged, Bassam Abu Sharif, a former spokesman for Yasser Arafat, wrote:

> The sad smile of the Virgin Mary as she shields her son, the Messiah, did not prevent the soldiers of the Israeli occupation from taking up positions to shoot at the face of this Palestinian angel, i.e., Jesus, and murder the smile so as to murder what they hadn't managed to murder throughout 2,000 years. In Bethlehem, a new crime was committed. . . . This, of course, was a failed attempt to murder peace, love, and tolerance, just as their forefathers tried to murder the prophetic message when they hammered their nails and iron stakes through the body of Jesus into the wooden cross.[47]

This thinking is contrary to Islamic belief, which teaches that Jesus was not murdered or crucified, but that Allah brought him to heaven, and a "likeness" of

Neturei Karta, a marginal, but vocal, fervently
Orthodox group of Jews, carrying anti-Israel signs.

In front of the Israeli Consulate, April 28, 2005
(Credit: Fred Askew Photography)

Jesus was crucified instead. This "likeness" is identified as the Jew the Romans forced to help Jesus carry the cross or as Judas Iscariot, who betrayed Jesus. The Qur'an speaks of the Jews' opposition to Jesus and the apostles, but also states clearly that the Jews did not kill or crucify Him.[48]

Jews Against Israel

Israel not only has to defend herself from non-Jews who question the legitimacy of the Jewish state, but from some Israelis and Jews as well. Most of them come from the left. Sometimes these anti-Zionist assaults are indistinguishable from those of non-Jews. Some justify their hostility by using their family's experiences in the Holocaust. Others defend their actions because they are Jews or have some connection with the Jewish state. Unfortunately, Arabs and their sympathizers who attack Israel use the statements these Jews make to provide legitimization for their negative views.[49]

These attacks are also used to demonstrate that the American Jewish community is divided on critical issues affecting Israel. The *Boston Globe*, for example, published two pictures of Israel's 55th Independence parade that illustrates the problem: one showed groups of pro-Israel participants carrying Israeli flags; the other was a picture of the Neturei Karta, a marginal, but vocal, fervently Orthodox group of Jews carrying anti-Israel signs. People could easily conclude that there was an equal number of each group at the parade.[50]

What distinguishes this form of Jew hatred from legitimate criticism of Israel? "Anti-Zionism . . . is a form of anti-Semitism when Zionism is described by the extreme right, the extreme left, and also by parts of Arab-Muslim circles as the evil of the world and therefore can be used easily as a wanted scapegoat. This implies the fight against the existence of Israel."[51]

In other words, reasonable criticism of Israel becomes antisemitism when "Israel and the Jews are reproached for replicating the most horrific crimes of the National Socialists — apartheid, ethnic cleansing, crimes against humanity, genocide."

In this case, "demonizing [sic] of the Jews is transferred to the state of Israel (striving for world power, the vindictiveness and cruelty of 'an eye for an eye,' the greed of capitalism and colonialism)." In judging statements critical of Israel, we must determine if "a double standard is being set, i.e., Israel is evaluated differently from other states, whether false historical parallels are drawn (comparison with the National Socialists), and whether anti-Semitic myths and stereotypes are used to characterize [sic] Israeli politics."[52]

Endnotes

1. Yehoshafat Harkabi, *The Palestinian Covenant and Its Meaning* (Portland, OR: Vallentine Mitchell, 1979), p. 117.

2. Y. Harkabi, *Arab Attitudes to Israel* (Jerusalem: Israel Universities Press, 1974), p. 175.

3. Harkabi, *The Palestinian Covenant and Its Meaning*, p. 12.

4. Ibid.; Shmuel Ettinger, "Anti-Semitism in Our Time," *The Jerusalem Quarterly* no. 23, (Spring 1982): p. 95–113.

5. Harkabi, *Arab Attitudes to Israel*, p. 171, 176.

6. Ibid. Dr. Fayez A. Sayegh, Senior Consultant to the Kuwait Ministry of Foreign Affairs is the expert quoted.

7. "Palestine Leader: Number of Jewish Victims in the Holocaust Might be 'Even Less Than a Million . . .' Zionist Movement Collaborated with Nazis to 'Expand the Mass Extermination,' " (Washington, DC: The Middle East Media Research Institute [MEMRI], Number 95, May 30, 2002), Online.

8. Ibid.

9. Arieh Stav, *Peace: The Arabian Caricature: A Study of Anti-Semitic Imagery* (Jerusalem: Gefen Publishing House, 1999), p. 18, 79, 183–184, 198–199, 240.

10. Ibid.

11. Ibid; Bernard Lewis, "The Arab World Discovers Anti-Semitism," *Commentary* (May 1986): p. 52.

12. Menahem Milson, "What Is Arab Antisemitism?" MEMRI Special Report Number 26 (February 27, 2004).

13. Ibid.

14. Ibid.

15. Quoted in Stave, *Peace: The Arabian Caricature*, p. 99; see also MEMRI Special Dispatch, Number 86 (April 12, 2000), Online.

16. "Palestinian Kids Collect Terrorist Cards," *Jerusalem Post* (December 25, 2003), Online; "Educating children for hatred and terrorism: encouragement for suicide bombing attacks and hatred for Israel and the Jews spread via the Internet on Hamas' online children's magazine (Al-Fateh)," *C.S.S.* (October, 2004); Matthew McAllester, "The Roots of Hatred: Decades after the Holocaust, a different anti-Semitism prevails," Newsday.com (January 18, 2004), Online; "Israel/Occupied Territories: Palestinian Armed Groups Must Not Use Children," Amnesty International (May 23, 2005), Online.

17. Joseph Dan, "Jewish Sovereignty as a Theological Problem," *Azure* (Winter 2004), Online.

18. "New PA Text Books Teach Anti-Semitic Forgery as History [Palestinian Authority Promotes "Protocols."] *Arutz*, 7 (April 11, 2005), Online.

19. Ibid.

20. Ibid.

21. Nina Shea, "This Is a Saudi Textbook (After the Intolerance Was Removed)," Washingtonpost.com (May 21, 2006), p. B01.

22. Ibid.

23. Joseph Dan, "Jewish Sovereignty as a Theological Problem," *Azure* (Winter 2004), Online.

24. Ibid; see also Manfred Gerstenfeld, "An Interview with Meir Litvak: The Development of Arab Anti-Semitism," Jerusalem Center for Public Affairs, Number 5 (February 2003), Online.

25. Milson, "What Is Arab Antisemitism?"

26. Norman Cohn, *Warrant For Genocide: The Myth of the Jewish World Conspiracy and the Protocols of the Elders of Zion* (London: Eyre and Spottiswoode, 1967); Hadassa Ben-Itto, *The Lie That Wouldn't Die: The Protocols of the Elders of Zion* (Portland, OR: Vallentine Mitchell); Steven Jacobs and Mark Weitzman, *Dismantling the Big Lie: The Protocols of the Elders of Zion* (Jersey City, NJ: KTAV Publishing House, Inc, 2003).

27. Yehoshafat Harkabi, "Arab Positions on Zionism," ed. Shmuel Almog, *Zionism and the Arabs* (Jerusalem: The Historical Society of Israel and the Zalman Shazar Center, 1983), p. 192; Daniel Pipes, "The Politics of Muslim Anti-Semitism," *Commentary* (August 1981): p. 41–45.

28. Lewis, "The Arab World Discovers Anti-Semitism," p. 30–33; Reuven Ehrlich, Part A "The Protocols of the Elders of Zion: The Renaissance of Anti-Semitic Hate Literature in the Arab and Islamic World," Hate Industry (C.S.S), Online.

29. Lewis, "The Arab World Discovers Anti-Semitism," p. 30–31.

30. "Arab Press Debates Antisemitic Egyptian Series 'A Knight Without a Horse,' " MEMRI Inquiry and Analysis Series, Number 109 (November 8, 2002), Online.

31. Ibid; In his weekly column in the London Arabic-language daily *Al-Hayat*, Mark Sayegh protested the series, which he acknowledged was founded on a forgery. "The historic truth does not interest some in the Arab and Egyptian 'elite,' " he claimed. "For example, instead of demanding that their government cancel the peace agreement with Israel — the agreement that has been carried out successfully for a quarter of a century — some Cairo artists turn to drums, microphones, and media idiocy that exacerbate the Palestinians' situation." "Arab Press Debates Antisemitic Egyptian Series 'A Knight Without a Horse,' " MEMRI Inquiry and Analysis Series, Number 113 (November 20, 2002), Online. Writing in Al-Hayat's movie column, Ibrahim Al-Arabi also objected to the airing of the series: ". . . By means of the series, the art of Arab television managed to place itself at the heart of a lengthy debate, going back over 150 years, about the book, which today is known with certainty to be a 'fabrication' by the Russian Czar's secret police aimed at justifying attacks on the Russian Jews. This book always served fascist, racist, and antisemitic regimes, for stepping up persecution of the Jews — with a more disastrous result for the Arabs than for the Jews, as it turned into a political and historic argument supporting the idea of a 'national homeland for the Jews' and the establishment of [the State of] Israel. . . ." "Arab Press Debates Antisemitic Egyptian Series 'A Knight Without a Horse,' " MEMRI Inquiry and Analysis Series, Number 109.

32. "Egypt's Response to Accusation of Arab Media Antisemitism." MEMRI (January 8, 2003), Online.

33. "Jewish Holy Books on Display at the Alexandria Library: Torah & the 'Protocols of the Elders of Zion,' " (MEMRI) Special Dispatch Series Number 619 (December 3, 2003).

34. "Al-Ahram on the Aftermath of a MEMRI Report about the Display of the 'Protocols of the Elders of Zion' at the Alexandria Library," MEMRI Special Dispatch Series, Number 671 (March 2, 2004).

35. Itamar Marcus, "The Protocols of the Elders of Zion and Denying Israel's Right to Exist — Today on Palestinian Authority Educational TV," *Palestinian Media Watch Bulletin* (December 28, 2003), Online.

36. Menahem Milson, *Countering Arab Antisemitism* (Jerusalem: World Jewish Congress), p. 12–13.

37. Menahem Milson, "The New Anti-Semitic Axis," *The International Jerusalem Post* (April 11, 2003): p. 12.

38. Nissan Ratzlav-Katz, "Egyptian TV Promoting Anti-Semitism and Child 'Martyrdom,' " Israel National Radio (July 4, 2006), Online.

39. Raphael Israeli, *Poison: Modern Manifestations of a Blood Libel* (Lanham, MD: Lexington Books, 2002), p. 4–31. A senior Arab doctor at the Hebron Hospital who examined dozens of girls and a teacher could not find any indication of physical illness, p. 15, 27.

40. MEMRI TV Project Special Report: "Iranian TV Drama Series about Israeli Government Stealing Palestinian Children's Eyes," MEMRI Special Dispatch Series, Number 833 (December 22, 2004), Online.

41. Milson, "Countering Arab Antisemitism," p. 11–12; "Anti-Semitic Blood Libel in Egypt's al-Ahram," *SRI* (October 2000); "Holocaust Denial in Egypt," *SRI* (October 14, 1998).

42. Stav, *Peace: The Arabian Caricature*, p. 232; "*The Damascus Blood Libel (1840)* as told by Syria's Minister of Defense, Mustafa Tlass," MEMRI. Inquiry and Analysis Series, No. 99 (July 27, 2002).

43. "Egypt's Response to Accusations of Arab Media Antisemitism," (MEMRI) Special Dispatch Series, No. 454 (January 3, 2003).

44. "French Legal Authorities Investigating Editor of Major Egyptian Daily for Antisemitism," MEMRI Inquiry and Analysis Series, Number 107 (September 6, 2002), Online.

45. "Egypt's Response to Accusations of Arab Media Antisemitism," (MEMRI) Special Dispatch Series; Bassam Za'za' and Tanya Goudsouzian, "America, Israel Waging Campaign to Blot Out Reality-Al Manar," *Gulf News* (October 10, 2003), Online.

46. Ibid.

47. Bassam Abu Sharif wrote this in his weekly column in the London-based Saudi Arabian daily,*Al-Sharq Al-Awsat,* MEMRI Special Dispatch Series, Number 362 (April 5, 2002); Milson, "The New Antisemitic Axis," p. 12; Stav, *Peace: The Arabian Caricature*, p. 19, 20–21, 29, 31, 34–35, 59, 71.

48. Qur'an 4: 157–158; Aluma Dankowitz, "Reactions in the Arab Media to *The Passion of the Christ,*"MEMRI Inquiry and Analysis Series, Number 171 (April 20, 2004).

49. Manfred Gerstenfeld, "Jews Against Israel," Jerusalem Center for Public Affairs, Number 30 (March 1, 2005), Online; see also, Matthew Rothschild, "Israel Isn't David . . . It's Goliath," *The Progressive,* Online; Anat Biletzki, Andre Draznin, Haim Hanegbi, Yehudith Harel, Michel (Micado) Warschawski, and Oren Medicks, "For Truth and Reconciliation, For Equality and Partnership," *The Olga Document* (July 2004), Online; Ari Packer, "Anti-Semitism from a Jewish pro-Palestinian Perspective," Jewish Friends of Palestine: An Online Initiative of Jewish Activists for a Free Palestine; Fiamma Nirenstein, *Terror: The New Anti-Semitism and the War Against the West* (Hanover: NH, Smith and Kraus Global, 2005); Phyllis Chesler, *The New Anti-Semitism: The Current Crisis and What We Must Do About It* (San Francisco, CA: Jossey-Bass, 2003); Just Peace UK, Online; Brian Whitaker, "Hate Mail," *The Guardian* (January 19, 2004), Online; Amira Hass, "No End to the Growing Settlements Insult," *Ha'aretz* (July 2, 2003); Amira Hass, "The Revolt of the Guinea-Pigs," *Ha'aretz* (February 21, 2001); Amira Hass, "All the Way from the Sea to the River," *Ha'aretz* (May 30, 2001); Tanya Reinhart, "Right For Both Peoples," *Yediot Aharonot* (March 27, 2001); Amos Elon, "Israelis and Palestinians: What Went Wrong?" vol. 49, no. 20 (December 19, 2002); Danny Rabinowitz, "Along with the Star of David," *Ha'aretz* (May 26, 2005); Steve Erlanger, "Israel's 'Mr. TV' Faults Settlements in Documentary," *NYT* (May 31, 2005), p. A3.

50. Gerstenfeld, "Jews Against Israel."

51. "Manifestations of Anti-Semitism in the European Union," unpublished EU Report, EU on Anti-Semitism in Europe (December 1, 2003), Online.

52. Ibid.

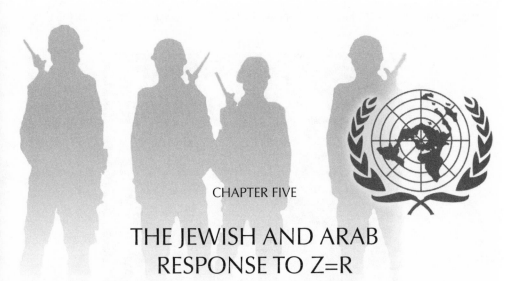

CHAPTER FIVE

THE JEWISH AND ARAB
RESPONSE TO Z=R

JEWISH RESPONSE

The Israeli government was outraged when the Third Committee passed the Z=R resolution. To dramatize the contempt Israel and the Jewish people had for the resolution, Chaim Herzog, the Israeli ambassador, stood up at the podium and shocked everyone, including the photographers, when he ripped the resolution to pieces. The inspiration for this dramatic gesture came from his late father, Chief Rabbi Isaac Yitzhak Halevy Herzog, who tore up the British White Paper in the Yeshurun Synagogue in Jerusalem in 1939.[1]

Immediately after the Third Committee passed the resolution and sent it to the full Assembly for approval, Moynihan strode over to Herzog and embraced him in a gesture of friendship and solidarity.[2]

The timing was eerie. In his speech before the members of the General Assembly, Herzog recalled how exactly 37 years earlier on that night of November 9 and 10, the Nazis had launched the first pogrom of the Holocaust in Germany and Austria. Z=R, he said, was the first "major international antisemitic attack on world Jewry since the days of the Third Reich." Quoting Abba Eban, a former UN Ambassador and Foreign Minister of Israel, Herzog described how the UN had begun "as an anti-Nazi alliance," but was becoming the "world center for anti-Semitism."[3]

When Z=R was first proposed in the Third Committee, the resolution infuriated and offended Jews and people of conscience around the world. There were demonstrations, meetings of world Jewish leaders in Jerusalem, plans to boycott the countries that supported the resolution, and crash programs in the United States to teach American Jews and the American public about Zionism. But American Jewish leadership feared that the resolution would require UN members to report on

Israeli UN Ambassador Chaim Herzog
(Courtesy of Israeli Government Photo Office)

U.S. efforts to eradicate racism and Zionism. The Soviet Union would have a UN-sanctioned excuse to destroy the movement of Jews seeking to immigrate to Israel. Brazil, one of the three Latin American countries that voted for the resolution in the Third Committee, thought it might curb the active Zionist groups there.[4]

Under the caption ". . . this is an obscene act," the Conference of Presidents of Major Jewish Organizations placed a full-page advertisement in the *New York Times* on Sunday, October 26, denouncing the attack on Zionism as "an assault against the values of democracy and civilization that all Americans cherish."[5] A coupon attached to the ad brought in thousands of dollars to the Presidents Conference from concerned individuals in every part of the United States and around the world. Each donor received a thank you letter with other suggestions on how they might help. The money the Conference received enabled it to place additional advertisements in other newspapers.[6]

Malcolm Hoenlein, executive director of the Greater New York Conference on Soviet Jewry (1971–1976) and then executive director of the Jewish Community Relations Council of Greater New York (1976–1986), worked behind the scenes with the UN missions and with Senator Moynihan and his staff. He also worked with Dr. David Luchins and the American Jewish community to fight the resolution publicly and privately.[7] The Presidents Conference held a seminar at the UN before the vote, but in the end nothing could be done to stop the resolution from being passed.[8]

Moynihan became the major public spokesman against the resolution. He visited the editorial offices of all the leading newspapers to ask for assistance in fighting Z=R. Soon Herzog was inundated with an avalanche of mail and cables. He received two sacks of mail a day from Jews and non-Jews; people wore buttons proudly proclaiming "I am a Zionist," and the resolution was constantly in the headlines.[9] The Israeli government and the World Zionist Organization (WZO) invited representatives of 27 countries to Jerusalem in early December 1975 to sign a declaration pledging aid to Israel "to fulfill its historic mission in the return to Zion." At the end of the two-day conference, Prime Minister Yitzhak Rabin told the delegates, "We have to undermine the moral right of this organization to pass judgment on us."[10]

The Conference of Presidents arranged a mass rally against racism and antisemitism on November 11 in anticipation of the presentation of the draft resolution

Malcolm Hoenlein
(Photo courtesy of Malcolm Hoenlein)

"...this is an obscene act."

With these words the U.S. Representative to the United Nations Third Committee denounced the vote equating Zionism with racism, a vote which he said put the UN "at the point of officially endorsing anti-Semitism."

How are Americans to respond to what our government's spokesman called "a supreme act of deceit...a massive attack on the moral realities of the world"?

1) We commend our government and our representatives at the United Nations—Ambassador Daniel Patrick Moynihan, Clarence Mitchell Jr., and Leonard Garment—for leading the struggle at the UN against the perversion of truth. We are proud of our country and its spokesmen for recognizing that Zionism, the national liberation movement of the Jewish people, derives from the very principles of liberty and justice for all that inspired the founding of our own country.

2) We welcome the action of those Western democracies and African and other states that resisted the threats and pressure of the Arab oil billionaires and refused to take part in the immoral act of condemning Zionism.

3) We will remember those totalitarian dictatorships—Arab, Communist and Fascist—that made Friday, October 17 a day of shame in the history of nations. We will not forget how Chile voted, nor that Cuba joined hands with the Arab states in sponsoring the resolution. We will not forget that East Germany voted for it; that Brazil, India, Mexico and Turkey went along; that Franco Spain and Soviet Russia joined Idi Amin's Uganda. All voted for anti-Semitism.

4) Finally, we will resist the obscene attempt to equate Zionism with racism as we defend democracy against religious bigotry and anti-Americanism in the United Nations and around the world. For we know that this anti-Zionism campaign is an attack against the State of Israel, against the Jewish religion, against the Jewish people. It is an assault against the values of democracy and civilization that all Americans cherish. It is a horrifying reminder of the Nazi campaign that began with words of hate and ended with acts of extermination.

In this struggle, we look for support to all men and women, of every race and religion, who love freedom. If you are moved to join with us in this effort, please use this coupon.

Conference of Presidents of Major Jewish Organizations ad in *New York Times*.
(Courtesy of Conference of Presidents)

to the General Assembly plenary. Designed to "voice the feelings of all Americans about the obnoxious and obscene display of anti-Semitism at the United Nations," the two-hour protest was scheduled to begin at noon at the Brotherhood-in-Action Plaza in the heart of the Garment Center.[11]

The protestors came from metropolitan New York and all along the Atlantic coast and the interior. They even came from Canada. The city was filled with 300 chartered buses from Pittsburgh, Baltimore, New Haven, Hartford, and Boston. Others came from Atlanta, Chicago, Maine, Montreal, and Toronto. Some people flew into the city on short notice.[12] Thousands of members from the Ladies Garment Workers Union, the Amalgamated Clothing Workers Union, attended the rally. Many other labor unions lent their support as well.

Speeches were made by men and women of note, including the then dean of the Senate, Jacob K. Javits (R-NY); Clarence Mitchell, deputy to Senator Moynihan; Leah Rabin, wife of Prime Minister Yitzhak Rabin; David M. Blumberg, president of B'nai B'rith; Bayard Rustin, president of the A. Philip Randolph Institute; the late Betty Friedan, founder of the National Organization of Women (NOW); the Right Reverend Paul Moore, Episcopal Bishop of New York; Monsignor James F. Rigney, rector of St. Patrick's Cathedral; Paul O'Dwyer, New York City Council president; Rabbi Israel Miller, chairman of the Conference of Presidents of Major Jewish Organizations; and Rabbi Arthur Hertzberg, president of the American Jewish Congress.[13]

Demonstrators spilling out from the Brotherhood-in-Action Plaza at the Conference of Presidents of Major Jewish Organizations rally against racism and antisemitism.

(Courtesy of Conference of Presidents)

Rallies were held at the same time in Chicago and Miami. News conferences to protest the resolution were held in Los Angeles, Detroit, Cleveland, Denver, and Baltimore.[14]

Most Israeli diplomats and government officials believed that the resolution was so outrageous and embarrassing to the majority of the UN member states that it would shortly cease to be an issue. Responding to the charges would only give the resolution undue weight and grant Z=R credibility. The failure to grasp the long-term threat to the State of Israel and Jews in the Diaspora helps explain Israel's reluctance to engage in the fight at the UN.

Israeli leaders did not want to know about the negative effects the resolution created. They believed no one could properly determine whether the damage to the Jews and to Israel was caused by the resolution or by all the other assaults on Zionism at the UN and elsewhere.[15]

Prime Minister Yitzhak Rabin stated the purpose of Z=R was "to deny Israel its right of existence," and "to prepare the ground for the establishment of an 'Arafatian state' in place of and on the ruins of the State of Israel."[16] Before the huge demonstration in New York, Herzog believed American Jews took the situation too lightly. Only after American diplomats, politicians, and writers were involved did Herzog see serious activity from American Jewish organizations. Leadership missed the point because they may have been dismissing the significance of Z=R by viewing it as yet just another ideological assault by the Soviets and the Third World against Israel in the UN.[17]

With the delayed American Jewish reaction and the noise in the press finally getting noticed, it dawned on the Israelis that something needed to be done to address the anti-Zionist resolution. Cultural minister Aharon Yadlin announced that education about Zionism would be a top priority and that Zionist values, history, and vision would be taught to counter the effects of Z=R. Israeli Defense Minister Moshe Dayan told a press conference in Skokie, Illinois, that the Jewish people had experienced expressions of hostility and lack of understanding for 4,000 years, and that the fate of Zionism would be determined by the Jewish people and not the UN.[18]

Herzog, said Yigal Allon, the Israeli Foreign Minister, was the only person who appreciated the danger, and was the one who told the Belgian Parliament that Zionism would protect its own interests, but that the UN itself was in extreme danger. Allon assumed that the resolution would inflict minimal and temporary damage on the Jewish people and Israel. To prevent voting blocs from passing resolutions contrary to the spirit of the UN Charter, Allon suggested the Charter be amended, and he was ignored.[19]

Recalcitrant Israeli Reaction to the Resolution

The Israelis were also reluctant to openly attack Z=R because they feared it would focus attention on the political rights of the Palestinians when they were not prepared to make any concessions. Political power struggles between the World Jewish Congress (WJC) and the World Zionist Organization (WZO) ensued. The disagreement centered on how to respond and what role WZO would assume in the conflict.

The World Jewish Congress is the representative body of Jewish communities and organizations in nearly 100 countries across six continents. Its mission is to assist Jews and Jewish communities around the world. As part of the Jewish Agency, the World Zionist Organization is responsible for working with youth in the Diaspora. Both organizations believed they were to lead in the fight against the UN resolution. The WJC recognized the insidious nature of the UN campaign against the Jews and Israel. They saw the increase in antisemitic acts, especially in the West, as isolated and disconnected, not as part of a serious resurgence of antisemitism, and decided to focus on fighting antisemitism, which contained "anti-Zionism in its anti-Semitic form," and viewed the WZO's program as superfluous.[20]

The WZO was not willing to concede its role in fighting anti-Zionism to anyone. As "the organization of the Zionist movement . . . there is no other organization," declared Eli Eyal, chairman of the Department of Information of the WZO. "There can be no situation in which the fight against anti-Zionism shall not be waged by the Zionist Movement and the Zionist Organization. . . . From the very moment that the word Zionism becomes synonymous with obloquy or odium in whatever form — it is a victory for our enemy."[21]

What he was saying was that just as Israel does not ask Americans or other foreign nationals to fight on its behalf, the WZO doesn't need anyone to fight its battles. They can manage themselves.[22] What especially disturbed Eyal was that the UN draft resolution was co-sponsored by Fidel Castro's Communist government with the right-wing government of Chile's General Augusto Pinochet — who allegedly traded his vote to the Arabs to forestall UN censure of his own genocidal acts. No other issue could have united the far left and the far right, and so clearly demonstrated that the Jews would be scapegoats, on international and personal levels.[23]

In 1982, Dr. Yohanan Manor, the WZO's Director General of Information, met with the heads of organizations fighting anti-Zionism in France, Canada, England, and the United States to learn what they were doing to combat anti-Zionism and present them with an update. He wanted to hold demonstrations everywhere to protest the defamation of Zionism, and lamented "the neglect of proper Zionist *hasbara* (public relations)."[24]

Manor asked Jewish organizations to support a WZO conference in Paris, where major personalities would be appointed to a task force to fight anti-Zionism. A number of distinguished Jews and non-Jews from across the political and religious spectrum agreed to sponsor "Anti-Zionism — Danger to the Democratic Process."[25]

Political infighting, ideological differences, organizational discord, personal resentments, and reluctance to raise issues about Palestinian policy doomed the conference from the beginning. In its place, the Zionist Congress held a special session on antisemitism, and almost no mention was made of Z=R or the suggested task force. American-Jewish leadership was also reluctant to engage in a campaign against Z=R. They either followed Israel's lead or were worried that dissenting Americans would accuse them of dual loyalty.

Manor believed the Jewish establishment wrongly assumed that ignorance of Zionism was the cause of the problem and didn't realize how serious it really was. He saw the debasement of Zionism as a unifying factor in a global campaign to eliminate the Zionist/Jewish example of autonomy and freedom as a model for oppressed peoples throughout the world. He understood that the goal of anti-Zionists was to weaken "the very foundations of the West," by undermining "international law and order." The resolution was an effective propaganda tool. And as long as the anti-Zionists did not declare their real objective — the destruction of Israel — their activities were [and are] viewed as legal and legitimate.[26]

The overwhelming majority of Middle East experts in Israel and overseas were reluctant to address the issue of Arab antisemitism. Despite a voluminous amount of antisemitic references in contemporary Arab publications, it was simply too difficult to accept that the level of hatred that had been left behind in Europe was now transmitted and transplanted in the Middle East.[27]

Being in a "state of chronic siege," Israelis are so desperate to remove themselves from this predicament that they engage in "wishful thinking divorced from reality." Many have tried to rationalize the Arab threat by supporting policies that appease the terrorists in the "delusional hope" of freeing Israel from the peril it faces. Israelis acknowledge positive signs and disregard or reject evidence that doesn't support their belief that all Israel needs to do to ensure peace is to provide more concessions. This, they say, would inevitably reduce Palestinian hostility and anger and bring them to resolve the conflict. In their view, the Israeli government and their supporters are seen as the obstacles to peace, not the Arabs.[28]

For nearly ten years, the Israelis chose not to fight for the abrogation of Z=R. Some worried that if they exposed Arab antisemitism, they would reinforce political intransigence and people wouldn't want to give up an inch of territory during the Oslo Peace Process. It was discouraging and disturbing to acknowledge that Arab antisemitism was a truly harmful hatred of Jews throughout the world created by the collaboration between Arab and Western antisemites.

ASSESSING THE DAMAGE

It took until 1984 for the Israeli embassies around the world to start assessing the effect the resolution was having on Israel's image around the world. So many in the Israeli diplomatic corps just didn't care, and in Europe, they didn't even bother to provide an impartial analysis.[29] When they looked, they discovered that in the 12 years since the passage of Z=R, the damage to Israel's image was undeniable, and the Israeli government finally launched the campaign to force the UN to abrogate the resolution, which took until December 16, 1991. Historian Jacob Talmon noted:

> . . . there was something horribly mean and spiteful in spokesmen of what is, in their language, always named "the noble Arab race" bamboozling representatives of states born yesterday, without even a word in their native tongues to describe the Jew, without the vaguest knowledge or understanding of the peculiar and distant roots and the worldwide aspects of the Jewish problem and the Middle East conflict, without any authentic information on what is going on in present-day Israel. No less repulsive was the plotting with Machiavellian regimes, whose cynical opportunism knows no bounds, to brand as racists the most tragic victims of racism for whom actually the very word had been coined, and upon whom it has been practiced most thoroughly. . . . Not so long ago anti-Semitism and racism were synonymous.[30]

But the racist label does not fit the Jews of Israel. Arabs and Jews in Israel do not have separate seats on public buses or separate public lavatories. Arabs are admitted to schools and universities in Israel. Liberal Jews are disturbed that there are no civil marriages, but this has to be seen within Israeli and Jewish historical perspective. Members of most religious denominations adhere to religious law in marriage ceremonies as "a matter of conscience."[31]

Israel is in a no-win situation. When Israel evacuated more than 70,000 persecuted and starving Falashas (Beta Israel-House of Israel) from the Gondar region of Ethiopia, a German news commentator asked why the Israelis had taken out only Jews. Instead of seeing this as the first group to have been brought out of Africa since the Exodus to enjoy freedom, this liberation of thousands from government oppression was seen as a racist act.[32]

Now the "old myth of Judeo-Marxist international plot" became the "myth of an international Zionist-American-Imperialist conspiracy," because of a "compulsive need" to see the world divided into a camp of imperialists and "a camp of those striving for national liberation."

Talmon did not characterize the relationship between Jews and Arabs as idyllic, but given the decades of war, the "clash over rights, traumatic memories," and "mutual suspicion and fear," the policies and attitudes of Israel . . .

> would stand any comparison with the treatment of Poles by the Second Reich, of the Ukrainians and Byelo-Russians in inter-war Poland, the attitude of the kingdom of Hungary toward its Slav and Romanian subjects,

the fate of the Irish under British rule, not to speak of the situation of the Jews of Eastern Europe — all cases of a dominant race set upon strengthening its hold, by methods which include settling members of its ethnic group in border areas inhabited by national minorities.[33]

Talmon asked why someone hadn't formally asked the UN Commission to investigate the then Soviet Union, whose policies in the Baltic countries were planned to "swamp those minorities with multitudes of Great Russians and members of other races, and to transfer large numbers of Lithuanians, Latvians, and Estonians into remote areas of Russia.

"All that Israel wants," Talmon concluded, is:

. . . to stay alive, afloat and tolerably safe, free to contribute in its own way to the wonderfully knit tapestry of world civilization and humanity's quest for a just society. . . . There still remains the fundamental truth that somehow the Jewish right to live and exist on a basis of genuine equality, as a right, and not on sufferance or in return for some excellence, is not yet taken for granted as natural and obvious by the world.[34]

ARAB REACTION TO PASSAGE OF Z=R

Arab sponsors of the resolution did not appear ecstatic with their success. Some Arab members and their supporters were disturbed when Secretary General Waldheim issued a statement about of the "gravity of the situation" resulting from the vote. Waldheim's remarks were an affront to them because, after the fact, once the deed was done and irrevocable, he dropped his neutral stance and sided with the West in condemning the vote.[35]

In an editorial, A.M. El-Messiri, UN advisor to the League of Arab States, defended Asian and African states for voting against Israel. He claimed they acted "not out of fear of Arab threats or blackmail, nor for love of Arab gold," but were exercising a concrete and legal form used to express their long-held views about Zionism. He said that Israel is a racist form of settler colonialism like those in Algeria, Rhodesia (now Zimbabwe), Angola, and South Africa. Of particular concern was the exclusionary nature of the state.[36]

If some Zionist pioneers viewed the settlement of Palestine as a fulfillment of biblical prophecy, "the displaced and evicted victims of this Zionist vision" saw the process quite differently. The Balfour Declaration of 1917, the "first European official sanction of the Zionist ideal, referred to the Arab Moslems and Christians of Palestine, who made up over 90 percent of the population, as the 'non-Jewish communities' — that is, the indigenous majority was already being ruthlessly relegated to the status of a minority." The Zionists did not share their culture and knowledge with the "native Palestinians." They were guided by ideals such as "Hebrew Labor or Conquest of Soil," which meant that the redemption of the land of Israel and the regeneration of the "Jewish character" could only be achieved by "Jewish labor" alone. The Zionists established institutions "that acquired, by necessity, military traits because they excluded the indigenous population."[37]

The exclusionist vision led all of the Afro-Asian countries represented at the UN in 1947 to vote against the establishment of a Jewish state in Palestine, except South Africa. Over the years, the attitude to "Zionist supremacist isolationism solidified." The Law of Return, granting the right of any Jew to become an Israeli citizen upon his arrival in the country while denying the same right to Palestinians born and raised there, further demonstrated the true nature of the Jewish State.[38]

Amnon Rubenstein, a former dean of the Tel Aviv Law School and chairman of the Knesset's Constitution, Law and Justice Committee, points out that the Law of Return can also be found in other countries. Most significant of these laws of repatriation is in Section 116 of the Federal Republic of Germany's constitution. Hundreds of thousands of ethnic Germans who were expelled from their homes in the former Soviet Union were automatically granted citizenship. The German law is stricter than Israel's because Germany refuses citizenship to millions of foreigners who were born in Germany.[39]

Some of these applicants were second- and third-generation immigrants, who are continually refused naturalization as German citizens. Even with the existence of the European Convention on Human Rights and the European Court for Human Rights, Germany has not been compelled to rescind its own "Law of Return" on the grounds that it violates "universal principles of equality," the argument advanced by those calling for Israel to repeal its Law of Return.[40]

States can differentiate between potential immigrants and citizens according to the UN Convention on the Elimination of All Forms of Racial Discrimination, ratified in 1965. The convention clearly states: "Nothing in this Convention may be interpreted as affecting in any way the legal provisions or States Parties concerning nationality, citizenship, or naturalization, provided such provisions do not discriminate against any." The German repatriation law is not atypical. Practically every Baltic and Balkan state has a repatriation law. Section 375 of Greek law, for example, confers automatic citizenship on an individual "of Greek nationality" who serves in the military. Section 25(1) of the Bulgarian constitution has a very simple process to allow a person of "Bulgarian origin" to become a citizen. Automatic citizenship is given to a "native Armenian" residing in the Armenian republic according to Section 13(3) of the Armenian constitution.[41]

In October 2001, the Council of Europe's Venice Commission of Jurists affirmed the right of states to allow preferential repatriation. This means, "nothing in these policies invalidates either citizenship or immigration laws that express certain preference for kinsmen returning to their homeland." The Council decided to accept "assistance given by kin states to their kin-minorities to preserve their cultural, linguistic, and ethnic identity," but the assistance must be "accepted by the states of which members of the kin-minorities are citizens." This is a multilateral attempt, Rubinstein observes, to "re-establish the legitimacy of nationalism within the framework of international jurisprudence," without discriminating against a particular people, which has significant "implications for national minorities living within its borders."[42]

This new form of nationalism is not the type that fosters "fanatical, insular, or patronizing tribalism," but one that respects civil, human, and minority rights. The modern state accepts dual allegiances and encourages them. An individual can be an Italian American, African American, or an Irish American, just as a Jew can be Jewish French, Jewish British, Jewish American, or a Zionist Jew.[43]

The European Council's affirmation of the right of the majority in a country to protect its demographic supremacy by controlling immigration and determining who should be granted citizenship justifies Israel's Law of Return. Austria, Bulgaria, Greece, Hungary, Italy, Romania, Russia, Slovakia, and Slovenia have laws conferring official status to "the connection between the nation and its ethnic or national brethren living abroad." Greece expects to grant dual citizenship to approximately 300,000 Albanians of Greek extraction. In 1999, Russia, which is not a nation state, passed a law stating that any person connected to Russian culture is a kinsmen, and can become a Russian citizen immediately if they return to the Russian Federation.[44] In light of this new evaluation, it is hard to claim that Israel's Law of Return harms the democratic nature of the state and principles of equality.[45]

But racism is not a political issue alone. Zionist leaders, including the "liberal Abba Eban," claimed the goal of Israel was not integration. In a book he wrote in 1957, Eban expressed his concerns that the Jews coming from Arab countries "would force Israel to equalize its cultural level with that of the neighboring world."[46] "It would be moral myopia," El-Messiri opined, "to try to solve Auschwitz by Deir Yassin[47] and in answer to the Occidental concentration camps, propose the dispersion of the Palestinians: Justice knows no discrimination." The resolution helped foster the quest for peace, according to El-Messiri, because if the Zionist State continued to "impose its racist policies," the Arabs and their supporters had "to fight for their human rights and dignity." Should Israel be willing to integrate, this would provide the foundation for a just and lasting peace, since in his mind, demographics would win the day.

A condemnation of Zionism does not imply an attack on Judaism, which is unrelated to land, El-Messiri cautioned. "The Jews have undoubtedly religious and spiritual ties with a land they consider holy, a feeling comparable to that of other people for many other lands; but that feeling is different" from a "political ideology that claims . . . a piece of land and dispossesses its people." We must remember, he concludes, "Not all Jews are Zionists and not all Zionists are Jews." Even in Israel there are non-Zionists and even anti-Zionist groups — some of whom are becoming quite critical of Zionism. "Are they, too, going to be muzzled by being labeled anti-Semites?" he asked.[48]

THE ARAB LEAGUE

The Arab League, founded in 1945 to strengthen ties among its 20 member states, coordinate their policies, and promote their common interests, rejected the charges that Arabs were motivated by anti-Jewish prejudice. "The Arabs have a deep and natural respect for Judaism as a universal religious faith and as spiritual values," the declaration said. The resolution dealt with "a concrete phenomenon — a political ideology, a political machinery based on it and the policies of a government."[49]

The Arabs took issue with calling Zionism a national liberation movement. An "authentic" liberation movement sees "its salvation through its liberation, but not through the enslavement of others. . . . No movement that seeks its ingathering through the dispersal of others can be a true national liberation movement."[50] What about the creation of nations in the Americas? That was ignored.

Saudi Arabian Ambassador Baroody was especially disturbed by Moynihan's characterization of Z=R as an "infamous act" and "a lie." "Are we liars, all the 72 member states that voted for the resolution?" he asked. Do the United States and the West have a "monopoly" on the truth? And if Z=R was an infamous act, "was the partition of Palestine a famous act? . . . The Palestinian people were sold down the Thames [river] by Mr. Balfour and down the Potomac [river] by Mr. Truman. What business had Mr. Balfour and Mr. Truman to create an imbroglio in our midst? . . . What have the Palestinians, and for that matter all the Arabs in the region, done to the United Kingdom and the United States?"

As to Jewish claims that God gave them Palestine because they are "exclusive," he wondered "since when is God in the real estate business . . . ? Show us the title deed. And since when did He give Mr. Balfour and Mr. Truman powers-of-attorney to transfer land that does not belong to them? . . . Does God parcel out land? . . . I don't think that any of the Zionists have direct or indirect communication with God Almighty."

Baroody acknowledged that Zion "allegedly is the site of King David's grave. This is why there is reverence for Mt. Zion and in the Psalms it is said: 'I look to the hills.' It is the spiritual Zionism that we thought at one time would prevail."

Annoyed that 76 U.S. senators opposed Z=R, Baroody explained they were controlled by the Zionists: "The Zionists own most of the mass media of information and political campaigns depend on mass media," and the president, senators, and congressmen need the media for their campaigns. "God help any candidate in this country who is not supported by the Zionists! God help him."[51]

The PLO political department declared the "Zionist ghetto of Israel must be destroyed." The state had "a racist theocratic ideology," which had to be replaced by the establishment of a democratic, secular Palestinian state."[52]

Yasser Arafat told Oriana Fallaci, the Italian journalist, that the conflict would continue: "We are just beginning to get ready for a long, long war, a war that will run for generations. Ours is not the first generation to fight . . . in the '20s our fathers were already struggling against Zionist invaders. . . . We will never stop until we can go back home and Israel is destroyed."

When Fallaci questioned Arafat about whether he was seeking peace, he replied: "We don't want peace, we want victory. Peace for us means Israel's destruction and nothing else. What you call peace is peace for Israel. . . . For us it is shame and injustice. We shall fight on to victory. Even for decades, for generations, if necessary."[53]

Z=R "clears the way for the historical demise of the rapacious Zionist entity," said Arab leaders. It sent "shock waves through the issue of Israel's right to exist, without having any practical effect on the right of the Jews to be present in Palestine. This adds legality and international consent to what the [Palestinian] revolution regards as a humane and proper substitute for Israel, that is the democratic secular state." In other words, a UN decision had created the State of Israel and the force of a similar resolution could ensure its demise.[54]

REPEAL OF THE RESOLUTION IN 1991

Eighty-five countries, a little more than half of the 166 members of the UN, co-sponsored the repeal, including the Soviet Union and all its former Eastern European Communist allies. Cuba, North Korea, and Vietnam were the only Communist countries to vote against the repeal. No Arab country voted for the repeal, but Bahrain, Egypt, Kuwait, Morocco, Oman, and Tunisia were absent when the vote was taken, a sign that the measure had split Islamic and nonaligned governments.[55]

Senator Moynihan noted that 16 years was a long period of time "to wait for the world to come to its senses." In 1975, practically no one cared, he said. One American who showed his profound concern was former Vice President Hubert Humphrey. Although suffering from cancer that would eventually kill him, he flew to New York on November 10, 1975, to sit in the UN hall. Moynihan portrayed him as "unannounced, unabashed, outraged, bearing witness." Humphrey would later proclaim "the continued efforts to repeal this resolution will tell us a lot about the United Nations and even more about the United States."[56]

Vice President Dan Quayle called for the repeal of the resolution in 1988, but the Israeli government was less than enthusiastic about the idea, fearing there would be a high price to pay for U.S. help. They were correct. By initiating a repeal, President George H. W. Bush attempted to finesse the pro-Israel lobby in the United States during an election year while pressuring Israel to acquiesce to its Arab neighbors.

European and other allies supported the repeal to give the president that leverage over the Jews and the Israelis.

Overtly, the Bush administration claimed that it did not reach this decision because of the presidential election, but because it finally had enough votes to repeal Z=R. But many political experts claimed that Bush's timing diverted criticism from his decision to withhold guarantees for Israeli loans for the resettlement of Soviet Jewish refugees in Israel. Bush did not want to be accused of insensitivity and harshness toward Israel, especially during such an important period.[57]

Shoshana Cardin, then chairman of the Conference of Presidents of Major American Jewish Organizations, said the attempt to fight the resolution "was initiated immediately after the vote in the UN with little enthusiasm or optimism, but with a sense of necessity."[58] On May 22, 1989, she said, Secretary of State James Baker called on the Arab world to "repudiate the odious line that Zionism is racism." In 1990, John R. Bolton [the present U.S. Ambassador to the UN] appeared before the Subcommittee on Near Eastern and South Asian Affairs of the Senate Foreign Relations Committee and publicly stated the determination of the Bush administration to overturn Resolution 3379 and invited Congress to engage in this effort.[59]

From 1990 on, administration officials and members of numerous national Jewish organizations contacted every foreign government to prepare for abrogation. They included the former Soviet Union, which had drafted and sponsored the Zionism=Racism 1975 vote with the Arab states, in their efforts.[60]

President Bush, Vice President Quayle, and Secretary Baker initiated a special effort to get the resolution repealed before the UN ended its 1991 session. When the UN met in September of that year, Bush announced that he would pursue the issue and informed all the members of the UN General Assembly of his intentions.[61]

When working in conjunction with the State Department, Jewish unity was a critical component of the successful campaign. Shoshana Cardin noted that "Jewish organizations assiduously targeted every country that could possibly vote for repeal or rescission, assigned contact personnel and maintained daily records of potentially positive and definite positive responses."[62]

On December 16, 1991, Deputy Secretary of State Lawrence Eagleburger introduced a one sentence resolution: "The General Assembly decides to revoke the determination contained in its Resolution 3379 of 10 November, 1975." The language was carefully crafted to meet "special needs" of various delegations.[63]

Though passage of the repeal was certain, Israel and American Jewry waited. "The victorious vote was 111-25, much greater than hoped for, and it was met with excitement, cries of joy, and some relief. But though it passed, there was no assurance that the member agencies of the UN would change their tone or lessen their

Shoshana Cardin
(Photo courtesy of Shoshana Cardin)

diatribes against Israel. The repeal was a result of the largest, most concerted and concentrated lobbying effort ever experienced at the UN, one that involved government and private sectors working together. And in the end, when all was said and done, a tremendous amount of damage had been done."[64]

THE EXTENT OF THE DAMAGE

Further research found that by the end of 1991, Z=R had done significant damage to Israel, and thus forced them to accept repeal. They had not realized how Z=R had conferred legitimacy on antisemitism. The systematic and deliberate dehumanization of Zionism in the West was succeeding.[65] Israel was "no longer among the ordinary evil-doers of this world, all of whom at one time or another attack and harm civilian populations, oppress minorities, and institute exclusive immigration laws and monopolistic religious laws." Israel's crimes were committed "as part of an entire ideological system" and therefore every Israeli government action was racist and "anti-humanistic." Israel had gone from being a legitimate national liberation movement to one that opposed the rightful aspirations of other nations and peoples.[66] The General Assembly had provided the stage and a guilt-free path for antisemites and antisemitism at the UN.[67]

Has much changed since the repeal? "Today, anti-Zionism is very much alive in some form" in the UN, "but it is more a slogan than an ideology. Anti-Zionism, anti-Israel, and anti-U.S. slogans are one of the few types of glue that somehow holds together the heterogeneous coalition against globalism. The major failure of anti-Zionism is that there are a growing number of sovereign states that recognize the Jewish state. Less than 60 countries accepted her in 1975; today there are more than 160. Israel's position at the UN is far better than it has been in the recent past. Since 2000, Israel is a member of a group, the Western Group, enabling her to be elected to all its institutions and bodies.[68]

Endnotes

1. "A Day of Infamy," *The Jerusalem Post* (November 16, 1985), Online.

2. "Protocols of Anti-Zionism," *Newsweek* (October 27, 1975), p. 40.

3. Chaim Herzog, *Who Stands Accused? Israel Answers Its Critics* (New York: Random House, 1978), p. 4; Paul Hoffman, "Palestine Issue Taken Up At U.N," *NYT* (November 4, 1975), p. 8; Joseph Lerner, "William Korey's Century of Hatred: Protocols Live to Poison Yet Another Generation," *IMRA Newsletter*, Online; see also, Malka Hillel Shulewitz, ed., *The Forgotten Millions: The Modern Jewish Exodus from Arab Lands* (London and New York: Continuum, 1999); Maurice M. Roumani, *The Case of the Jews from Arab Countries: A Neglected Issue* (Tel Aviv: World Organization of Jews from Arab Countries, Fourth printing, 1983), p. 1–36; Terence Prittie, "Middle East Refugees" in *The Palestinians: People, History, Politics*, eds. Michael Curtis, Joseph Neyer, Chaim I. Waxman, and Allen Pollack (New Brunswick, NJ: Transaction Books, 1975), p. 58–66.

4. Paul Hoffman, "U.N. Vote Today Worrying Jews," *NYT* (November 10, 1975), p. 1, 10. For a discussion of Christian response to the beginning of the Jewish return to Palestine see Egal Feldman, *Dual Loyalties: The Jewish Encounter with Protestant America* (Urbana and Chicago, IL: University of Illinois Press, 1990), p. 162–174.

5. Report from the Conference of Presidents of Major Jewish Organizations, Conference Archives (1975), p. 12.

6. Ibid.

7. Interview with Rabbi Michael Monson in late 2005; interview with Malcolm Hoenlein January 18, 2006. Despite this significant activity, Herzog openly complained that the American Jewish community should be doing more. Both Hoenlein and Monson felt this was unfair given the efforts being made. Monson was especially effusive in praising the role played by Hoenlein. When this critique was reported in the pages of the *Times*, the Israeli cabinet suggested that Herzog return to Israel to explain what happened at the UN. "Statement by Ambassador Chaim Herzog Permanent Representative of Israel to the United Nations at Conference of Presidents of Major American Jewish Organizations," *CZA*, S/110/47 (October 24, 1975), p. 14–15; "A Day of Infamy."

8. Report from the Conference of Presidents of Major Jewish Organizations, p. 12.

9. "Statement By Ambassador Chaim Herzog," p. 16; "A Day of Infamy."

10. "Jews of 27 Countries pledge Support for Zionism," *NYT,* December 6, 1975, p. 10.

11. Report from the Conference of Presidents of Major Jewish Organizations, p. 12.

12. "Huge Rally Here Assails U.N. Anti-Zionism Move," *NYT*, November 12, 1975, p. 16.

13. Ibid.

14. Report from the Conference of Presidents of Major Jewish Organizations, p. 13.

15. Yohanan Manor, *To Right a Wrong: The Revocation of the UN General Assembly Resolution 3379 Defaming Zionism* (New York: Shengold Publishers, Inc., 1996), p. 268–269.

16. Thomas Mayer, "The U.N. Resolution Equating Zionism with Racism: Genesis and Repercussions" (London, England: Institute of Jewish Affairs), Research Report Number 1 (April 1985), p. 8; "The United Nations Versus Zionism," November 11, 1975, Washington, D.C.: The Israeli Embassy, Washington, D.C, AJC File U.N.-Nazism.

17. Ibid.

18. Manor, *To Right a Wrong*, p. 89, 87–88.

19. Ibid., p. 89.

20. Ibid., p. 87–88, 92, 104-115; Eli Eyal to Steve J. Roth (April 18, 1982) CZA File S110/4.

21. Steve J. Roth, CZA File S110/4 (April 18, 1982).

22. "The Fight Against Anti-Zionism: Opening Speech by Eli Eyal, Chairman of the Department of Information," CZA S110/2.

23. "The Fight Against Anti-Zionism," CZA S110/2.

24. Yohanan Manor, "The Real Arena: The Struggle Against Anti-Zionism," October 1981, CZA S110/2.

25. Manor, op. cit., p. 108; Manor, *To Right a Wrong*, p. 104–115; Yohanan Manor, "Report on the Study Mission Re International Conference for the Fight Against Anti-Zionism," no date, CZA S 110/4.25; among the presenters and committee members were Daniel Bell, professor emeritus of the Social Sciences, Harvard University; Saul Bellow, the Nobel Laureate for Literature; Sir Isaiah Berlin, first president of Oxford's Wolfson College; Leonard Bernstein, the American-Jewish conductor and composer; Father Thomas Drinan, professor of Georgetown University Law School; Joseph Lane-Kirkland, president of the U.S. AFL-CIO; U.S. Senator Daniel Patrick Moynihan; Bayard Rustin, head of the NAACP; Albert Sabin, inventor of the oral polio vaccine; Simone Veil, former president of the European Parliament, and Harold Wilson, the former British Prime Minister.

26. Manor, "Report on the Study Mission Re International Conference for the Fight Against Anti-Zionism," p. 1–4.

27. Menahem Milson, *Countering Arab Antisemitism* (Jerusalem: World Jewish Congress), p. 3, 8; Arieh Stav, op. cit., p. 271–273.

28. Kenneth Levin, *The Oslo Syndrome: Delusion of a People Under Seige* (Hanover, NH: Smith and Kraus, Inc, 2005), p. viii, 277, 280, 289, 346.

29. Manor, *To Right a Wrong*, p. 268.

30. J.L. Talmon, "The New Anti-Semitism," *The New Republic* (September 18, 1976), p. 21.

31. Ibid.

32. David Landes and Richard Landes in "Zionism at 100," Martin Peretz, ed., *The Australia / Israel Review*, September 12–30, 1997, p. 17.

33. Talmon, "The New Anti-Semitism," p. 21.

34. Ibid., p. 21, 23.

35. Kathleen Teltsch, "Assembly Head Deplores Action," op. cit.

36. A.M. El-Messiri, "Zionism and Racism," *NYT* (November 13, 1975), p. 41.

37. Ibid.

38. Ibid.

39. Amnon Rubenstein, "The Problem Is How to Become an Israeli," *Haaretz* (January 4, 2000), Online.

40. Amnon Rubenstein, *From Herzl to Rabin: The Changing Image of Zionism* (New York: Holmes and Meier, 2000), p. 198–199.

41. Rubenstein, "The Problem Is How to Become an Israeli."

42. Amnon Rubinstein, "Zionism's Compatriots," *Azure* no. 16 (Winter 2004), Online.

43. Ibid.

44. Ibid.

45. Ibid.

46. This is a reference to a quote in Abba Eban's book *Voice of Israel* (New York, Horizon Press, 1957), p. 74–77. It is a distortion of Eban's statement. Here is what he did say: "Let us examine this idea of integration in its individual components. Do we seek to be economically integrated into the Near East? Our very mission is to establish a society which will bear no resemblance to the forms of social exploitation characteristic of Arab and Moslem society. Do we aspire to the same forms of political organization as those which engage the sentiment of the Arab world? Surely we are attracted neither by the theocratic monarchies of the Arabian peninsula nor by the protectorates or sheikdoms of the Persian Gulf, nor by those forms of republicanism in the Levant states in which assassination is the conventional method of changing prime ministers and in which the parliamentary procedure reflects no public interest or educated popular concern. Neither the monarchies nor the republics of the Middle East offer us a form of political organization in which we can seek integration.

"In the sphere of culture, while paying all honor to the potentiality of the Arab tradition, we come to Israel with the purpose of reviving and maintaining the Hebrew tradition. Moreover, Israel possesses unique interests, the paramount one of which is the network of connections with the Jewish world in all the countries of the Dispersion. This is something exclusive to the State of Israel. . . . The slogan should not be integration, but good neighborliness; not Israel as an organic part of the Middle East, but Israel as a separate and unique entity at peace with the Middle East. What we aspire to is not the relationship which exists between Lebanon and Syria; it is far more akin to the relationship between the United States and the Latin-American continent: relations of good neighborliness, of regional cooperation, of economic interaction, but across a frankly confessed gulf of historic, cultural, and linguistic differences. The things which divide Israel from the Arab world are very often the most positive things which Israel exemplifies in its region. Nor should this interpretation be understood as equivalent to a desire for Israel to be regarded as an alien bridgehead in the area. There is a form of cooperation which falls far short of organic integration.

"If Israel wishes to seek the most congenial world for its political relations and its cultural links, I suggest that that orientation be found in the word Mediterranean-Israel not as a Middle Eastern country, but as a Mediterranean country. The Mediterranean is the only channel of intercourse and contact between Israel and the rest of the world. All Israel's commerce, all its connections, pass across that sea. If this is true as a geographical fact, it is even more true as a historic and cultural fact."

47. On April 8, 1948, units of Menachem Begin's *Etzel* (*Irgun Tzvava Leumi*, National Military Organization) and Yitzhak Shamir's *Lechi* (*Lochamai Herut Yisra'el*, Freedom Fighters For Israel), launched an attack against Deir Yassin, an Arab village west of Jerusalem. Between 100 and 110 people were killed. The incident created a panic, fueled in large part by exaggerated claims on both sides about the number of dead. This resulted in many Arabs fleeing their homes. See Uri

Milstein, *History of Israel's War of Independence: Out of Crisis Came Decision*, Vol. IV (New York: University Press of America, Inc. 1998), p. 343–396; Yoav Gelber, *Palestine 1948* (Portland, OR: Sussex Academic Press, 2001), p. 98–99, 101; Benny Morris, *The Birth of the Palestinian Refugee Problem Revisited* (New York: Cambridge University Press, 2004), p. 91, 97–99, 116.

48. El-Messiri, "Zionism and Racism"; see also "The U.N. Resolution on Zionism," *Journal of Palestine Studies*, vol. 5, issue ½ (Autumn 1975–Winter 1976): p. 252–254.

49. Paul Hoffman, "Arabs Hope Anti-Zionism Vote Will Lead to Vast Reappraisals," op. cit.

50. "Excerpts From Remarks Pro and Con on Zionism Text," *NYT* (November 12, 1975), p. 16

51. Baroody, Saudi Arabia Statement in the U.N. General Assembly A/PV.2400, 192–211, CZA S110/47; see also "The Birth of a Nation," *Newsweek* (November 24, 1975), p. 52.

52. *Newsweek* (November 17, 1975).

53. Oriana Fallaci, "An Oriana Fallaci Interview: Yasir Arafat," *The New Republic* (November 16, 1974), p. 10.

54. Quoted in Yehoshafat Harkabi, "Arab Positions on Zionism," ed. Shmuel Almog, *Zionism and the Arabs* (Jerusalem: The Historical Society of Israel and the Zalman Shazar Center, 1983), p. 190–191.

55. Paul Lewis, "U.N. Repeals Its '75 Resolution Equating Zionism With Racism," *NYT,* (December 17, 1991), p. 1, 12; "The U.N. Expunges a Smear," *NYT* (December 17, 1991); "Repealing United Nations General Assembly Resolution 3379," Congressional Record Volume 137, Number 140 (October 3, 1991). On the same day, the U.N. voted 152-1, with the United States abstaining, to urge Israel to revoke a resolution declaring Jerusalem as its capital. David Harsanyi, "The United Nation's War Against Israel," *Capitalism Magazine* (May 27, 2002), Online.

56. "Daniel Patrick Moynihan to Dear Friend," Conference of Presidents Archives (December 17, 1991).

57. Paul Lewis, "For Israel the Zionism Vote Has a Dark Lining," *NYT* (December 22, 1991), Section 4, p. 4.

58. Correspondence from Shoshana Cardin, (January 6, 2006), author's archive.

59. Ibid.

60. Ibid.

61. Ibid

62. Ibid

63. Ibid.

64. Ibid.

65. Ehud Sprinzak, "Anti-Zionism: From Delegitimation to Dehumanization," *Forum-53* (Fall 1984), p. 5–7.

66. Ibid.

67. Manor, op cit, p. 272; Thomas A. Idinopulos, "The Zionism and Racism Controversy: Historical Perspective on the Issues," *The Christian Century* (January 28, 1976), p. 68–72; David Harsanyi, "The United Nation's War Against Israel," *Capitalism Magazine* (May 27, 2002), Online.

68. Yohanan Manor, Communication, "Daily Highlights-World Conference against Racism," (August 31–September 7, 2001), Online.

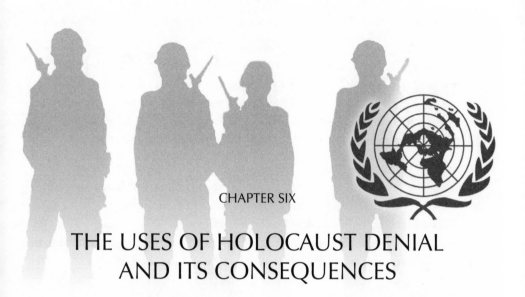

CHAPTER SIX

THE USES OF HOLOCAUST DENIAL AND ITS CONSEQUENCES

HOLOCAUST DENIAL AS A WEAPON

D enial of the Holocaust is an attempt to reject the connection of the Jewish people to their immediate history, erode the legitimacy of Israel, and allow the Arabs "to appropriate the role of historical victim and . . . apply it to themselves. Television and modern technology have provided authoritative vehicles for defaming and denying the Jewish people, their religion, history, nation, and land — in order to sever contemporary Jews from their past and the land of Israel."[1] The Jews have "succeeded in [winning] world sympathy by playing on the Holocaust and Nazi atrocities," says Dr. Abdul Wahid Al-Humaid, Secretary General of the Manpower Council in Saudi Arabia. For French Holocaust denier Robert Faurisson, "The alleged 'Holocaust' of the Jews is the sword and the shield of the Jewish tyranny all over the world. Destroy it."[2]

Articles in the Arab media and Internet continually question the existence of gas chambers and crematoria in the camps. They proclaim the number of Jews who died during the war was exaggerated and deny the systematic Nazi policy to annihilate the Jews of Europe. According to Arab propagandists, the Zionists and Israel invented the Holocaust to extract compensation from Germany and Western countries to use against anti-Zionists.[3]

The current grand mufti of Jerusalem of the Al-Aqsa Mosque — the leading Palestinian religious authority — gives his imprimatur to Holocaust denial. On March 24, 2000, just before the pope's historic visit to the mosque, he gave an interview to the Italian newspaper *La Republica*: "Too Many Lies about the Holocaust, [Pope] Wojtyla Free Us from the Jews." He said:

Six million Jews dead? No way, there were much fewer. Let's stop with this fairy tale exploited by Israel to capture international solidarity. It is not my fault if Hitler hated Jews; indeed, they were hated a little everywhere. Instead, it is necessary to denounce the unjust occupation endured by my people. Tomorrow I will ask John Paul II . . . to support our cause.[4]

In denying the Holocaust, the Egyptian daily paper *Al-Akhbar* defended Hitler's revenge against the Jews. After he discovered that the Zionists in Germany "were a fifth column" who betrayed the country to the Allies in order to "realize their aspirations" for a Jewish state, Hitler retaliated against them.[5]

Another *Al-Akhbar* column proclaimed Hitler's innocence but complained that, "If only you had done it, brother, if only it had really happened, so that the world could sigh in relief [without] their evil and sin."[6]

The Arabs accused Zionist leaders of conspiring with the Nazis, including the SS, to terrorize the Jews in order to force them to go to Palestine. They say the Zionists devised a plan to massacre thousands of Jews in the "detention camps" in Budapest, and when the Zionists realized that Jews fleeing Europe were going to the United States instead of Palestine, they "plotted" to sink a ship in the Atlantic to demonstrate the danger of crossing the ocean, encouraging the refugees to use the safer route to Palestine.[7]

In a controversial article in the Egyptian government daily *Al-Liwaa Al-Islami,* "The Lie about the Burning of the Jews," they claim the Zionists fabricated the gas chambers to "blackmail the West" and to ensure "the realization of the Zionist project." Muhammad Al-Zurqani, the editor-in-chief who resigned after the article appeared, said that he and the author were "educated from childhood that the Holocaust is a big lie."[8]

The purpose of the article was to focus attention on the "current Holocaust that we are experiencing in Palestine and which does not cause the West the same pain that it feels about an event that was, at the very least, falsified or exaggerated." The "true Holocaust is occurring from Rafah to Jenin, Nablus, Baghdad, Nafaj." According to him, Palestinian prisoners suffer more under the Israelis than the Jews did in Nazi camps.

This suffering has reached such a level that it has been said that all of the experiments conducted in the Abu Ghraib prison on Iraqi prisoners or in Guantanamo were first conducted on the Palestinian prisoners, whose numbers reach 8,000, and among them 300 women and 300 children. Some of them suffered from experiments that turned their bodies into germ laboratories and turned them into human guinea pigs. . . . They have made germ laboratory mice out of these heroic prisoners.

He also compared the Holocaust to the alleged half a million olive trees that were "annihilated" by the Israelis. "Is this not Nazism? Is this not a modern Holocaust?" he asked.[9]

Al-Ahram acknowledged that Treblinka was real, and that there was a great massacre at Auschwitz, but there were also camps in Southern Lebanon where constant Israeli massacres were carried out. What, he asked, is the difference between Zionism and antisemitism? If Jews suffered brutally at the hands of the Nazis, how can they adopt discriminatory practices against Palestinians?[10]

Another Arab columnist opposed Holocaust denial because it would be used by the Israelis to "show the West that the Arabs don't want peace, and if they had the chance, they would finish what the Nazis couldn't."

Al-Hayat expressed the view that if the Arabs and Israelis are to reach some type of understanding, they had to accept each other's history.

Al-Ahram Centre for Political and Strategic Studies reverted to moral equivalence and suggested that Arabs and Jews should "reject all types of oppression, regardless of whether it came from Nazi Germany or Israeli occupation."[11]

The Holocaust and "The Occupation" Are Not Equal

Equating Palestinian suffering to the Holocaust and Israeli military actions to the Nazis is a distortion of history. The Holocaust was the intentional, systematic, and bureaucratic attempt to destroy European Jewry using various means, including gas chambers and crematoria.

The Israelis have never engaged in any effort to exterminate the Arabs or any group anywhere. Refugee camps housing Arabs are not concentration or extermination camps. People are not starved to death, forced to work as slave laborers, nor are they methodically liquidated. Israeli military responses are not retribution, but reprisals, or more accurately, acts of deterrence against acts of terrorism.[12] The Israelis are fighting heavily armed terrorists who attack unarmed civilians — men, women, and children — in their homes, buses, schools, discos, cafes, malls, and supermarkets.

Ironically, despite Arab claims for redress under international standards, the very same international laws and customs of war that shield civilians from combat are completely ignored by the Arabs.[13] Reprisal "is the act or practice in international law of resorting to force short of war to produce redress of grievances." Deterrence restrains and dissuades "crime by fear." The impetus "for revenge is hatred for an act that caused real or perceived anguish, pain, or suffering. The response has to be comparable to or greater than the wrong inflicted for emotional satisfaction. Moral limits are rarely observed."[14]

Determining *jus in bello* (justice in warfare) is not as difficult to establish or as subjective as it might appear. Deterrence and reprisal are just acts; revenge is criminal. Civilians and those not engaged in fighting are not to be killed in acts of reprisal or deterrence. There has to be a "causal connection between the target and the military goal." If reprisals and deterrence succeed, it should end the iniquity causing the response, and the parties should be able to resolve their differences in peace.[15]

The Arabs accuse the Zionists of using the Holocaust to extract money from Germany to fund the State of Israel. The amount of reparations Israel received was not based on the number of Jews killed, but on the cost to Israel of absorbing and assimilating Jews who survived the war in Europe. Absent from Arab consideration is the fact that the money received from Germany in the post-Holocaust era is just a fraction of what the Germans had stolen from the Jews. To date, the Conference on Material Claims Against Germany and the Holocaust survivors, including the State of Israel, have received a mere $50 billion to make up for between $240–$330 billion that was looted and stolen, without considering the costs of the lives of each of the six million people murdered. Moreover, Israel did not begin to receive reparations until the 1950s. The Arabs are Holocaust deniers, and they are trying to have it both ways — denying that there ever was a Holocaust while complaining about Germany making reparations for its own acknowledged culpability.[16]

Holocaust denial and accusations about "the money" have become so much a part of Arab mainstream political propaganda that they are taken for granted. This is seen as an Arab "retreat from historical reality and societal responsibility into fundamentally antidemocratic politics of the irrational," and demonstrates the absence of "a rational, democratic culture" in the Arab world. It means that when empirical evidence disproves common beliefs or conspiracies against the Arab world, it is not accepted.[17]

Instead of dealing with domestic issues such as illiteracy, overpopulation, or sluggish economies, an Arab League's think tank conference in Abu Dhabi in August 2002 chose to focus on denying the Holocaust. An article in the Jordanian paper *Al-Arab Al-Yom* explained that Arabs have become the victims of European imperialism and the Zionists: "The Holocaust is not what happened to the Jews in Germany, but rather the crime of the establishment of the State of Israel on the ruins of the Palestinian people."[18]

This message forms the foundation for much of what the Arab population thinks about Israel and the United States. By claiming that the Americans are part of a Zionist and Jewish conspiracy, Arab intellectuals have been able to incorporate Holocaust denial and anti-Americanism into a world view that is a "virulent strain of irrational politics." This approach leads to totalitarianism, making the issue of the denial of history more than a Jewish issue. Holocaust denial threatens the ability of Arab societies to develop democracy, endangers the West, and the political well-being of the Arab world.[19]

DENYING THE JEWISH CONNECTION TO THE LAND

Denying the Holocaust makes it easy to deny Jews any connection to the land of Israel. Two key elements of this myth involve debasing and denying Jewish biblical history and transforming it into the history of the Muslims/Arabs by claiming that the Arabs are descendents of the Canaanites. By turning ancient Israelites and Canaanites into Arabs, the propagandists turn Jewish history into the history of the Palestinian Authority. Take out the word Jew and substitute the word Arab and thousands of years of documented Jewish life disappear.[20]

Why is it necessary to appropriate thousands of years of Jewish connection to the land and claim it for the Arabs? Because the PA needs to invent a historic bond to the land in order to invent a Palestinian national history. The only way for the PA to do that is by stealing the history of the Jewish people. They appropriated the term "Palestine," which has nothing historically to do with Arab identity. Most of the Arab population in the region migrated during the last century to take advantage of the improved working and living conditions in areas created by Jewish land development, investment, and activities.[21]

When Jordan and Israel signed an armistice agreement on April 3, 1949, the Jordanians guaranteed "free access to the Holy Places and cultural institutions and use of the cemetery on the Mount of Olives."[22] But until Jews returned to the area in 1967, they were not permitted to pray at the Western Wall, visit the cemetery, or go anywhere in East Jerusalem. Under Jordanian control, the Western Wall was turned into a slum. Fifty-eight synagogues in the Jewish Quarter, including Khurvat Rabbi Yehuda Hehasid from the 13th century, were destroyed. Either they were torn down, used as stables and chicken coops, or converted into refuse dumps.[23]

The Mount of Olives cemetery, with tombstones dating back to the first century B.C., was ravaged. (The cemetery has a significant place in Judaism as it is located in the Valley of the Dry Bones and is the place Jews believe resurrection of the dead will happen. This was a concern for some who wanted to be buried at the cemetery so they would be among the first to be resurrected with the arrival of the Messiah.[24]) Approximately 38,000 tombstones were stolen and used to build military bunkers and for paving latrines. An asphalt road was cut through the cemetery, and a hotel was built at the top of the mountain. When the Israelis captured the city in 1967, they found open graves with large holes in them with bones scattered throughout the area.[25]

In June 2004, the Knesset Interior Committee met to discuss illegal Arab buildings built on graves, the destruction of gravestones, and using the site as a garbage dump and a marketplace for drugs and prostitution. Anti-Jewish graffiti — slogans, symbols, and insignia of terror gangs — were found throughout the cemetery, and mourners are stoned even now.[26]

The Palestinians have attempted to obliterate Jewish archeological sites in Jerusalem, Jericho, Nablus, and elsewhere that provide physical evidence of the Jewish connection to the land of Israel. This demonstrates radical Islam's contempt for the religious traditions of other groups, as evidenced by the Taliban's destruction of the

The Mount of Olives Cemetery

ancient Buddahs in Afganistan.[27] The Palestinian Ministry of Information asserts that the archaeology in Jerusalem shows "nothing Jewish . . . no tangible evidence of any Jewish traces or remains." Other officials claim Jerusalem is not a Jewish city, "despite the biblical myth implanted in some minds."[28]

Under the Oslo Accords, the Arabs regained control of Nablus and Shechem in 1995, where, according to Jewish tradition, the biblical patriarch Joseph was buried, near the city of Nablus.[29] Israeli soldiers were stationed at the tomb to protect it and the Od Yosef Chai Yeshiva located at the site. Then on October 7, 2000, Prime Minister Ehud Barak ordered the Israeli army to leave the compound after securing an agreement from the Arabs to protect its security. Within hours, Torah scrolls, prayer books, and other holy objects were burned as the Palestinian guards looked on. Using hammers, crowbars, and pickaxes, the mob began to demolish the building. They razed the tomb and the yeshiva, turned the tomb into a mosque and brutally murdered American-born Rabbi Hillel Lieberman, the head of Od Yosef Chai, on his way to protect the site after hearing it was being vandalized.[30] The desecration was broadcast live on PA TV making "it infinitely more potent and destructive."[31] Five days later, Palestinian youths torched the ancient Shalom al Yisrael synagogue in Jericho.

After September 2000, the Muslim Waqf authorities relieved the Israel Antiquities Authority from overseeing archaeological activities on the 36-acre Temple Mount. Since then, the Muslims have removed thousands of tons of material while they build underground mosques at the site. Included in these ruins were the archaeological remains — masonry stones, blocks, floor tiles, and pottery — from the period of the

First and Second Temples. Decorations and inscriptions on stones were removed, as were Hebrew lettering and five-pointed stars, a Hasmonean symbol.[32]

To prove their claim that the Temple Mount is really the site of a mosque dating back to the time of Adam and Eve, they are transforming the area into holy places, leaving nothing to justify Israeli claims to the area. More importantly, a result of the extensive removal of so much from the site is that the southern wall of the Temple Mount is in danger of collapse. Israel is already being blamed for the predicted catastrophe.[33]

The Palestinian Authority broke the treaty again in Bethlehem by failing to protect the synagogue and guarantee Jewish access. Rachel's Tomb has come under repeated attacks. In 1965, the Israelis had found a synagogue mosaic in Gaza from the Byzantine period showing King David wearing a crown and playing lyre, identified by an inscription in Hebrew. Not long after they found the mosaic, David's face was gouged out. During the 1967 Six-Day War, the Israelis captured Gaza and took what remained of the mosaic to the Israel Museum in Jerusalem.[34] The Great Mosque of Gaza was originally built as a Crusader church, but was later converted into a mosque. As one archaeologist explained:

> Some of the upper columns were taken from an ancient synagogue. We know this because on one of these columns were engraved Jewish symbols, the same ones that appeared on the mosaic floor of the Jericho synagogue. . . . Enclosed in a circular wreath near the top of the column was a three-footed menorah, a shofar, and a lulav. Below the wreath was a Hebrew and Greek inscription memorializing a donor to the synagogue. . . . When [he] visited the mosque in 1973, this was all still on the column. . . . When [he] returned to Gaza in 1996, it had all been erased and the stone smoothed over. This could not have been done easily; it obviously required great effort.[35]

IRANIAN HOLOCAUST DENIAL

The Iranians are using Holocaust denial to advance their own agenda. Mahmoud Ahmadinejad, who was appointed president of the Islamic Republic of Iran in August 2005, has brought Holocaust denial to a high art on the international scene. In a televised address on December 14, 2005, he said, "They have created a myth in the name of the Holocaust and consider it above God, religion, and the prophets. . . . If someone were to deny the existence of God . . . and deny the existence of prophets and religion, they would not bother him. However, if someone were to deny the myth of the Jews' massacre, all the Zionist mouthpieces and the governments subservient to the Zionists tear their larynxes and scream against the person as much as they can."[36]

"On the basis of this myth," he noted a couple of months later, "the pillaging Zionist regime has managed, for 60 years, to extort all Western governments and to justify its crimes in the occupied lands — killing women and children, demolishing homes, and turning defenseless people into refugees."[37]

Why has Ahmadinejad become such an advocate of Holocaust denial? One plausible explanation is that he understands the West's fixation with "multiculturalism, moral equivalence, and relativism," and thus appreciates the importance of victimology. If he wants to annihilate Israel, Iran has to be seen as the victim — not Israel.[38]

Ahmadinejad turns to the Europeans with a question: "So we ask you: If you indeed committed this great crime, why should the oppressed people of Palestine be punished for it? If you committed a crime, you yourselves should pay for it."[39]

He knows that there are millions of educated people in the West who do not hold their culture in high regard. If the West can have nuclear weapons, why can't Iran? "Your arsenals are full to the brim, yet when it's the turn of a nation such as mine to develop peaceful nuclear technology you object and resort to threats."[40]

Ahmadinejad also knows that relativism has become part of Western thought. In this environment, who can be sure that the Holocaust was not overstated, the facts embellished or even made up in order to steal Palestinian land?[41]

Their success in analyzing "Western malaise" has persuaded them that they can create "a Holocaust-free reality," enabling the Muslims to become the victims and "Jews the aggressors deserving punishment. And thus Ahmadinejad's righteously aggrieved (and nuclear) Iran can, after 'hundreds of years of war,' finally set things right in the Middle East. And then a world that wishes to continue to make money and drive cars in peace won't much care how this divinely appointed holy man finally finishes a bothersome 'war of destiny.' "[42]

Endnotes

1. Author interview with Itamar Marcus, PMW.

2. "French Holocaust Denier on Ban of Al-Manar: 'The Big Lie of the Alleged Holocaust . . . Is the Shield of Jewish Tyranny . . . Destroy It,' " MEMRI Special Dispatch Series, Number 831 (December 20, 2004).

3. "Anti-Semitism in the Egyptian Media: Part I: Holocaust Denial," MEMRI Special Dispatch Series Number 77 (March 16, 2000); "Holocaust Denial in the Syrian Media," MEMRI Special Dispatch Number 71 (February 2, 2000); "Gas Chamber Denial in the Palestinian Media," MEMRI Number 33 (May 20, 1999); "Anti-Holocaust a Myth, Says Syrian Newspaper," Update SRI (February, 2000); "Holocaust Deniers Plan Conference in Beirut, Update SRI (February 2001); "Which Is Worse — Zionism or Nazism," Update SRI (August 26, 2003); "Radio Iran — A Forum for Holocaust Denial," Update SRI (February, 2000); "PA Newspaper Article: The Fable of the Holocaust," *Al-Hayat Al-Jadida* PMW (April 1, 2001); "Egyptian Journalists on Sharon and the Holocaust," MEMRI Special Dispatch Series Number 188 (February 22, 2001); see also Henry L. Feingold, "The Roots and Meaning of Holocaust Denial," *Jewish Frontier* (Summer/Fall 2001); Mark Glenn, "One Less Than Six Million," Palestinian National Authority State Service International Press Centre (January 24, 2004), Online; Kenneth R. Timmerman, "In Their Own Words: Interviews with Leaders of Hamas, Islamic Jihad and the Muslim Brotherhood," Simon Wiesenthal Center Reports on the Middle East (1994), p. 13–21; Reuven Paz, "Palestinian Holocaust Denial," (April 22, 2000), Online.

4. "[Pope] Wojtyla Free Us from the Jews. An interview with the Grand Mufti of Jerusalem about the Pope's Visit," MEMRI, Special Dispatch Series, Number 82 (March 29, 2000).

5. "The Egyptian Government Paper *Al-Akhbar* Once Again Defends Hitler," MEMRI Special Dispatch Series, Number 231 (June 20, 2001), Online.

6. "Columnist for Egyptian Government Daily to Hitler: 'If Only You Had Done It, Brother,' " MEMRI Special Dispatch Series, Number 375 (May 3, 2002).

7. "Anti-Semitism in the Egyptian Media: Part I: Holocaust Denial."

8. "Former Editor-in-Chief of Egyptian Government Paper: 'We Were Educated from Childhood That the Holocaust Is a Big Lie,' " MEMRI (September 10, 2004) Special Dispatch Series, Number 782.

9. Ibid.; see also "Egyptian Columnist: Guantanamo Is the Real Auschwitz," MEMRI, Special Dispatch Series, Number 351 (March 5, 2002); Goetz Nordbruch, "The Socio-Historical Background of Holocaust Denial in Arab Countries: Reactions to Roger Garaudy's The Founding Myths of Israeli Politics," (The Vidal Sassoon International Center for the Study of Antisemitism, 2001), p. 9–10; see also, "Palestinians Debate Including the Holocaust in the Curriculum," MEMRI Special Dispatch Series, Number 187 (February 21, 2001); "Anti-Semitism in the Egyptian Media: Part I: Holocaust Denial"; "Egyptians Justify Holocaust Denial and the Use of Antisemitic Motifs," SRI (August 2003); "Egyptian Politician Distances Party from Anti-Semitic Article," Haaretz (August 27, 2004).

10. Ray Hanania, "Holocaust Denial Is Wrong and Injures a Righteous Palestinian Cause," Arab Media Syndicate (September 24, 1998), Online; "Anti-Semitism in the Egyptian Media: Part I: Holocaust Denial."

11. Nadia Abou El-Magd, "Debating Holocaust Denial," *Al-Ahram Weekly* no. 481 (May 11–17, 2000), http://weekly.ahram.org.eg/2000/481/eg12htm; "An Arab Voice Rejects Holocaust Denial," MEMRI Number 89 (April 28, 2000); "David Irving Case," Online.

12. Yaacov Lozowick, *Right to Exist: A Moral Defense of Israel's Wars* (New York: Random House, 2003), p. 119.

13. Ibid., p. 120.

14. Ibid.

15. Ibid.

16. Michael Shermer and Alex Grobman, *Denying History: Who Says the Holocaust Never Happened and Why Do They Say It?* (Berkeley, CA: University of California Press, 2000), p. 104–105; "Jews Lost between $240–330b. During the Holocaust," *The Jerusalem Post* (April 20, 2005), Online.

17. Jonathan Eric Lewis, "The Dangers of Holocaust Denial," *Midstream* (April 2003), p. 20–21.

18. Ibid.

19. Ibid., p. 21.

20. "PA Historians: Israel's Biblical History Is Arab Muslim History," PMW (August 8, 2004); see David Hazony, "Memory in Ruins," *Azure* (Winter, 2004), Online.

21. Ibid.

22. Raphael Israeli, *Jerusalem Divided: The Armistice Regime, 1947–1967* (Portland, OR: Frank Cass, 2002), p. 40.

23. Jeff Jacoby, "When Jerusalem Was Divided," *The Boston Globe* (January 8, 2001), Online.

24. Ibid.

25. Ibid; Hazony notes that PA TV broadcasts stress that Israel has no right to exist and that it has no historical connection or claims to the land. On one program, Dr. Issam Sissalem, senior historian and former head of the history department of PA University, and Dr. Jarir Al-Qidwah, head of

the PA public library and Arafat's advisor on education, asserted that Hebrews in the Bible have no connection with Jews living today. Arabs are the Hebrews referred to in the Bible; the prophets were Muslims; the idea that the Temple Mount was located in Jerusalem is a lie; King Solomon was an Arab prophet, and Zionism is racism. Hazony, "Memory in Ruins"; see also Matthew Kalman, "Archeologist Draws Fire for Doubting Biblical Accounts," *Salt Lake City Tribune* (November 6, 1999), Online; Hershel Shanks, "Nor Is It Necessarily Not So," *Haaretz* (November 5, 1999), Online; Hershel Shanks, *The City of David: A Guide to Biblical Jerusalem* (Washington, DC: The Biblical Archaeology Society, 1999).

26. "Outrage Over Illegal Arab Building on Mt. Olives," *Arutz* 7 (June 2, 2004), Online; "A New Plan for Mt. of Olives Cemetery," *Arutz* 7 (November 29, 2004), Online.

27. "The Destruction of the Temple Mount Antiquities," *Jerusalem Letter/Viewpoints*, Jerusalem Center for Public Affairs Number 483 (August 1, 2002), Online.

28. Jacoby, "When Jerusalem Was Divided."

29. "Trouble in the Holy Land: Arab Vandals Desecrate Joseph's Tomb," WorldNetDaily (February 25, 2003), Online; Geoffrey R. Watson, *The Oslo Accords: International Law and the Israeli-Palestinian Peace Agreements* (New York: Oxford University Press, 2000), p. 106.

30. Margot Dudkevitch, "Murdered Joseph's Tomb Teacher to be Buried Tomorrow," *Jerusalem Post* (October 10, 2000), Online; "Palestinians Set Fire to Joseph's Tomb," *Jerusalem Post* (October 16, 2003), Online.

31. David Landau, "Desecration of Holy Places Could Prove to be Most Fateful Acts," *JTA* (October 20, 2000), Online.

32. Ami-El, Jerusalem Center for Public Affairs, August 1, 2002.

33. Ibid; Daniel Pipes, "Nightmare on Temple Mount," *New York Post* (September 4, 2002), Online; Etgar Lefkovits, "Temple Mount Access May Be Limited for Fear of Collapse," *Jerusalem Post* (September 27, 2004), Online.

34. Hershel Shanks, "Holy Targets — Joseph's Tomb Is Just the Latest," *Biblical Archeology Review* (January/February 2001) quoted in "The Arab Campaign to Destroy Israel," American Jewish Committee (June 2000–January 2002), Online.

35. Ibid.

36. Karl Vick, "Iran's President Calls Holocaust 'Myth' in Latest Assault on Jews," Washingtonpost. com (December 15, 2005), p. A01, Online; "Iranian Leader: Holocaust a 'Myth,'" *CNN* (December 14, 2005), Online; "Iran TV Discussion on the Myth of the Gas Chambers and the Truth of Protocols of the Elders of Zion; 'The Only Solution for This Cancerous Tumor [Israel] is Surgery" MEMRI Special Dispatch Series Number 1072 (January 18, 2006), Online.

37. "Iranian President Ahmadinejad on the 'Myth of the Holocaust' & Message to 'Aggressive European Governments . . . and the Great Satan,'" MEMRI Special Dispatch Series No. 1091 (February 14, 2006), Online; "Iranian Leader: Holocaust a 'Myth' "; "Iran's Leader Renews Doubt of Holocaust: Germans Should Shed Guilt, He Tells Magazine," Washingtonpost.com (May 29, 2006), p. A14, Online.

38. Victor Davis Hanson, "The Not-So-Mad Mind of Mahmoud Ahmadinejad," Victorhanson.com (January 23, 2006), Online.

39. Ibid.

40. Ibid.

41. Ibid.

42. Ibid.

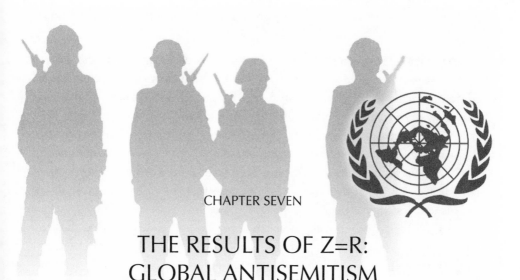

CHAPTER SEVEN

THE RESULTS OF Z=R: GLOBAL ANTISEMITISM

How Words Create Violence

The constant attacks against Israel at the UN and in Europe continue to take their toll. There is a significant increase in antisemitism in Europe, as well as in Afro-Asia, Asia, and all Muslim countries. According to former Israeli Prime Minister Ariel Sharon, this is a direct result of the 17 million Muslims who have inundated the European Union (EU) and incite violence against Jewish people and Israel. These Muslims, he said, endanger the lives of the Jews of Europe.[1] Muslim influence can be seen in an opinion poll taken in October 2003 that found that 59 percent of the approximately 7,000 Europeans surveyed view Israel as the biggest threat to world peace.[2]

Another poll taken in Italy, France, Belgium, Austria, Spain, the Netherlands, Luxembourg, Germany, and Britain found that 46 percent of those polled believed that Jews had a "mentality and lifestyle" different from others, and 35.7 percent said the Jews should cease being victims of the Holocaust. Fifteen percent thought "it would be better if Israel did not exist." In Italy, 17 percent expressed this view. More than 71 percent of the respondents said Israel should leave Judea and Shomron. More than 68 percent acknowledged Israel's right to exist, but that Prime Minister Ariel Sharon's government "was making the wrong choices."[3]

As a consequence of such pervasive anti-Israel (anti-Jewish) antipathy, in France, Belgium, the Netherlands, and the United Kingdom there were physical attacks, verbal abuse, and vandalism against synagogues, stores, and cemeteries. Greece experienced desecration of cemeteries and memorials by elements of the far right.

Adding to the no-win situation, Israel was accused of exaggerating the extent of antisemitism in the EU, but then, in late 2003, the French government acknowledged the danger to the "stability" of France caused by the radicalization of its own estimated seven million member Muslim community.[4]

Not long after Sharon made his remarks about Muslims in Europe, professors Werner Bergman and Wolfgang Benz, authors of a 112-page study commissioned by the EU-sponsored European Monitoring Centre on Racism and Xenophobia (EUMC), charged that the report was buried for fear of a civil war. American lawmakers and Jewish leaders in Europe and in the United States wanted to see the report and were angry, especially after the European poll showed Israel as the greatest threat to world peace. The professors concluded that the wave of antisemitic violence sweeping through Europe is committed by "either right-wing extremists or radical Islamists or young Muslims mostly of Arab descent, who are often themselves potential victims of exclusion and racism." [5]

Antisemitic pronouncements, often disguised as attacks on Israeli policies, were reported in the mass media and expressed in statements by politicians and pundits. In Spain, France, Italy, and Sweden, Arab Muslims and elements of the political left held joint pro-Palestinian rallies, resulting in assaults on Jews and their institutions. In Germany, and to a lesser degree in Austria, there were public discussions about the connection between Israeli policy and antisemitism.[6]

A June 2006 Pew Global Attitudes survey found that almost 37 percent of Germans now support Israel, while 18 percent sympathize with the Palestinians. In March 2004, the Germans were evenly divided between the Arabs and Israelis. The French are also more supportive of Israel than they were in 2002. Then they sympathized with the Arabs by 36 percent to 19 percent.[7] Perhaps the change was caused by Muslim riots in France in the autumn of 2005 and the murder of Dutch filmmaker Theo van Gogh in November 2004 — after his controversial film criticizing Muslim culture was shown on Dutch TV.[8]

ANTI-ZIONISM AND 9/11

Since September 11, 2001, Islamist terrorism is viewed by some as a direct result of the failure to resolve the Middle East conflict for which Israel alone is held accountable. At the same time, Jews are held responsible for America's pro-Israel policies. This creates the environment for anti-American and antisemitic attitudes to consolidate into conspiracy theories about Jews controlling the world. Israel and the United States aren't enemies, so many use that as an excuse to express antisemitism. Anti-globalization forces may rebuke Israel for being overly aggressive, as colonialists and imperialists — which may not be antisemitic — but if they compare Israeli behavior to Nazi behavior, it is outright antisemitism. Demonizing Israel shifts to demonizing the Jewish people. That's how conventional antisemitism is transformed into a legitimate model acceptable to the European political mainstream.[9]

Foreign Policy noted:

> Not since Kristallnacht, the Nazi-led pogrom against German Jews in 1938, have so many European synagogues and Jewish schools been desecrated. This new antisemitism is a kaleidoscope of old hatreds shattered and rearranged into random patterns at once familiar and strange. It is the medieval image of the Christ-killing Jew resurrected on the editorial pages of cosmopolitan European newspapers. It is the International Red Cross and Red Crescent movement refusing to put the Star of David on their ambulances. It is Zimbabwe and Malaysia — nations nearly bereft of Jews — warning of an international Jewish conspiracy to control the world's finances. It is neo-Nazis donning checkered Palestinian kaffiyehs and Palestinians lining up to buy copies of *Mein Kampf*.[10]

On Britain's National Holocaust Remembrance Day in 2003, a cartoon was published in the British daily *Independent*, on the day before Israeli elections, showing Prime Minister Ariel Sharon eating a Palestinian baby. Reflecting the acceptance of such anti-Israel bias, Dave Brown, the *Independent*'s cartoonist won the Political Cartoon of the Year Award from the national newspaper cartoonists and the Political Cartoon Society.[11]

In Edinburgh, an Episcopalian church painted a mural showing "a crucified Jesus flanked by Roman soldiers — and modern-day Israeli troops." An Episcopalian clergyman defended the mural by claiming that it was intended to force the congregation to think about the Arab/Israeli conflict.[12]

With Jews in powerful and highly visible positions in international financial institutions, with financial uncertainty, dislocation, and globalization, a number of developing countries are looking for scapegoats for their failures as leaders. Malaysian Prime Minister Mahathir Mohamad's explanation for his country's financial chaos was that Jews were responsible for determining "our currency levels and bring[ing] about the collapse of our economy."

A spokesman for the Jamaat-i-Islami political party in Pakistan reached the same conclusion: "Most anything bad that happens, prices going up, whatever, this can be attributed to the IMF and the World Bank, which are synonymous with the United States. And who controls the United States? The Jews do."[13]

In Darfur, the Islamic Sudanese government is blaming the Jews for causing the genocide there. Sudanese President Omar al-Bashir refused to allow UN peacekeepers into Darfur, claiming that their real objective is "to colonize Africa, starting with the first sub-Saharan country to gain its independence. If they want to start colonization in Africa, let them choose a different place." Who is behind this push for deployment? "It is clear that there is a purpose behind the heavy propaganda and media campaigns" al-Bashir said. "If we return to the last demonstrations in the United States, and the groups that organized the demonstrations, we find that they are all Jewish organizations."[14]

Antisemitic Attacks

Antisemitic statements routinely made against Israel and Zionism at the UN and in the Arab and Israeli media would never be tolerated if they were directed toward other UN member states. Thousands of complaints about human rights abuses in Bahrain, Chad, Liberia, Malawi, Mali, Pakistan, Saudi Arabia, and Syria have been made to the UN throughout the years, but Commission meetings are not open to the public, and the offending countries are never censured.[15]

At the same time, the Commission consistently prohibited the use of anti-semitism — "one of the most poisonous forms of racism" — from all appropriate resolutions, but allowed it to be recorded in the chambers.

At the March 17, 1997, session of the UN Commission on Human Rights, Israel was accused of "inject[ing] 300 Palestinian children with HIV virus during the years of the Intifada." An apology was issued, but the complaint that the Israeli health minister "permitted Israeli pharmaceutical companies to conduct dangerous tests on more than 4,000 Palestinian prisoners" was never withdrawn.[16]

The issue of AIDS was raised in Gaza on May 15, 1997, in the official PA newspaper *Al-Hayat Al-Jadidap*. It claimed that the Israelis "brought Russian Jewish girls with AIDS to spread the disease among Palestinian youth,[17] and that "Israel is distributing food containing material that causes cancer and hormones that harm male virility and other spoiled food products in order to poison and harm the Palestinian population."[18]

In 1999, Secretary-General Kofi Annan acknowledged that in the Jewish community "it has sometimes seemed as if the United Nations serves the interests of all peoples but one: the Jews." He was encouraged that for the first time the General Assembly had included antisemitism among the types of racism it wanted to eliminate.

"The United Nations will never forget its origins in the fight against fascism, and that its Charter was drafted as the world was learning the full horror of the Holocaust," he said. "This history makes it especially sad that such a gulf has developed" between the UN and the world Jewish community.[19]

The Durban Conference

During the summer of 2001, many NGOs met at the UN World Conference Against Racism in Durban, South Africa, and removed most references to antisemitism from its final declaration. No mention was made of the Holocaust or the need to study this event, even though it had insisted that those inciting racial hatred be brought to justice. The only references to the Holocaust were with regard to the Middle East, in which Palestinians were proclaimed the victims of Israeli racism.[20]

Irwin Cotler viewed the proceedings in Durban as a "Festival of Hate," with a clear mandate for the future: "Just as the struggle against racism in the 20th century required the dismantling of South Africa as an apartheid state, so the struggle against racism in the 21st century requires the dismantling of Israel as an apartheid state."

Cotler acknowledges that Israel is not above the law. She is as accountable for any contravention of international human rights and humanitarian law as any other nation. "But Israel is being systematically denied equality before the law" and is being "singled out. . . for discriminatory indictment while granting the real human rights violators exculpatory immunity."

The UN's Kofi Annan said that it is not possible that the whole world is against Israel, yet Israel is right; but Cotler concludes, "History has shown that a minority of one can be right."[21]

FAILURE OF DURBAN

In spite of the atmosphere of vilification against Zionism and Israel nurtured by various organizations during the NGOs' Durban Conference, which was held just before the UN official member states conference, the final declaration did not contain attacks against or condemnation of Israel and Zionism.

Article 63 states its concern for the plight of Palestinian people "under foreign occupation" and mentions "the inalienable right of the Palestinian people to self-determination and to the establishment of an independent State." It also "recognizes the right to security for all States in the region, including Israel and calls upon all States to support the peace process and bring it to an early resolution."[22]

When a correspondent at the conference asked Kofi Annan whether approving language critical of Israel would tarnish the image of the UN as an impartial mediator in the Arab/Israeli conflict, he replied that the conference document and declaration had to be fair. "The question of Zionism versus racism is dead," he said, noting that the UN had abrogated it a decade earlier. "I think the delegations understand that and those who don't are beginning to get that very clearly."[23]

When asked whether he wanted all specific references to Israel removed from the draft declaration, the secretary-general said the Middle East was not the only area in which people were suffering.

"I would hope that we would come up with language, whether in a generic form or whatever, that will speak to every situation and will respond to the feelings and the pain that vulnerable people are feeling around the world," he added.[24]

CONDONING VIOLENCE

On April 15, 2002, six European states — Austria, Belgium, France, Portugal, Spain, and Sweden — approved a UN Human Rights Commission resolution condoning "all available means, including armed struggle" to establish a Palestinian state.[25] It was clearly understood in UN code language that "by all available means" meant making terrorism legitimate. Before the vote, Ambassador Alfred Moses, chairman of UN Watch, the Geneva-based institute of the American Jewish Committee said:

> A vote in favor of this resolution is a vote for Palestinian terrorism. An abstention suggests ambivalence toward terror. Any country that condones — or is indifferent to — the murder of Israeli civilians in markets, on buses, and in cafes, has lost any moral standing to criticize Israel's human rights record.[26]

The resolution also contradicted Security Council resolutions 1397 and 1402, that demand an "immediate cessation of all acts of violence, including all acts of terror," and Kofi Annan's statement to the Commission on April 12: "The killing of innocent civilians violates international law and undermines the legitimacy of the cause it purports to serve. That, of course, applies also to suicide bombings aimed at civilians, which are as morally repugnant as they are politically harmful."[27]

In 2002, the General Assembly published 22 reports on the state of the Palestinians and other Arabs living under Israeli occupation.[28] Under the heading of human rights organizational structure on the UN's website, there is only one country-specific mandate: the "Special Committee to Investigate Israeli Practices Affecting the Human Rights of the Palestinian People and Other Arabs of the Occupied Territories," including Jerusalem and the "Syrian Arab Golan."

JENIN: THE MASSACRE THAT WASN'T

The behavior of the UN in April 2002 was a key factor in creating the near-hysteria about the alleged "massacre" in the Jenin refugee camp in the West Bank by the Israel Defense Forces (IDF), who were accused of murdering hundreds of unarmed civilian Palestinian men, women, children, and elderly.

The IDF had entered the refugee camp to root out terrorists in what members of Fatah called "the capital of the suicide martyrs." Fatah claimed that the camp of 14,000 people had fighters who would not allow anything to defeat or faze them.[29] Of the 107 suicide bombers who had killed hundreds of Israelis, 23 were from Jenin or its environs.[30]

For eight days, Israeli soldiers fought house-to-house against hundreds of armed Arabs in a very crowded, populated urban area that had been extensively booby-trapped. According to one resident, explosives were placed in the streets, "inside cupboards, under sinks, inside sofas," and in cars and dumpsters.

The refugee camp where the fighting occurred is a very small part of the city of Jenin, but it was turned into a minefield by the time the IDF arrived. On one street, they found 124 explosives, some weighing 250 kilograms (550 lbs.). More were found in the camp itself.

After the Israelis razed buildings where Palestinian gunmen were hiding, the resistance ended and the true scope of the damage became known. The UN reported the death of 23 Israeli soldiers and 52 Palestinians, more than half of them armed fighters. Hundreds of houses were either destroyed or seriously damaged.[31]

Touring the refugee camp after the Israelis withdrew, Terje Roed-Larsen, the UN's Special Coordinator for the Middle East, said the devastation was so absolute that "it looks like an earthquake has hit it," and that was "totally unacceptable and horrific." Israeli refusal to permit search-and-rescue teams to come to the camp was morally repugnant.[32]

Kofi Annan wanted to send a commission headed by Marti Ahtisaari, the former president of Finland, to investigate the allegations against Israel. His colleague, Cornelio Sommaruga, the former president of the International Committee of the Red Cross, had once compared the Star of David to the Nazi swastika.

The Weekly Standard viewed the idea of "a UN fact-finding mission to Jenin" as "scandalous to begin with" and "an assault on Israel's honor, even its basic legitimacy as an independent nation, that no similarly situated democracy would ever be expected to endure."[33]

The *Standard* then asked, if the death toll had been a hundred times higher than the 52 Palestinians killed, would that have justified a UN fact-finding mission? In 1993, a two-week U.S. bombing campaign against Mogadishu killed a thousand Somali civilians. During the entire Intifada, which at that point had been six months old, far fewer Palestinians than that had died as Israel confronted a far greater and more immediate national security threat than any America faced in East Africa. But did the UN convene an inquiry into the human catastrophe in Somalia? It did not.[34]

UNRWA (United Nations Relief and Works Agency), the *Standard* continues, finances and runs schools in Jenin, where children are told that all of Palestine, from the Jordan River to the Mediterranean Sea, is theirs. During the summer months, the schools teach students the arts of kidnapping, throwing rocks, manufacturing bombs, and blowing themselves up. UNRWA also provides buses to take local residents on tours of Israel to show the property stolen from them by the Jews.

In addition, UNRWA permits its food warehouses to serve as weapons depots. It also feigns ignorance about explosives and counterfeit money factories operating in the public shelters it built in Jenin. UNRWA cannot fathom how its administrative offices are decorated with "graffiti celebrating some of the world's most notorious terrorist organizations. Or how some of the world's most notorious terrorists might have found their way onto the agency's payroll — to the point where the Popular Front for the Liberation of Palestine, extreme even in the context of Palestinian extremism, now openly controls the UNRWA workers' union."[35]

Arab diplomats make groundless charges about the UN favoring Israel that are accepted as facts. During the debate on Iraq in May 2002, for example, the Syrian, Iraqi, and Arab League representatives complained that the UN had imposed sanctions against Iraq for failing to comply with UN resolutions, but when Israel ignored UN resolutions they were not punished for their violations. This is a false comparison since the UN distinguishes between resolutions adopted by the General Assembly and the Security Council. General Assembly resolutions have political (and in the public mind, even moral) authority, but are not legally binding.[36]

Human Rights Violations

On April 15, 2003, at the 59th session of the UN Commission on Human Rights, four resolutions criticizing Israel were passed. During heated debates preceding the votes, Israelis were charged with being worse than the Nazis. One resolution criticized Israeli policy "including the illegal installation of settlers in the occupied territories." It condemned the limits on the freedom of movement of Palestinians, the security fence, and "indiscriminate terrorist attacks."

Another resolution condemned "the gross violations of human rights and international humanitarian law, in particular, acts of extra-judicial killing, closures, collective punishments, the persistence in establishing settlements, arbitrary detentions, the besieging of Palestinian towns and villages, the shelling of Palestinian residential districts from warplanes, tanks, and Israeli battleships, the conducting of incursions into towns and camps and the killing of men, women, and children there." It condemned the "acts of mass killing perpetrated by the Israeli-occupying authorities against the Palestinian people." Yet another asserted the "inalienable, permanent, and unqualified right of the Palestinian people to self-determination, including their right to establish their sovereign and independent Palestinian state." The last resolution called on Israel to stop altering the physical character and legal status of the Syrian Golan Heights it occupied in the 1967 war.[37]

In a letter, and later in a meeting with Sergio Vieira de Mello, the High Commissioner of the Human Rights Commission, representatives of the International Association of Jewish Lawyers and Jurists said they expected the High Commissioner to explicitly condemn statements made at the annual session of the Commission calling for the elimination of Israel. That condemnation also applied to statements and resolutions made against Israel, Jews, antisemitism, and Holocaust denial. Vieira de Mello assured the representatives that he had expressed his concerns to the appropriate members, but the High Commissioner did not respond to repeated requests for a clear public reprimand.[38]

Antisemitic publications were printed in the tens of thousands; at other times in the hundreds of thousands. The deputy director of the International Department of the Central Committee of the Soviet Communist Party wrote that Zionism would be "condemned as a serious international offense."[39]

In December 2003, Foreign Minister Brian Cowen of Ireland promised Israeli Foreign Minister Silvan Shalom that he would introduce a specific resolution against antisemitism if Israel agreed not to have it included in the religious intolerance resolution that was coming to a vote. After the Third Committee adopted the resolution on intolerance without reference to antisemitism, Cowen reneged on his agreement.

"At the heart of the UN's problem with anti-Semitism lies rejection of the very idea of Jewish victimhood," wrote Anne Bayefsky. "Instead of ensuring that victimhood brooks no discrimination, on November 26 a resolution condemning terrorist attacks on Israeli children failed to make it through the General Assembly, while one on Palestinian children was adopted with only four states opposed. Israel was forced to withdraw its resolution because Egyptian amendments deleting 'Israeli' before every mention of the word 'children' were guaranteed an automatic U.N. majority."[40]

CHILDREN AS CANNON FODDER

Since the Intifada began in September 2000, Palestinian terrorist organizations used increasingly larger numbers of children to perpetrate acts of violence against Israelis. Palestinian children, some as young as seven or eight years old, serve as human shields — a clear contravention of international law and their basic rights. The Palestinian Authority took no steps to prevent this abuse and exploitation.[41]

The PA is part of the problem:

> The cynical use of children as pawns . . . begins in the Palestinian education system. Palestinian textbooks — many of which have been recently published by the PA itself — openly teach hatred of Israel and Israelis. Materials published and broadcast in the official Palestinian media reinforce these lessons, aiming much of its incitement at children. Such programs encourage Palestinian children to hate Israelis and take part in the violence. Children are urged by television advertisements to "drop your toys and take up arms," while Palestinian educational television . . . glorifies martyrdom in the struggle against Israel. . . . These children will design the nature of our coexistence in the next generation.

At the same time, Palestinian terrorists killed more than a hundred Israeli children, and many more were maimed, injured, and permanently disabled.[42]

From 2000 through 2004, Palestinian TV continuously broadcast music videos to entice young children into becoming *shahids* — martyrs for Allah. In July 2006, Palestinian TV re-broadcast the most "sinister" of these videos in which a child actor played Muhammad al-Dura — the child died during a battle between Palestinians and Israelis and was discovered to have been callously shot by the Palestinians for public relations purposes. The film urges Palestinian children to join him in Child Martyrs' Heaven.[43]

ASSASSINATIONS, EXTRAJUDICIAL KILLINGS, AND SELF-DEFENSE

In 2004, the UN Human Rights Commission composed primarily of African and Asian states including Cuba, China, Saudi Arabia, Sudan, and Zimbabwe, adopted five resolutions against Israel, then spent three hours mourning the death of Sheikh Ahmad Yassin, the Hamas terrorist. The sheikh had authorized suicide bombings and urged his followers to violence against Israelis and Jews wherever they might be.[44]

The commission and Kofi Anan denounced the Israeli action as an "extrajudicial killing," which was provocative and wrong. Yassin and Abdel Aziz Rantissi — a Hamas terrorist who succeeded Yassin as head of Hamas in the Gaza strip — were assassinated by the Israelis as combatants involved in a war against Israel.

PREVENTING TERROR

Though it sounds callous, the matter of extrajudicial killings has long been studied and adjudicated. Stopping terrorist leaders from implementing their murderous objectives is a justifiable military goal, as long as the number of civilians killed in the process is not out of proportion with the objective. Although they were civilians, they were not entitled to prior judicial process. Manuals of the International Committee of the Red Cross clearly state that civilians directly involved in conflicts relinquish their immunity from attack. Combatants are legitimate military targets who can be eliminated wherever they are and whenever they are found under international law. This can be while asleep or engaged in a military operation. Their only recourse from being killed is to surrender.

Thus, any attempt to employ the judicial process would have endangered Palestinian civilians and the IDF. According to the Geneva Convention, the rule in targeting combatants is based on proportionality. "Incidental loss of civilian life" should not be "excessive." In both assassinations, the civilian losses were kept at a minimum.[45]

Israel is perfectly within her legal rights to seek out leaders of Hamas for assassination. No distinction is made by Hamas between the political and military wings of the organization. Its official goal is the mass murder of Jewish civilians, a decision that was made by its political leaders.[46]

Military law dictates that civilian casualties be kept to a minimum, and the United States and Israel are very careful to avoid them. When the IDF first targeted Yassin, they used a 500-pound bomb to reduce collateral damage, and he escaped with minor harm. If Israel had no concern for civilians, a larger bomb would have been dropped. Alan Dershowitz wrote, "Any democracy facing threats to its civilian population comparable to those faced by Israel would respond in much the same way Israel is now responding to the terrorism being conducted by Hamas and other terrorist groups."[47]

If the UN were equally concerned about extrajudicial killings in other countries, Israel would not be in a position to complain. While the UN commission was condemning Israel, it received a report about more than 3,000 extrajudicial killings of civilians in Brazil by the military and police, and never reacted. The UN Rapporteur on Extrajudicial, Summary or Arbitrary Executions brought information to the commission about poorly disguised extrajudicial assassinations with the lethal shots fired from behind the victims at close range. Two of his sources were then shot and killed after he left the country, but the Human Rights Commission of Brazil did nothing about it.[48]

Ambassador Ya'akov Levy, permanent representative of Israel to the United Nations Office in Geneva, said this "forum has clearly reached its nadir by lending a hand and moral standing for supporting the most despicable and horrendous of evils — that of terrorism — while denying Israel the right of self-defense against that evil."

(When Israelis assassinated Yassin, acknowledged as a terrorist by the United States and the EU, the UN called a special session to condemn them. The resolution passed by 31-3, with 18 abstentions.)

Everything these terrorists do, Levy continued,

> . . . turns to hatred and bloodshed: ambulances which should be protecting the sick become vehicles for terrorists and bombs; mosques and churches, places of worship and contemplation, become fortresses for terrorist killers who shoot from their shelter; and places of incitement for murder and brutality. Ultimately, the sacredness of life is distorted by these terrorists to become a glorification of death and so-called "martyrdom."[49]

THE SECURITY FENCE

On July 9, 2004, the UN International Court of Justice issued a non-binding resolution asking Israel to demolish its security fence. The UN Ambassador from the United States, John Danforth, noted that in the ruling the court had modified the right of nation-states to defend themselves in a way that caused concern:

So the Court opinion, which this resolution would accept, seems to say that the right of a state to defend itself exists only when it is attacked by another state, and that the right of self-defense does not exist against non-state actors. It does not exist when terrorists hijack planes and fly them into buildings, or bomb train stations, or bomb bus stops or put poison gas into subways. I would suggest that if this were the meaning of Article 51, then the United Nations Charter could be irrelevant in a time when the major threats to peace are not from states, but from terrorists.[50]

The court ruling, which the UN General Assembly endorsed, opposed military retaliation against non-state terrorist organizations unless the government that shelters the terrorists grants their enemies permission to do so.[51]

Misplaced Priorities

Jean Ziegler, the UN Special Rapporteur on the Right to Food, acknowledged that practically a billion people were malnourished, but instead issued a report on the "food crisis" in the "occupied Palestinian territory." He faulted the "apartheid wall" and never noted the recurrent terrorist attacks responsible for the disruption of the flow of goods and workers, or the millions of dollars Yasser and Suha Arafat took from the Palestinian people.[52]

Ziegler, known for his anti-Israel bias, urged the EU to freeze Israel's trade partner status to pressure her to deliver food to the Palestinians, and never acknowledged the danger of sending anything, including food and medicine, into the West Bank and Gaza. The Geneva-based UN Watch asked Kofi Annan to dismiss him, and filed a legal brief outlining his condemnation of Israel on matters not related to food.[53]

The Commission Rapporteur on Freedom of Religion or Belief wrote a report about hate in the world, and never mentioned antisemitism. A report on the status of Muslims and Arabs around the globe is required. When the Rapporteur suggested a report on antisemitism, his idea was disregarded.[54]

UN Conference on Antisemitism

In June 2004, the UN convened the first conference on antisemitism in its history. UN expert Anne Bayefsky remarked that the UN provides a "platform for those who cast the victims of the Nazis as the Nazi counterparts of the 21st century. The UN has become the leading global purveyor of anti-Semitism — intolerance and inequality against the Jewish people and its state."[55]

Palestinian self-determination is justified, she said, but demonizing Israel while sanctifying Palestinians demonstrates that the fundamental issue is not Palestinian suffering. If that were the case, the UN would have adopted resolutions abhorring the active promotion of Palestinian children as suicide bombers and venerating them as holy martyrs. There would be resolutions against using Palestinians as human shields and against Arab states that won't allow Palestinian refugees to integrate into their societies or become citizens.[56]

The UN's "big lie" — that the occupation of Palestinian land is the primary reason for the Arab-Israeli conflict — helps fuel antisemitism.

> According to UN revisionism, the occupation materialized in a vacuum. In reality, Israel occupies land taken in a war [sic] which was forced upon it by neighbors who sought to destroy it. It is a state of occupation which Israelis themselves have repeatedly sought to end through negotiations over permanent borders. It is a state in which any abuses are closely monitored by Israel's independent judiciary. But ultimately, it is a situation which is the responsibility of the projectionists of Jewish self-determination among Palestinians and their Arab and Muslim brethren who have rendered the Palestinian civilian population hostage to their violent and anti-Semitic ambitions.[57]

Whether the conference on antisemitism marked a change in the UN's attitude would be determined if the General Assembly adopts a resolution against antisemitism, appoints a special Rapporteur, and issues an annual report on global antisemitism. If the UN is really serious about fighting antisemitism, they must be challenged to condemn those who violate human rights even if they live in Damascus or Riyadh; to stop censuring Israel when the Jewish people defend themselves against their killers; to give a name to the terrorists who murder Jews simply because they are Jews, and not to stand for a minute of silence to honor individuals who sought to destroy Israel. If they do that, only then can they send a message that it will no longer tolerate antisemitism anywhere.[58]

The answers were not long in coming. In November 2004, the General Assembly voted on a resolution concerning religious intolerance in which antisemitism was mentioned in only one paragraph. Fifty-four Member States — out of 153 who voted — did not support the resolution. Instead of being a positive effort, the conference became just one more part in the UN's attempt to separate antisemitism and the Jewish people from Israel. As Anne Bayefsky noted, "Put the Jews on one side, Israel on the other, and divide and conquer."[59]

Before the vote on religious intolerance, the same states declined to back a resolution "to ensure effective protection of the right to life . . . and to investigate . . . all killings committed for any discriminatory reason, including sexual orientation." In other words, antisemitism and murdering people because of their sexual preferences were permissible to practically every one of the 56 members of the Organization of the Islamic Conference (OIC).[60]

THE UN MUST DEFINE TERRORISM

Resolution 1373, adopted by the Security Council on September 28, 2001, obligates the UN to find ways to combat terrorism. But it has yet to do so. The UN acknowledges "the question of a definition of terrorism has haunted the debate among states for decades. . . . The lack of agreement on a definition of terrorism has been a major obstacle to meaningful international countermeasures. Cynics have often commented that one state's terrorist is another state's freedom fighter.[61]

The resolution's legal requirements are imposing: to "refrain from providing any form of support, active or passive, to entities or persons involved in terrorist acts"; to "take the necessary steps to prevent the commission of terrorist acts"; to "deny safe haven to those who finance, plan, support, or commit terrorist acts"; and to "prevent those who finance, plan, facilitate, or commit terrorist acts from using their respective territories for those purposes against other States or their citizens."[62]

The Organization of the Islamic Conference adamantly maintains that the definition of terrorism never include "armed struggle for liberation and self-determination," so that when Arab terrorists blow up Jewish men, women, and children in synagogues, cafes, shopping centers, pizza shops, buses, and discotheques, it is acceptable and justifiable.[63]

UN OFFICIALS CONTRIBUTE TO CONFUSION
ABOUT ISRAEL AND ANTISEMITISM

In March 2002, Kofi Annan called the lands Israel obtained in the 1967 Six-Day War "illegal." George P. Fletcher, a professor at Columbia University School of Law, feared "that Palestinians will dig in with a new feeling of righteousness and believe that the international community will force Israel to withdraw from its 'illegal occupation.' . . . Injecting the word 'illegal' into the conversation will only shift the focus from calming the situation and increase intransigence of the Palestinians . . . [and it] is a perilous threat to the diplomatic search for peace."[64]

"In Middle Eastern politics," he said, "memory enables each side to nurture its grievances, but there is little collective memory that might facilitate negotiations on the basis of shared assumptions. Few seem to care anymore that the 1967 war was a war of self-defense for Israel or that United Nations Security Council Resolution 242 referred to withdrawal from 'territories' rather than from 'the territories' — a crucial distinction that shows that the resolution does not necessarily require withdrawal from all of the land occupied in 1967. In this time of crisis and forgetfulness, using the term 'illegal' is destructive and dangerous. For the uninformed, the discussion will start with the secretary general's labeling of the occupation as a violation of law."[65]

". . . Resolution 242, passed right after the 1967 war, envisions a just resolution of the conflict and calls for withdrawal and mutual recognition, but it says nothing about legality. Resolution 338, passed after the 1973 Yom Kippur War, imposes an obligation on Israel and the Arabs to negotiate peace. Because it insisted that the Palestinians negotiate an end to the Israeli presence, the Security Council could not have thought the occupation itself violated international law. Later Security Council resolutions — numbered 446, 452, and 465 — do indeed condemn Israel's policy of building settlements in the occupied territories and declare that these settlements have 'no legal validity.' Yet these rebukes against Israeli policy were about the settlements — not about the legality of the occupation. And even then, the Security Council stopped short of actually saying that all settlements are illegal. Some of the settlements might be acceptable under the language of Resolution 242, which recognizes that Israel has the right to live within 'secure and recognized boundaries.' "[66]

There is room for debate about Israel's support for the settlements and whether that violates the prohibition in the Fourth Geneva Convention wherein "the occupying power shall not deport or transfer parts of its own civilian population into the territory it occupies." Until a peace treaty can be negotiated between the Israelis and Palestinians, it is not illegal for the Israelis to occupy the land. The Palestinians refuse to acknowledge this.[67]

UN special envoy to Iraq Lakhdar Brahimi
with UN Secretary General Kofi Annan.
(Credit: UN Photo)

THE UN VIEW

In April 2004, a UN special envoy to Iraq, Lakhdar Brahimi, told a French television network that Israel is "the great poison in the region." He said his task of forming an Iraqi government was being made difficult by "the Israeli policy of domination and the suffering imposed on the Palestinians."

Blaming Israel for the absence of democracy, the lack of human rights, and poverty in Muslim countries is routine. After a meeting with French President Jacques Chirac in Paris, Brahimi affirmed his earlier statement saying, "that, [it] is the feeling of everyone in the region and beyond and I think this is a statement of fact, not an opinion."[68]

In response, American Jewish leaders asked Kofi Annan to appoint a special advisor on Jewish affairs to serve as a link to the American Jewish community. The secretary-general is surrounded by Muslim assistants and advisors who are antagonistic toward Jews, and they make it difficult for Jews to meet with him. Brahimi is one of the people who advise him, and Kofi Annan's Pakistani chief of staff is known for his anti-Jewish attitude.[69]

The UN view of Israel is probably best described by the UN Special Rapporteur on Israel, John Dugard. He told the commission, ". . . after the necessary disclaimer of sympathy for terrorism, the report will focus on two issues that . . . most seriously demand the attention of the international community — the unlawful annexation of Palestinian territory and the restrictions on freedom of movement." He has described Palestinian terrorists as tough and their efforts as determined, daring, and successful.[70]

MORAL CLARITY

No one questions the need for sympathy and action on behalf of the oppressed said Natan Sharansky. But the absence of moral clarity in the world, he writes, is what allows "dictators to speak about human rights even as they kill thousands, tens of thousands, millions, and even tens of millions of people. It is a world in which the only democracy in the Middle East is perceived as the greatest violator of human rights in the world. It is a world in which a human rights conference in Durban . . . can be turned into a carnival of hate."[71]

Waiting for Arab dictatorial regimes to reform or getting the support of international organizations is futile, said Sharansky. Non-democratic leaders will not be moved to alter their ways. Countries that exercise power in international associations are too often non-democratic and refuse to provide freedom to their own citizens. They can hardly be expected to champion freedom in other parts of the globe.[72]

Free nations cannot be created without the active support of countries that understand the overwhelming moral discrepancy between freedom and intimidation, and they must challenge the hypocrites. To defeat oppression requires that we believe that "all people are created equal but also that all *peoples* are created equal."[73]

Kofi Annan and the members of the UN understand that the Commission on Human Rights has an image problem. In December 2004, the United Nations criticized the commission for eroding the credibility and professionalism of the UN and for being controlled by states whose concern is "not to strengthen human rights but to protect themselves against criticism or to criticize others."

Hillel Neuer, executive director of UN Watch in Geneva, asked the most fundamental question of those seeking a reform of the organization: "How can the objective enforcement of human rights, an apolitical task, be pursued by a body made up entirely of governments which are inherently political? That is the crucial question confronting the U.N. Commission on Human Rights."[74]

IS THE UN WORTH IT?

In 1975, Senator Moynihan argued that the United States should remain in the opposition to the UN. Syndicated conservative columnist Charles Krauthammer rejected that argument, positing that it was not worth saving and that the United States should "let it sink." The United States derives some moral satisfaction for attacking some of the more outrageous resolutions, he said, but this is a self-defeating policy: "It seeks to diminish the moral and political victories of its adversaries, but instead — inadvertently but necessarily — it blames them."[75]

The UN has failed in its primary responsibility, which is to ensure the peace. There are times when its actions worsen the conflicts over which it still has some influence. The UN is more than a failed institution. "It is a bad instrument."[76]

In an attempt to reform the Commission, Kofi Annan established the UN Human Rights Council to replace the discredited Human Rights Commission. The Council met in June 2006 with the first session focusing on the "human rights situation in the occupied Arab Territories, including Palestine." The balance of power on the Council is held by the OIC.[77]

In July 2006, a special session of the Council was called to discuss Israel's incursion into the Gaza Strip. In August 2005, 8,000 Israeli civilians and soldiers left Gaza, leaving the area completely under Palestinian control. Since then, the Palestinians have fired more than 500 Qassam rockets into Israeli cities of Sderot, Netivot, and Ashkelon, killing Israeli civilians. When Israel sought to defend itself against these attacks and rescue a soldier abducted by the Palestinians, the Human Rights Council sprang into action to condemn Israel.[78]

Endnotes

1. "Ariel Sharon, Prime Minister of Israel," EUPoliyix.com, (November 24, 2003).

2. "Poll Controversy as Israel and U.S. Labeled Biggest Threats to World Peace" (October 23, 2003), Online; "Prodi Reassures U.S. Jewish Leaders After Poll," (November 5, 2003), Online; Omer Taspinar, "Europe's Muslim Street," *Foreign Policy* (March/April 2003), Online; Mark Lilla, "The End of Politics," *The New Republic* (June 23, 2003), Online; Jonah Goldberg, "Israel Isn't Peaceful," *Jewish World Review* (November 5, 2003), Online; Judy Weil, "Jews in Europe Cannot Lead a Normal Life," *Maariv* (April 4, 2004), Online.

3. "European Poll; 46% Say Jews Are Different," *Haaretz* (January 1, 2004), Online.

4. Marc Perelman, "Envoy Says Antisemitism Threatens France," *Forward* (December 5, 2003), Online.

5. Werner Bergman and Juliane Wetzel, "Manifestations of Anti-Semitism in the European Union," Berlin, Germany, Center for Research on Antisemitism Technische Universitat Berlin, March 2003, p. 5–10.

6. Ibid.

7. "America's Image Slips, But Allies Share U.S. Concerns Over Iran, Hamas," Pew Global Attitudes Project (June 6, 2006), Online.

8. "Spiegel Interview with Ayaan Hirsi Ali: Everyone Is Afraid to Criticize Islam," *Der Spiegel* (February 6, 2006), Online; "Gunman Kills Dutch Film Director," *BBC News* (November 2, 2004).

9. Ibid; Marc Perelman, "E.U. Accused of Burying Report on Antisemitism Pointing to Muslim Role," *Forward* (November 28, 2003), Online; Sharon Sadeh, "Researchers Blast EU for Burying Anti-Semitism Study," (November 11, 2003).

10. Mark Strauss, "Antiglobalism's Jewish Problem," *Foreign Policy* (November/December 2003), Online.

11. "Independent Cartoonist Wins Award for Sharon Cartoon," *Independent* (November 27, 2003), Online; see also, "Fears of Anti-Semitism Sweep Europe: Leftists, Intellectuals Blaming Israel for World's Ills," SFGate.com (December 14, 2003).

12. Werner Bergmann and Juliane Wetzel, "Manifestations of Anti-Semitism in the European Union," First Semester 2002 Synthesis Report on behalf of the EUMC European Monitoring Centre on Racism and Xenophobia Zentrum für Antisemitismusforschung / Center for Research on Antisemitism Technisch Universität Berlin Vienna, March 2003.

13. Strauss, "Antiglobalism's Jewish Problem"; see also, "Furor over Antisemitic Remarks of German MP," (Tel Aviv: Tel-Aviv University, The Stephen Roth Institute for the Study of Antisemitism and Racism), http://www. tau.ac.il/Anti-Semitism/updates/i00061.html.

14. "Sudan President Blames the Jews for Encouraging Peacekeeping Efforts," ADL Press Release (June 21, 2006), Online; "Sudan Blames Jews for U.N. Peacekeeper Push," MSNBC (June 21, 2006), Online.

15. "President's Message," The International Association of Jewish Layers and Jurists," (n.d. 2003), http://www.intjewishlawyers.org/html/president.html.

16. Moshe Zak, *Maariv,* March 23, 1998, p. B6, Online; see also Raphael Israeli, *Poison: Modern Manifestations of a Blood Libel* (Lanham: MA, Lexington Books, 2002); "Palestinian Authority Quotes," Online.

17. David Blewett, "Israel's Unfriendly Neighborhood," National Christian Leadership Conference for Israel (1999), Online.

18. In a newspaper interview of David Blewett by the Israeli newspaper *Yediot Aharonot,* June 25, 1997, Online.

19. "U.N. Secretary-General Kofi Anan Calls for Partnership between Jewish Community and U.N.," *Charity Wire* (December 13, 1999), Online.

20. Anne Bayefsky, "The UN and the Jews," *Commentary* (February 2004): p. 43; see also Fiamma Nirenstein, "Worst Fears Conformed," WorldNetDaily (September 14, 2001), Online; Nirenstein, "Written on the Walls of Durban," WorldNetDaily (September 20, 2001), Online; "Hanan Ashrawi's Address to World Conference Against Racism," (August 28, 2001), Online; see also Fiamma Nirenstein, "Dead Jews Walking," WorldNetDaily (July 12, 2002), Online; Gary Mc-Dougall, "The Durban Racism Conference Revisited: The World Conference on Racism Through a Wider Lens," *The Fletcher Forum of World Affairs Journal* (Fall 2002); Jerry V. Leaphart, "The Durban Racism Conference Revisited: The World Conference Against Racism: What Was Really Accomplished," *The Fletcher Forum of World Affairs Journal* (Fall 2002); Tom Lantos, "The New World Order: The Durban Debacle: An Insider's View of the UN World Conference Against Racism," *The Fletcher Forum of World Affairs Journal* (Fall 2002); Charles Krauthammer, "Disgrace in Durban," *The Weekly Standard* (September 17, 2001), p. 15.

21. "Prof. Irwin Cotler: Beyond Durban," Jewish Agency for Israel (2001), Online; Irwin Cotler, "Why Is Israel Singled Out?" *The Jerusalem Post* (January 16, 2002), Online.

22. Yohanan Manor, Communication, "Daily Highlights-World Conference against Racism," (August 31–September 7, 2001), Online.

23. "World Conference against Racism, Racial Discrimination, Xenophobia and Related Intolerance," Department of Public Information-News Media Services Division-New York (August 31–September 7, 2001), Online; Herb Keinon, "Annan: Zionism Is Racism — A Dead Issue," *Jerusalem Post* (September 2, 2001), Online.

24. Ibid.

25. Michael Rubin, "The U.N.'s Refugees: The International Body Gives Aid and Comfort to Terrorists," *Opinion Journal* (April 18, 2002), Online.

26. "Six European States Vote for Palestinian Terrorism," *Charity Wire* (April 15, 2002), Online.

27. Ibid.

28. Anne Bayefsky, "General Emergency Special Sessions," December 11, 2003.

29. Yagil Henkin, "Urban Warfare and the Lessons of Jenin," *Azure* (Summer 2003), Online.

30. Jonathan Fighel, "Jenin Al Kassam: A Hothouse of Terrorism," *ICT* (June 30, 2002), Online.

31. Yagil Henkin, "Urban Warfare and the Lessons of Jenin," *Azure* (Summer 2003), Online; Jonathan Fighel, "Jenin Al Kassam: A Hothouse of Terrorism"; "Anatomy of anti-Israel Incitement: Jenin, World Opinion and the Massacre That Wasn't," Anti-Defamation League (June 2002), p. 1–30; Nina Gilbert, "Compromise Reached on Burying Jenin Dead," *The Jerusalem Post* (April 15, 2002), Online.

32. "U.N. Envoy Says Jenin Camp 'Horrific Beyond Belief,' " Common Dreams News Center (April 18, 2002) by Agence France Presse, Online; Charmaine Seitz, "Investigating Jenin," *The Nation* (May 1, 2002), Online.

33. David Tell, "The U.N. Israel's Obsession," *The Weekly Standard* (May 6, 2002), Online; "Engel Says U.N. Team to Investigate Jenin Is Biased Against Israel" (April 29, 2002),Online.

34. Ibid.

35. Ibid.

36. Julian Schvindlerman, "Israel Faces Rampant Discrimination at the United Nations," *The Miami Herald* (November 1, 2002), Online; Julius Stone, *Israel and Palestine: Assault on the Law of*

Nations (Baltimore, MD: The Johns Hopkins University Press, 1981), p. 2–3; see also Michael J. Glennon, "Why the Security Council Failed," *Foreign Affairs* (May/June 2003), Online.

37. "U.S. Opposes Human Rights Commission Criticizing Israel," (April 16, 2003), Online; "U.N. Human Rights Panel Assails Israel for 'Mass Killings,' " Associated Press (April 16, 2003), Online.

38. "President's Message."

39. Yohanan Manor, *To Right a Wrong: The Revocation of the UN General Assembly Resolution 3379 Defaming Zionism* (New York: Shengold Publishers, Inc., 1996), p. 9.

40. Anne Bayefsky, "The U.N.'s Dirty Little Secret," *The Wall Street Journal* (December 8, 2003), Online.

41. "Right of Reply by Mr. Ze'ev Luria to the Palestinian Observer," Third Committee Permanent Mission of Israel to the United Nations (October 21, 2003), Online.

42. Ibid; Margot Dudkevitch, "Peace with Israel Is Not to be Found in PA Schoolbooks," *The Internet Jerusalem Post* (November 2001); Ted Lapkin, "The War Crimes of the Palestinians," *FrontPageMagazine* (February 27, 2004), Online; Matthew McAllester, "The Roots of Hatred" Newsday.com (January 18, 2004), Online.

43. Itamar Marcus and Barbara Cook, "Seducing Children to Martyrdom," *The Jerusalem Post* (July 4, 2006), Online; "Egyptian Cleric Sheik Muhammad Nassar Tells a Group of Children about Child Martyrdom in the Early Days of Islam Al-Nas TV (Egypt)" MEMRI video clip Number 1185 (June 15, 2006); Eva Chen, "French TV Sticks By Story That Fueled Palestinian Intifada," CNSNews.com (February 15, 2005); Gerard Van der Leun, "The Weaponization of Children," *American Digest* (July 31, 2006), Online; "Hezbollah's Human Shields," *The Washington Times* (July 31, 2006), Online; Steven Stalinsky, "Islamic Leaders Urge Children to Be Bombers, the MEMRI Report," *The New York Sun* (August 16, 2006), Online.

44. Anne Bayefsky, "Business as Usual: No Love for Israel in Geneva," *National Review* (April 26, 2004), Online; "Brahimi's Israel Comments Draw Annan, Israeli Ire," *Haaretz* (April 24, 2004), Online. Since September 2000, when the second Intifada began, Hamas arranged for 52 suicide bombings against Israeli civilians, resulting in the death of hundreds and the wounding of thousands. Daniel Mandel, "Ambiguous Response: Disturbing Reaction to Yassin's Death," *Washington Times* (March 25, 2004), Online.

45. Bayefsky, "Business as Usual"; Michael Walzer, *Just and Unjust Wars: A Moral Argument With Historical Illustrations* (New York: Basic Books, 2006); Joshua Brook, "Human Rights Advocates Embarrass Themselves," New Republic Online (July 28, 2006); Mark Mellman, "The Case Against Proportionality (Israel vs Hezbollah)," *Free Republic* (July 16, 2006), Online; Yashiko Sagamori, "The Disproportionate People," Middleeastfacts (August 11, 2006), Online.

46. Alan Dershowitz, "Assassinating Terrorists — Is It Legal?" *Toronto Globe and Mail* (September 16, 2003), Online.

47. Ibid.

48. Ibid.

49. Herb Keinon, "Israel Blasts UN Human Rights Panel," *Jerusalem Post* (March 24, 2004), Online; Shlomo Shamir, "U.S. Vetoes UN Resolution Censuring Israel for Yassin Killing," *Jerusalem Post* (March 26, 2004), Online; "Australia Opposes Israel Censure Over Yassin Killing," ABC Online (March 25, 2004).

50. Patrick Cox, "The UN's Attack on Self-Defense," Tech Central Station (July 30, 2004), Online.

51. Ibid.

52. Bayefsky, "Business as Usual"; "UN Rights Body Issues Three Condemnations of Israel," *Haaretz* (March 15, 2004), Online.

53. Hillel C. Neuer, "The UN's Food Politics," *The National Post* (Canada), Comment Page, (September 6, 2004), Online; Shlomo Shamir, "UN Figure Calls on EU to Freeze Israel's Special Trade Status," *Haaretz* (October 14, 2004); "UN Watch Files Proceedings at UN Commission on Human Rights to Remove Special Rapporteur Jean Ziegler for Abuse of Mandate," *UN Watch* (July 21, 2004), Online.

54. Anne Bayefsky, "Business as Usual."

55. Anne Bayefsky, "One Small Step: Is the U.N. Finally Ready to Get Serious about Anti-Semitism?" *The Wall Street Journal* (June 21, 2004), Online; Shlomo Shamir, "Arabs Shock Europeans, Refuse to Condemn Anti-Semitism," *Haaretz* (July 28, 2004), Online; Jeff Jacoby, "Anti-Semitism and the UN," *JewishWorldReview* (June 25, 2005), Online; Barbara Victor, *Army of Roses, Inside the World of Palestinian Women Suicide Bombers* (Emmaus, PA: Rodale), 2003.

56. Ibid.

57. Ibid

58. Ibid; Shlomo Shamir, "Jews Must Feel UN Is Their Home," *Haaretz* (June 21, 2004), Online.

59. Anne Bayefsky, "Fatal Failure: The U.N. Won't Recognize the Connection Between Anti-Zionism and Anti-Semitism," *National Review Online* (November 30, 2004); "The United Nations: Leading Global Purveyor of Anti-Semitism: An Interview with Anne Bayefsky," Jerusalem Center For Public Affairs Number 31 (April 1, 2005), Online.

60. Ibid.

61. "Definitions of Terrorism," www.unodc.org/odccp/terrorism_definitions.html (March 10, 2005).

62. www.un.org/News/Press/docs/2001/sc7158.doc.htm.

63. Anne Bayefsky, "U.N.derwhelming Response: The U.N.'s Approach to Terrorism," *National Review* (September 24, 2004), Online.

64. George P. Fletcher, "Annan's Careless Language," *NYT* (March 21, 2002).

65. Ibid.

66. Ibid.

67. Ibid; see also, "Annan Urges Israel to Withdraw from All Occupied Palestinian Territories," *Al-Jazeerah* (March 6, 2004), Online.

68. Bayefsky, "Business as Usual"; "Brahimi's Israel Comments Draw Annan, Israeli Ire," *Haaretz* (April 24, 2004), Online; "Report: UN Envoy to Iraq Calls Israeli Policy 'Biggest Poison,'" *Haaretz* (April 23, 2004), Online.

69. Shlomo Shamir, "U.S. Jews Suggest Special Advisor for UN Chief Annan," *Haaretz* (May 24, 2004), Online.

70. Bayefsky, "One Small Step."

71. Natan Sharansky, *The Case for Democracy* (Green Forest, AR: Balfour Books, 2006), p. xviii–xix.

72. Ibid., p. 278.

73. Ibid., p. 279; see also *Amir Taheri, "Eye of the Storm: The London and Paris 'Street' Is Still Roiling,"* *The Jerusalem Post* (March 9, 2005), Online.

74. Hillel C. Neuer, "Rights and Wrong," *The New Republic Online* (February 18, 2005); see also Max M. Kampelman, "A Caucus of Democracies," *The Wall Street Journal* (January 6, 2004), Online. At the annual Geneva session of the Sub-Commission on Human Rights on August 17, 2006, the UN refused to define terrorism once again. "The United Nations, Human Rights and Terrorism," *UN Watch Newsletter* (August 17, 2006), Online.

75. Charles Krauthammer, "Why the U.S. Should Bail Out of the U.N.: Let It Sink," The New Republic Online (August 24, 1987).

76. Ibid.

77. Anne Bayefsky, "Discrimination and Double Standards: Anti-Israeli Past Is Present at the U.N.'s Human Rights Council, " *National Review Online* (July 5, 2006).

78. Ibid; "The Human Rights Council," Special Session of the Human Rights Council, July 5–6, 2006, Office of the U.N. High Commissioner for Human Rights, Online.

CONCLUSION

After World War II, it appeared that antisemitism was in remission except at the UN. From the establishment of Israel to the Z=R resolution in November 1975, Jews experienced a brief respite from hatred for about 25 years. During this grace period, Jews seemed to be accepted in the community of nations. As long as the memory of the Holocaust was fresh, and Arabs were viewed as the aggressors, Jews were seen as the underdog and victim of Arab belligerence. Calls for the annihilation of the Jewish people by Arab leaders so soon after the destruction of the six million Jews of Europe fortified the determination of the Israelis to resist and aroused the conscience of the West.[1]

The Z=R resolution precipitated intense protests in the United States and Europe, and questions about the efficacy of the UN. There were those who dismissed the importance of the resolution by suggesting it was nothing more than a piece of paper. Historian and journalist Paul Johnson warned that this piece of paper was dangerous because "paper majorities tended to grow into real policies: the corrupt arithmetic of the Assembly, where . . . votes could be bought by arms or even personal bribes to delegates, tended to become imperceptibly the conventional wisdom of international society."[2]

Johnson also felt "the melancholy truth is that the candles of civilization are burning low. The world is increasingly governed not so much by capitalism or communism, or social democracy, or even tribal barbarism, as by a false lexicon of political cliches, accumulated over a half century and now assuming a kind of degenerate sacerdotal authority." All one had to do was "to peer into the otherwise empty head of the fascist Left" to see that:

> . . . men with colored skins can do no wrong, and those with white ones no right — unless of course they call themselves communists; that murdering innocent people for political purposes is acceptable providing you call yourself a guerilla; that, in the right political circles a chunk of gelignite is morally superior to rational argument. [The underlying assumption

is that a rifle has] a spiritual life of its own, depending upon whether it is in the hands of an American (bad) or a South East Asian (good).[3]

Johnson wondered how many delegates the Arab governments had bribed to vote against Israel, but conceded it could only be a matter of speculation. He also said Israel's bloodthirsty neighbors were clamoring for her extinction. Without exception, the majority of those who voted for Z=R were states noted for racist oppression. Iraq, for example, had just murdered or expelled more than 300,000 Kurds. Other common characteristics these states shared are totalitarian governments, large-scale corruption, political assassinations, controlled media, concentration camps, an impoverished population, and no rule of law.[4]

In contrast, he wrote, Israel is a social democracy whose people and government have "a profound respect for human life, a thriving culture, and flourishing technology. . . . The extermination of the Israelis has long been the prime objective of the Terrorist International; they calculate that if they can break Israel, then all the rest of civilization is vulnerable to their assaults."[5]

U.S. Ambassador Daniel Patrick Moynihan strongly believed, as did others, that the resolution would revive antisemitism: "A great evil has been loosed upon the world. The abomination of anti-Semitism . . . has been given the appearance of international sanction." That the democratic state of Israel had been singled out by the UN, whereas oppressive, religious, racial, political, and religious nondemocratic member regimes were ignored was especially reprehensible.[6]

As far back as the 1960s, resolutions against Israel were continually raised, but many never passed. Even when Israel was engaged in serious negotiations with the Arabs, the UN refused to prevent some 20 anti-Israel resolutions from being voted on.[7]

The Arabs have never hidden their ultimate goal of destroying the Jewish state. Professor Fayez al-Sayegh, the main Arab propagandist in the United States, and a member of the Executive Committee of the Palestine Liberation Organization, made this clear: "Peace in the land of Palestine and with its neighbors is our fondest desire. The primary condition for this is the liberation of Palestine, that is, the condition is our return to an Arab Palestine and the restoration of Palestine to us as Arabs."[8] For Chaim Weizmann, Israel's first president, "The real opponents of Zionism can never be placated by any diplomatic formula: their objection to the Jews is that the Jews exist, and in this particular case, they exist in Palestine."[9]

To achieve the demise of the Jewish State, the Arabs have attempted to delegitimize Israel by denying that it is a nation, which is historically inaccurate. Throughout their history, Jews have viewed themselves as a nation and been recognized as such. By defining the Jews as a religion, and not a nation and a people, the Arabs assert that Jews therefore have no right of a state for themselves. Palestine cannot be an entity as long as Israel exists, they proclaim, and have "adopted as a fundamental tenet . . . the basic rejection of any claim to Jewish sovereignty." They have also shaped the dispute to "one between a thieving state and a people striving to be free itself." And their propaganda successes play a key role in "strengthening their military resolve."[10]

Arabs also accuse Israel of failing to recognize Arab national existence. The opposite has been the case. It recognized Arab national identity when it agreed to partition Mandate Palestine into a Jewish and an Arab state in 1947 and in 2000 when it agreed to establish an Arab state on the West Bank and Gaza. The Arabs have rejected both offers by responding with force and violence against the Jews, so that by Arab choice, there is now no official Arab state called Palestine.

So what then is Zionism? Zionism is the "most recent chapter in an ancient story, an attempt by Jews to define their place in the modern world, and a refusal of the Jews to cease being, to die out, to fade away."[11] Significantly, Israel is the only national movement in the 19th and 20th centuries to modernize the society it established. The majority of the Third World failed to do this, including those with extraordinary natural resources like Brazil, Uganda, and others with large oil reserves in the Middle East. Without those assets, and besieged by enemies seeking to destroy her, in a single generation Israel went from being a poor agricultural nation to a world-class economy.[12]

The dispute between Israel and the Arabs is not racial. Zionism is not a racial or a discriminatory movement any more than any other national liberation movement in Europe in the 19th century or in Africa and Asia in the 20th century. Jews do not constitute a separate race, even though Nazi pseudoscience labeled them as such. Arabs are not a separate race and are not seen as being different than Jews. If anything, Zionism is less discriminatory and racist than most other movements, because it is defined in religious terms — not ethnic ones.

Rabbinical law proscribes that the mother determines the religion of the child regardless of the race or religion of the father — even if he was a non-Jew and was not converted according to Jewish law. An individual who converts to Judaism is recognized as a Jew, and a Jew who converts from Judaism is regarded as a non-Jew.[13]

Practically every member-state of the UN practices some form of discrimination against those not in the dominant group — whether according to race, language, culture, religion, sex, or origin. Some members of hate-driven societies are more active and destructive than others.[14] Citizenship in Arab countries, for instance, is determined by native parentage. Immigrants from one Arab state to another find it is nearly impossible to become naturalized citizens, particularly in Saudi Arabia, Algeria, and Kuwait. Those Arab countries allowing foreign Arabs to be naturalized reject Arabs from Israel.

Whereas the Arabs posit the elimination of a religion-oriented Israel and the creation of a secular state, this flies in the face of Arab laws that prohibit Jewish settlement. Jordan, for example, prohibits Jews from living there. In 1954, Jordan passed a law conferring citizenship to all former residents of Mandate Palestine — except Jewish ones. Civil Law No. 6 that governed the West Bank under Jordanian occupation stated: "Any man will be a Jordan subject if he is not Jewish."[15]

Anyone who visits Israel is struck by the array of different types and color of Jews. There are Jews from the West, the East, and Africa who are white, black, brown, and olive, who live and work wherever they want in the country. To suggest that Israel is an apartheid state based on race defies logic and empirical evidence. Israeli policies are a result of the need to protect its citizens from Arabs bent on their destruction, and have nothing to do with race.[16]

Significantly, Arabs living in Israel are guaranteed equality. Israel's Proclamation of Independence declares that the state

> will promote the development of the country for the benefit of all its in-habitants; will be based on the precepts of liberty, justice, and peace taught by the Hebrew Prophets; will uphold the full social and political equality of all its citizens, without distinction of race, creed, or sex; will guarantee full freedom of conscience, worship, education, and culture . . . and will dedicate itself to the principles of the Charter of the United Nations.

Although the infant state was embroiled in a war for its own survival, its leaders called "upon the Arab inhabitants of the State of Israel to return to the ways of peace and play their part in the development of the State, with full and equal citizenship and due representation in its bodies and institutions, provisional or permanent."[17]

The country's resolute determination to remain an explicitly Jewish state "does not make it any more racist than countries like Pakistan, Saudi Arabia, or Mauritania, which constitutionally call themselves Islamic States," the *London Observer* noted a day before the UN passed the Z=R resolution.[18]

Aharon Barak, chief justice of Israel's Supreme Court, explains that Zionism was not based on discrimination against non-Jews, but on their integration into the Jewish national home. Treating individuals differently does not always imply discrimination. Nor does treating individuals in an identical manner automatically imply equality. Equality is not absolute and may be infringed upon. But that is only in the context of a law that maintains the value of public safety, which is a valid purpose and does not exceed that which is necessary for the survival of the State of Israel.[19]

Israel was created in 1948 in one-sixth of the area allotted by the Balfour Declaration. The Allies had gained a vast area from the Turks during the war, and the British took one percent of the land the Great Powers acquired from the Turks to establish a Jewish homeland. In appreciation for having liberated them from the "tyranny of a bestial conqueror," and providing them with independent states, Lord Balfour hoped the world would not begrudge the Jews "that small notch in what are now Arab territories being given to the people who for all these hundreds of years have been separated from it." The Arabs found this small accommodation to the Jews abhorrent.[20]

Blaming Israel has become a way of life at the UN because antisemitism has proven to be an effective political ploy to divert attention from the main domestic problems they face at home. Just as a magician uses a hand or prop to distract the audience from what he is doing with his other hand, antisemitism serves the same purpose for many members of the UN.

In making Israel the culprit, politicians avoid dealing with their own failed domestic policies. So much creative energy is spent trying to purge the Jewish presence from their midst, that they fail to address their own serious failings. Adolf Hitler effectively used the same tactic in Germany by employing antisemitism to assume political power. Jews were a corrupting influence in society, he said, which justified them being removed from every area of German life, taking everything they owned away from them, and sending them to death factories.

Few ask Arab leaders some obvious questions: Why do they continue to refuse to officially recognize Israel's existence? And with 23 Arab states, if Israel didn't exist, who would they use as their scapegoat — and how would they use it?[21]

Is peace possible or even achievable under autocratic regimes? A peace settlement would deprive Arab dictators of a vital "safety valve" — hatred of Israel and Jews — and would expose them to the violence of their own bitter citizens, including those under Palestinian Authority rule. Israel protects these regimes simply by existing. Continual failure to reach peace agreements just when they seem certain to succeed suggests that Arabs want the conflict unresolved, but at low levels instead of all-out war. That way their minions are "usefully controllable." True peace in the region may only be possible with democratic governments that are accountable to their constituents.[22]

Dore Gold, a former Israeli ambassador to the UN, reminds us that the UN was created to keep global peace, yet it has a problem of distinguishing victims of aggression and the aggressors.[23] One example of this occurred in the early afternoon of October 7, 2000, five months after the Israeli military withdrew from Lebanon. In a clear breach of international law, Hizballah terrorists crossed the Lebanese border, ambushed three Israeli soldiers who were patrolling along the Israeli-Lebanese fence near the border gate, and abducted them.

The United Nations Interim Force in Lebanon (UNIFIL) observation post was on a hill 400 yards from the gate, enabling the observers to see what was happening. The *Daily Star* of Beirut confirmed this when it reported on October 11, 2000 that "interviews with UNFIL troops who witnessed the snatch. . . ." Two hours after the kidnapping, the Israel Defense Forces (IDF) informed UNFIL of the seizure of their wounded soldiers by Hizballah. No roadblocks were set-up by the UN peacekeepers to apprehend the terrorists.[24]

On June 28, 2001, Major General Gabi Ashkenazi, head of the Northern Command of the IDF, questioned Terje Roed-Larsen, UN Special Coordinator for peace negotiations in the Middle East, on whether UNFIL had a videotape of the kidnapping. He suspected UNIFIL Commander General Kofi Obeng of Ghana of having the tape, and that UN headquarters in New York knew about its existence. Roed-Larsen allegedly claimed that there was no tape. In May 2001, Obeng turned over the tape to the UN, but did not want to show it to Israel since it would be conceding its "impartiality." UN officials noted, "UNIFL had to maintain a delicate balance and could not simply share sensitive information about one side with the other."[25]

Strict impartiality was supposed to be observed by the Israelis and the Lebanese, not Hizballah, Gold pointed out.[26] He warned that the UN's continued betrayal of Israel is a measure of the organization's overall failure. Among its members, authoritarian and totalitarian regimes greatly outnumber Western democracies like Israel, who are vulnerable because Islamic and Arab states are eager to attack her. She has no protection from regional alliances, having been frozen out of the European Union and the African Union and any Asian regional groups. She is thereby at risk in many UN forums. In this, she is not alone. After the Gulf War in 1991, the UN ignored the plight of the Iraqi Kurds and Shiite Muslims. The UN offered no assistance to Christian communities in Sudan, Lebanon, and Indonesia who were persecuted by Muslims for years. Tibetan Buddhists were also "sacrificed."[27] With its 2001 World Conference Against Racism in Durban that provided NGOs with a protective shield that lent credibility to their virulent antisemitic charges that Israel has no right to exist,[28] the UN once again revealed its essential failure. The UN record shows it is incapable of serving as the "ultimate protector of international peace and security" because it fails to halt aggression or ensure order in the world.[29]

Though Z=R has been rescinded, the effects of the resolution continue to resonate, and the NGOs continue to create problems for Israel. Instead of helping the Arabs, some NGO's make it more difficult to obtain an accurate picture of the daily suffering the average Arab in the West Bank and Gaza endures. How can an objective observer know whether Arabs or Israelis are the cause of the plight of the Arabs when NGOs exaggerate and distort events? How can the corruption of the leadership, which does great damage to the Arabs who aspire to a state called Palestine, be exposed when Israel alone is portrayed as the source of their misery? If the NGOs are truly concerned about the anguish of those people, why don't they confront the PA leadership with questions about the billions of dollars in aid for infrastructure and schools that were diverted to pay suicide bombers' families, buy weapons, and contribute to the chaos? Why don't they ask why the leadership names educational institutions and sports sites after terrorists and murderers?[30]

Why is there no accounting for the billions that have been poured into the area, with nothing to show but the aggrandizement of the politically well-connected?

There are Arabs in Gaza and the West Bank who want to live in peace, who want to realize their dreams and aspirations for themselves and their families. This will only be possible when terrorism is renounced, and recognition of the need to coexist with Jews becomes the only viable alternative. The NGOs should and could create a better environment for a dialogue to begin, if they weren't so busy spreading the hate.[31]

The Arab/Israeli conflict has consumed much time and energy and life. When will it be resolved? When the UN debated the question of Palestine in 1947, two delegates made remarks that are worth recalling. Quo Tai-chi, Chinese representative to the Security Council, prophetically warned that unless Arabs and Jews "learn to love their neighbors as themselves, there will be no peace in the Holy Land, or indeed, in any land." Historical and legal procedures, political and economic considerations will never provide a solution for peace until Jews and Christians "return to the teachings of the prophets and the saints of the Holy Land . . . no parliament of man, no statement, no legal formula, no historical equation, no political and economic programme can singly or together themselves solve the problem."[32]

For Asaf Ali, Indian ambassador to the United States in 1947, Palestine had:

> become the acid test of human conscience. The United Nations will find that upon their decision will depend the future of humanity, whether humanity is going to proceed by peaceful means or whether humanity is going to be torn to pieces. If a wrong decision flows from this august Assembly . . . the world shall be cut in twain and there shall be no peace on earth.[33]

Endnotes

1. Ruth R. Wisse, *If I Am Not for Myself: The Liberal Betrayal of the Jews* (New York: The Free Press, 1992), p. 117; Moshe Shemesh, "Did Shuqayri Call for 'Throwing the Jews Into the Sea'?" *Israel Studies* vol. 8, no. 2 (Summer 2003): p. 70–81.

2. Paul Johnson, *Modern Times: The World from the Twenties to the Nineties* (New York: Perennial Classics, 2001), p. 690.

3. Paul Johnson, "The Resources of Civilization," *New Statesman* vol. 90, no. 2338 (October 31, 1975): p. 532.

4. Ibid.

5. Ibid.

6. "As Split Widens at the U.N., U.S. Starts Hitting Back," *U.S. News and World Report* (November 24, 1975): p. 39.

7. Shlomo Shamir, "The U.N. Still a Stage for Anti-Israel Incitement," *Haaretz* (November 9, 2003), Online.

8. "Israel and the Palestinians: A Discussion," *Midstream* (April 1970): p. 44, 48; Yehoshaphat Harkabi, "The Palestinians in the Israel-Arab Conflict," *Midstream* (March 1970): p. 8–9.

9. Chaim Weizmann, *Trial and Error: The Autobiography of Chaim Weizmann* (New York: Harper and Brothers Publishers, 1949), p. 290.

10. "Israel and the Palestinians: A Discussion"; Harkabi, "The Palestinians in the Israel-Arab Conflict," p. 8–9, 12.

11. Yaacov Lozowick, *Right to Exist: A Moral Defense of Israel's Wars* (New York: Random House, 2003), p. 306.

12. David S. Landes and Richard A. Landes, in "Zionism At 100," Martin Peretz, ed, op. cit., p. 16. Among the most technologically innovative nations, Israel is ranked 18th according to the world economic forum. (15:22 Guysen, Israël, News), Online.

13. "Zionism At 100," p. 18.

14. Bernard Lewis, *From Babel to Dragomans: Interpreting the Middle East* (New York: Oxford University Press, 2004), p. 275.

15. Jordanian Nationality Law, Article 3(3) of Law No. 6 of 1954, Official Gazette, Number 1171, (February 16, 1954), Online.

16. Phyllis Chesler, *The New Anti-Semitism: The Current Crisis and What We Must Do About It* (San Francisco, CA: Jossey-Bass, 2003), p. 167.

17. Itamar Rabinovich and Jehuda Reinharz, eds., *Israel in The Middle East: Documents, and Readings on Society, Politics and Foreign Relations, 1948–Present* (New York: Oxford University Press, 1984), p. 14-15.

18. Quoted in Martin Gilbert, *Israel: A History* (New York: William Morrow and Company, Inc.), p. 468.

19. Aharon Barak, "Some People Say a State That Is Both Jewish and Democratic Is an Oxymoron, But the Values Can Work Together," *Forward* (August 23, 2002), Online.

20. Marie Syrkin, "Who Are the Palestinians?" *Midstream* (January, 1970), p. 8, 10.

21. Adina Levine, "Harvard Prof Condemns 'Misguided' Political Attacks Against Israel," *The Record-News* (December 4, 2003), Online.

22. Lewis, *From Babel To Dragomans*, p. 378–380; Fawaz A. Gerges, "Empty Promises of Freedom," *NYT* (July 18, 2003), Online. See also David Barsamian, "Edward Said," *The Progressive* (April 1999), Online.

23. Dore Gold, *Tower of Babble: How the United Nations Has Fueled Global Chaos* (New York: Crown Forum, 2004), p. 228–229.

24. Ibid., p. 203.

25. Ibid., p. 203–205.

26. Ibid, p. 205.

27. Ibid., p. 230.

28. Ibid., p. 230.

29. Ibid., p. 230–231; USHMM.com.

30. Ibid., p. 229–230, 238.

31. Ibid.; Frank Luntz, "America 2020: How the Next Generation Views Israel," (Washington, D.C.: The Israel Project, 2005), p. 33–37.

32. Jacob Robinson, *Palestine and the United Nations: Prelude to Solution* (Westport, CT: Greenwood Press, Publishers, 1947), p. 199.

33. Ibid., p. 201.

BIBLIOGRAPHY
BOOKS

Abdullah of Jordan, King. *My Memoirs Completed.* Translated by Harold W. Glidden. London: Longman, 1978.

Abu-Lughod, I. *The Transformation of Palestine.* Chicago, IL: Northwestern University Press, 1971.

Aburish, Said K. *A Brutal Friendship: The West and the Arab Elite.* London: Indigo, 1997.

Ajami, Fouad. *The Arab Predicament: Arab Political Thought and Practice Since 1967.* Cambridge: Cambridge University Press, 1992.

Adler, Joseph. *Restore the Jews to Their Homeland: Nineteen Centuries in the Quest for Zion.* Northvale, VT: Jason Aronson, 1997.

Almog, Oz. *The Sabra: The Creation of the New Jew.* Berkeley, CA: University of California Press, 2000.

Almog. Samuel, ed. *Zionism and the Arabs.* Jerusalem: Zalman Shazar Institute Press, 1983.

_____. *Zionism and History: The Rise of a New Jewish Consciousness.* New York: St. Martin's Press, 1987.

Aronson, Shlomo. *Conference and Bargaining in the Middle East: An Israeli Perspective.* Baltimore and London: The John Hopkins University Press, 1974.

Al Roy, Gil Carl, ed. *Attitudes Toward Jewish Statehood in the Arab World.* New York: American Academic Association for Peace in the Middle East, 1971.

Antonius, Georges. *The Arab Awakening, the Story of the Arab National Movement.* New York: Capricorn Books, 1965.

Arens, Moshe, *Broken Conflict: American Foreign Policy and the Crisis Between the U.S. and Israel.* New York: Simon and Schuster, 1995.

Armstrong, Karen. *The Battle for God.* New York: Alfred A. Knopf, 2000.

_____. *Jerusalem: One City, Three Faiths.* New York: Ballantine, 1997.

Aruri, Naseer. *Palestinian Refugees: The Right of Return.* London: Pluto Press, 2001.

Ashrawi, Hanan. *This Side of Peace.* New York: Simon and Schuster, 1995.

Ateek, Naim Stifan, and Rosemary Radford Ruether. *Justice and Only Justice: A Palestinian Theology of Liberation.* London, England: Orbis Books, Ltd., 1990.

Atiyah, Edward. *The Arabs: The Origins, Present Conditions, and Prospects of the Arab World.* Baltimore, MD: Penguin Books, Inc., revised edition, 1958.

Auron, Yair. *The Banality of Indifference: Zionism and the Armenian Genocide.* Piscataway, NJ: Transaction Publishers, 2000.

Avineri, Shlomo. *The Making of Modern Zionism: The Intellectual Origins of the Jewish State.* New York: Basic Books, 1981.

Avishai, Bernard. *The Tragedy of Zionism: Revolution and Democracy in the Land of Israel.* New York: Farrar Straus Giroux, 1985.

Avnery, Uri. *Israel without Zionists: A Plea for Peace in the Middle East.* New York: The Macmillan Company, 1968.

Baldwin, Neil. *Henry Ford and the Jews: The Mass Production of Hate.* New York: Public Affairs, 2001.

Ball, George W., and Douglas B., *The Passionate Attachment: America's Involvement with Israel, 1947 to the Present.* New York: W. W. Norton, 1992.

Bard, Mitchell G. *The Complete Idiot's Guide to Middle East Conflict.* New York: Alpha Books, 1999.

Bauer, Yehuda. *From Diplomacy to Resistance: A History of Jewish Palestine 1939–1945.* Philadelphia, PA: Jewish Publication Society, 1970.

_____. *The Jewish Emergence from Powerlessness.* Toronto and Buffalo: University of Toronto Press, 1979.

Beker, Avi. *The United Nations and Israel: From Recognition to Reprehension.* Lexington, MA: Lexington Books, 1988.

Begin, Menachem. *The Revolt: Story of the Irgun.* Jerusalem: Steimatzky's Agency Limited, 1951.

Ben, Alex. *Arthur Ruppin: Memoirs, Diaries, Letters.* London: Weidenfeld and Nicolson, 1971.

Ben-Ami, Yitshaq. *Years of Wrath, Days of Glory: Memoirs from the Irgun.* New York: Robert Speller and Sons, 1982.

Ben-Gurion, David. *Letters to Paula.* Pittsburgh, PA: University of Pittsburgh Press, 1971.

_____. *Memoirs.* New York: The World Publishing Company, 1970.

_____. *Rebirth and Destiny of Israel.* New York: Philosophical Library, Inc., 1954.

Ben-Zvi, Abraham. *The United States and Israel: The Limits of the Special Relationship.* New York: Columbia University Press, 1993.

_____. *John F. Kennedy and the Politics of Arms Sales to Israel.* London and Portland, OR: Frank Cass, 2002.

Berger, Earl. *The Covenant and the Sword: Arab Israeli Relations 1948–56.* London: Routledge and Kegan Paul Ltd., 1965.

Berman, Aaron. *Nazis, the Jews and American Zionism 1933–1948.* Detroit, MI: Wayne State University Press, 1990.

Bethell, Nicholas. *The Palestine Trial: The Struggle for the Holy Land, 1935–48.* New York: G.P. Putnam's Sons, 1979.

Ben-Meir, Atalia. *Failure or Folly.* Shaarei Tikva: Ariel Center for Policy Research, 2003.

Benvenisti, Meron. *Sacred Landscape: The Buried History of the Holy Land Since 1948.* Berkeley, CA: University of California Press, 2000.

_____. *City of Stone: The Hidden History of Jerusalem.* Berkeley, CA: University of California Press, 1996.

_____, and Thomas L. Friedman. *Intimate Enemies: Jews and Arabs in a Shared Land.* Berkeley, CA: University of California Press, 1995.

_____. *Conflicts and Contradictions.* New York: Villard Books, 1986.

Bilby, Kenneth W. *New Star in the East.* New York: Doubleday and Company, 1950.

Black, Edwin. *The Transfer Agreement: The Dramatic Story of the Pact Between the Third Reich and Jewish Palestine.* New York: Carroll and Graf Publishers, Inc., 2001.

Blum, Yehuda. *For Zion's Sake.* New York: A Herzl Press Publication, 1987.

_____. *The Juridical Status of Jerusalem.* Jerusalem: The Leonard Davis Institute for International Relations, 1974.

Bovis, Eugene H. *The Jerusalem Question, 1917–1968.* Stanford, CA: Hoover Institution Press, Stanford University, 1971.

Bronner, Stephen Eric. *A Rumor about the Jews: Reflections on Antisemitism and the Protocols of the Learned Elders of Zion.* New York: St Martins Press, 2000.

Brown, George. *In My Way: The Political Memoirs of Lord George-Brown.* London: Victor Gollancz Ltd., 1971.

Brown, Michael. *The Israeli-American Connection: Its Roots in the Yishuv.* Detroit, MI: Wayne State University Press, 1996.

Browning, Christopher S. *The Origins of the Final Solution: The Evolution of Nazi Jewish Policy, September 1939–March 1942.* Lincoln, NE: University of Nebraska Press, 2004.

Buckley, William F. Jr. *United Nations Journal: A Delegates Odyssey.* New York: G.P. Putnam's Sons, 1974.

Buehrig, Edward H. *The UN and the Palestinian Refugees: A Study in Non Territorial Administration.* Bloomington, IN: Indiana University Press, 1971.

Cattan, Henry. *Palestine, the Arabs and Israel: The Search for Justice.* London: Longman Group Limited, 1969.

Caplan, Neil. *Palestine and the Arab Question 1917–1925.* London: Frank Cass, 1978.

_____. *Futile Diplomacy: Early Arab-Zionist Negotiation Attempts 1913–1931.* Vol. 1. London: Frank Cass, 1983.

_____. *Futile Diplomacy: Arab — Zionist Negotiations and the End of the Mandate.* Vol. 2. London: Frank Cass, 1986.

_____. *The Lausanne Conference, 1949: A Case Study in Middle East Peacemaking.* Tel-Aviv: The Moshe Dayan Center for Middle Eastern and African Studies, 1993.

Charters, David. *The British Army and Jewish Insurgency in Palestine, 1945–1947.* Houndsmills and London: Palgrave Macmillan Press, 1989.

Cheshin, Amir, Bill Hutman, and Avi Melamed. *Separate and Unequal: The Inside Story of Israeli Rule in East Jerusalem.* Cambridge, MA: Harvard University Press, 1999.

Chesler, Phyllis. *The New Anti-Semitism: The Current Crisis and What We Must Do About It.* San Francisco, CA: Jossey-Bass, 2003.

Clarke, Thurston. *By Blood and Fire: The Attack on the King David Hotel.* London: Hutchinson, 1981.

Clifford, Clark M., Eugene V. Rostow, and Barbara W. Tuchman. *The Palestine Question in American History.* New York: Arno Press, 1978.

Cobban, Helena. *The Palestinian Liberation Organization: People, Power and Politics.* New York: Cambridge University Press, 1984.

Cohen, Michael J. *Palestine: Retreat from the Mandate.* New York: Holmes and Meier Publishers, Inc., 1978.

_____. *Palestine to Israel: From Mandate to Independence.* London: Frank Cass, 1988.

_____. *Truman and Israel.* Berkeley, CA: University of California Press, 1990.

Cohen, Naomi W. *American Jews and the Zionist Idea.* Hoboken, NJ: KTAV Publishing House, Inc., 1975.

_____. *The Year After the Riots: American Response to the Palestine Crisis of 1929–30.* Detroit, MI: Wayne State University Press, 1988.

Collins, Larry, and Dominique Lapierre. *O Jerusalem.* New York: Touchstone Books, 1988.

Chomsky, Noam, and Edward W. Said. *Fateful Triangle: The United States, Israel, and the Palestinians.* Cambridge MA: South End Press, 1999.

_____. *The Umbrella of U.S. Power: The Universal Declaration of Human Rights and the Contradictions of U.S. Policy.* New York: Seven Stories Press, 1999.

Christison, Kathleen. *Perceptions of Palestine: Their Influence on U.S. Middle East Policy.* Berkeley, CA: University of California Press, 1999.

Cristol, A. Jay. *The Liberty Incident: The 1967 Israeli Attack on the U.S. Navy Spy Ship.* Washington, DC: Brassey's, Inc., 2002.

Crum, Bartley C. *Behind the Silken Curtain.* New York: Simon and Schuster, 1947.

Davis, Moshe, ed. *The Yom Kippur War: Israel and the Jewish People.* New York: Arno Press and Herzl Press, 1974.

_____, and Yehoshua Ben-Arieh, eds. *With Eyes toward Zion. Western Societies and the Holy Land.* New York: Praeger, 1991.

Dayan, Moshe. *Diary of the Sinai Campaign.* New York: Schocken Books, 1965.

DeNovo, John A. *American Interests and Policies in the Middle East, 1900–1939.* Minneapolis, MN: Minneapolis University Press, 1963.

Dershowitz, Alan. *The Case For Israel.* Hoboken, NJ: John Wiley and Sons, 2003.

_____. *Why Terrorism Works: Understanding the Threat and Responding to the Challenge.* New Haven, CT: Yale University Press, 2002.

Eban, Abba. *Personal Witness: Israel Through My Eyes.* New York: G.P. Putnam, 1992.

_____. *Voice of Israel.* New York: Horizon Press, 1957.

Elath, Eliahu. *Zionism in the UN: A Diary of the First Days.* Philadelphia, PA: Jewish Publication Society, 1976.

Edelheit, Abraham J. *History of Zionism: A Handbook and Dictionary.* Boulder, CO: Westview Press, 2000.

Eisenberg, Laura Zittrain. *My Enemy's Enemy: Lebanon in the Early Zionist Imagination, 1900–1948.* Detroit, MI: Wayne State University Press, 1994.

Elishakoff, Isaac, and Louis Rene Beres. *The Israel That Can Say No to Self-Annihilation.* Bloomington, IN: 1st Books Library, 2000.

Elpeleg, Zvi. *The Grand Mufti: Haj Amin Al-Hussaini, Founder of the Palestinian National Movement.* London and Portland Oregon: Frank Cass, 1993.

Eveland, Wilbur Crane. *Ropes of Sand: America's Failure in the Middle East.* London and New York: W.W. Norton and Company, 1980.

Evensen, Bruce J. *Truman, Palestine, and the Press: Shaping Conventional Wisdom at the Beginning of the Cold War.* Westport, CT: Greenwood, 1992.

Evron, Boas, and James Diamond. *Jewish State or Israeli Nation?* Bloomington, IN: Indiana University Press, 1995.

Eytan, Walter. *The First Years: A Diplomatic History of Israel.* New York: Simon and Schuster, 1958.

Ezrahi, Yaron. *Rubber Bullets: Power and Conscience in Modern Israel.* Berkeley, CA: University of California Press, 1998.

Fallodon, Viscount Grey of. *Twenty-Five Years, 1892–1916.* New York: Frederick A. Stokes Company, 1925.

Farsoun, Samih K., and Christina Zacharia. *Palestine and the Palestinians.* Boulder, CO: Westview Press, 1998.

Feller, Erika, Volker Turk, and Frances Nicholson. *Refugee Protection in International Law: UNCHCR's Global Consultations on International Protection.* New York: Cambridge University Press, 2003.

Findley, Paul. *Silent No More: Confronting America's False Images of Islam.* Washington, DC: American Educational Trust, 2001.

_____. *Deliberate Deceptions: Facing the Facts About the U.S.-Israeli Relationship.* Washington, DC: American Educational Trust, 1995.

_____. *They Dare to Speak Out: People and Institutions Confront Israel's Lobby.* Westport, CT: Lawrence Hill & Co., 1985.

Finger, Seymour Maxwell, and Arnold A. Saltzman. *Bending with the Winds: Kurt Wald-heim and the United Nations.* New York: Praeger, 1990.

Finkelstein, Norman G. *Image and Reality of the Israel-Palestine Conflict.* New York: Verso Books, 1995.

_____. *Beyond Chutzpah: On the Misuse of Anti-Semitism and the Abuse of History.* Berkeley, CA: University of California, 2005.

Fischbach, Michael R. *Records of Dispossession: Palestinian Refugee Property and the Arab-Israeli Conflict.* New York: Columbia University Press, 2003.

Fleischmann, Ellen L. *The Nation and Its "New" Women: The Palestinian Women's Move-ment 1920–1948.* Berkeley CA: University of California Press, 2003.

Frankel, Glenn. *Beyond the Promised Land: Jews and Arabs on the Hard Road to a New Israel.* New York: Touchstone Books, 1994.

Friedland, Roger, and Richard Hecht. *To Rule Jerusalem.* Berkeley, CA: University of California Press, 2000.

Friedlander, Saul, and Mahmoud Hussein. *Arabs and Israelis: A Dialogue.* New York: Holmes and Meier, 1975.

Friedman, Thomas L. *From Beirut to Jerusalem.* New York: Anchor Books, 1990.

_____. *Longitudes and Attitudes: Exploring the World After September 11.* New York: Farrar Straus Giroux, 2002.

Friedman, Isaiah. *Palestine: A Twice-Promised Land? Vol. 1: The British, the Arabs, and Zionism, 1915–1920.* Piscataway, NJ: Transaction Publishers, 2000.

_____. *The Question of Palestine: British-Jewish-Arab Relations: 1914–1918.* Pis-cataway, NJ: Transaction Publishers, 1991.

Friedman, Yohanan. *Tolerance and Coercion in Islam: Interfaith Relations in the Muslim Tradition.* New York: Cambridge University Press, 2003.

Fromkin, David. *A Peace to End All Peace: The Fall of the Ottoman Empire and the Creation of the Modern Middle East.* New York: Avon Books, 1989.

Furlonge, Sir Geoffrey. *Palestine Is My Country: The Story of Musa Alami.* New York: Praeger, 1969.

Garcia-Granados, Jorge. *The Birth of Israel: The Drama As I Saw It.* New York: Alfred A. Knopf, 1948.

Gelber, Yoav. *Palestine 1948: War, Escape and the Emergence of the Palestinian Refugee Problem.* Portland, OR: Sussex Academic Press, 2001.

Gerson, Allan. *The Kirkpatrick Mission: Diplomacy without Apology: America at the Unit-ed Nations 1981–1985.* New York: The Free Press, 1991.

_____. Israel, *The West Bank and International Law.* London: Frank Cass. 1978.

Gertz, Nurith. *Myths in Israeli Culture: Captives of a Dream.* London: Vallentine Mitch-ell, 2000.

Gervasi, Frank. *To Whom Palestine?* New York: D. Appleton-Century Company, Inc. 1946.

_____. *The Case for Israel.* New York: The Viking Press, 1967.

Gil, Moshe. *A History of Palestine, 634–1099.* Cambridge, England: Cambridge University Press, 1992.

Gilbert, Martin. *A History of the Twentieth Century: 1952–1999.* Vol. 3, New York: William Morrow & Co, 1999.

_____. *Israel: A History.* New York: William Morrow & Company, 1998.

_____. *Exile and Return: The Struggle for a Jewish Homeland.* Philadelphia and New York: J.B. Lippincott, 1978.

Givet, Jacques. *The Anti-Zionist Complex.* Englewood, NJ: SBS Publishing Company, Inc., 1982.

Goldberg, Brett. *A Psalm in Jenin.* Israel: Modan Publishing House, 2003.

Gold, Dore. *Tower of Babble: How the United Nations Has Fueled Global Chaos.* New York: Crown Forum, 2004.

_____. *Hatred's Kingdom: How Saudi Arabia Supports the New Global Terrorism.* Washington, DC: Regency Publishing, Inc., 2003.

Goitein, S.D. *Jews and Arab: Their Contacts Through the Ages.* New York: Schocken Books, Inc., 1955.

Gonen, Rivka. *Contested Holiness: Jewish, Muslim and Christian Perspectives on the Temple Mount in Jerusalem.* Jersey City, NJ: KTAV, 2003.

Gorenberg, Gershom. *The End of Days: Fundamentalism and the Struggle for the Temple Mount.* New York: The Free Press, 2000.

Gorny, Yosef. *The British Labour Movement and Zionism 1917–1948.* London: Frank Cass, 1983.

_____. *Zionism and the Arabs, 1882–1948: A Study of Ideology.* New York: Oxford, 1987.

_____. *The State of Israel in Jewish Public Thought: The Quest for Collective Identity.* New York: New York University Press, 1994.

Greenberg, Haim. *The Inner Eye.* New York: Jewish Frontier Association, 1953.

Grose, Peter. *Israel in the Mind of America.* New York: Random House, 1981.

Gutman, Stephanie. *The Other War: Israelis, Palestinians and the Struggle for Media Supremacy.* San Francisco, CA: Encounter Books, 2005.

Guyat, Nicholas. *The Absence of Peace: Understanding the Israeli Palestinian Conflict.* New York: Palgrave, 1998.

Haber, Eitan. *Menachem Begin: The Legend and the Man.* New York: Delacorte Press, 1978.

Hadawi, Sami. *Bitter Harvest: Palestine between 1914–1967.* New York: The New World Press, 1967.

Haim, Sylvia G., ed. *Arab Nationalism: An Anthology*. Berkeley, CA: University of California Press, 1962.

Hairn, Yehovada. *Abandonment of Illusions: Zionist Political Attitudes Toward Palestinian Arab Nationalism*. Boulder, CO: Westview Press, 1983.

Halabi, Rabah. ed. *Israeli and Palestinian Identities in Dialogue: The School for Peace Approach*. New Brunswick, NJ: Rutgers University Press, 2000.

Halpern, Ben, and Jehuda Reinharz. *Zionism and the Creation of a New Society*. New York: Oxford University Press. 1998.

_____. *The Idea of a Jewish State*. Cambridge, MA: Harvard University Press, 1969. 2nd ed.

_____. *A Clash of Heroes: Brandeis, Weizmann, and American Zionism*. New York: Oxford University Press, 1987.

Halevi, Yossi Klein. *Memoirs of a Jewish Extremist: An American Story*. Boston, MA: Little, Brown and Company, 1995.

Halkin, Hillel, *Letters to an American Jewish Friend: A Zionist's Polemic*. Philadelphia, PA: Jewish Publication Society, 1977.

Halperin, Samuel. *The Political World of American Zionism*. Detroit, MI: Wayne State University Press, 1961.

Harkabi, Yehoshafat. *The Palestinian Covenant and Its Meaning*. Portland, OR: Vallentine Mitchell, 1979.

_____. *Arab Strategies and Israel's Responses*. New York: The Free Press, 1977.

_____. *Arab Attitudes to Israel*. Piscataway, NJ: Transaction Publishers, 1974.

_____. *Palestinians and Israel*. New York: John Wiley and Sons, 1974.

Hart, Alan. *Arafat: A Political Biography*. Bloomington and Indianapolis: Indiana University Press, 1989.

Hattis, Susan Lee. *The Bi-National Idea in Palestine During Mandatory Times*. Haifa: Shikmona, 1970.

Hazony, Yoram. *The Jewish State: The Struggle for Israel's Soul*. New York: Basic Books, 2000.

Heller, Joseph. *The Stern Gang: Ideology, Politics, and Terror, 1940–1949*. London: Frank Cass, 1995.

Heller, Mark A. *A Palestinian State: The Implications for Israel*. Cambridge, MA: Harvard University Press, 1983.

Hertz, Eli E. *Reply*. New York: Myths and Facts Inc., 2005.

Hertzberg, Arthur. *The Fate of Zionism: A Secular Future for Israel and Palestine*. New York: HaperSanFrancisco, 2003.

_____. *A Jew in America: My Life and a People's Struggle for Identity*. San Francisco, CA: HarperSanFrancisco, 2002.

_____. *The Zionist Idea: A Historical Analysis and Reader.* Philadelphia, PA: Jewish Publication Society, 1997.

_____. *Jewish Polemics.* New York: Columbia University Press, 1992.

Hertzberg, Arthur, and Aron Hirt-Manheimer. *Jews: The Essence and Character of a People.* San Francisco, CA: HarperSanFrancisco, 1998.

Herzog, Chaim. *Who Stands Accused? Israel Answers Its Critics.* New York: Random House, 1978.

Herzog, Yaacov. *A People that Dwells Alone.* New York: Sanhedrin Press, 1975.

Heschel, Abraham Joshua. *Israel: An Echo of Eternity.* New York: Farrar, Straus and Giroux, 1969.

Hiroyuki, Yanagihashi, ed. *The Concept of Territory in Islamic Law and Thought: A Comparative Study.* London and New York: Kegan Paul International, 2000.

Hoffman II, Michael A. *Judaism's Strange Gods.* Coeur d'Alene, ID: Independent History, 2000.

Horowitz, David. *State in the Making.* New York: Alfred A. Knopf, 1953.

Hourani, Albert. *A History of the Arab Peoples.* Cambridge MA: The Belknap Press of Harvard University Press, 1991.

_____. *The Emergence of the Modern Middle East.* Berkeley, CA: University of California Press, 1981.

Huneidi, Sarah. *A Broken Trust: Herbert Samuel, Zionism and the Palestinians 1920–1925.* London: I B Tauris & Co Ltd., 2001.

Huntington, Samuel P. *The Clash of Civilizations and the Remaking of World Order.* New York: Touchstone, 1998.

Hurewitz, J.C. *The Struggle for Palestine.* New York: Greenwood Press Publishers, 1968.

_____. *Middle East Politics: The Military Dimension.* New York: Praeger, 1969.

_____. *Diplomacy in the Near and Middle East, a Documentary Record.* New York: Van Nostrand, 1956.

Israeli, Raphael. *Green Crescent Over Nazareth: The Displacement of Christians by Muslims in the Holy Land.* London: Frank Cass Publishers, 2002.

_____. *Jerusalem Divided: The Armistice Regime: 1947–1967.* London: Frank Cass Publishers, 2002.

_____. *Poison: Modern Manifestations of a Blood Libel.* Lanham, MD: Lexington Books, 2002.

Jochen, Hippler, and Andrea Lueg. *The Next Threat: Western Perceptions of Islam.* London: Pluto Press, 1995.

Johnson, Paul. *Modern Times: The World from the Twenties to the Nineties.* New York: Perennial Classics, 2001.

Karsh, Efraim. *Arafat's War: The Man and His Battle for Israeli Conquest.* New York, Grove Press, 2003.

_____. *The Arab-Israeli Conflict: The Palestine War 1948.* Botley, Oxford: Osprey Publishing Limited, 2002.

_____, and Inari Karsh. *Empires of the Sand: The Struggle for Mastery in the Middle East 1789–1923.* Cambridge, MA: Harvard University Press, 2001.

_____. *Fabricating History: The "New Historians."* Second Edition. London: Frank Cass, 2000.

Katz, Amnon. *Israel: The Two Halves of the Nation.* Northport, AL: Inverted-A, 1999.

Katz, Samuel. *Battleground: Fact and Fantasy in Palestine.* Revised Edition. New York: Taylor Productions, Ltd., 2002.

_____. *Days of Fire.* New York: Doubleday and Company, 1968.

_____. *The Hollow Peace.* Jerusalem: Dvir and The Jerusalem Post, 1981.

Katz, Yossi. *Partner to Partition: The Jewish Agency's Partition Plan in the Mandate Era.* London: Frank Cass, 1998.

Kaufman, Menahem. *The Magnes-Philby Negotiations, 1929: The Historical Record.* Jerusalem: The Magnes Press, Hebrew University, 1998.

Kedourie, Elie. *In the Anglo-Arab Labyrinth: The McMahon-Husayn Correspondence and Its Interpretations 1914–1939.* London and Portland, Oregon: Frank Cass, 2000.

_____, and Sylvia Haim, eds. *Zionism and Arabism in Palestine and Israel.* London: Frank Cass, 1982.

_____. *Palestine and Israel in the 19th and 20th Centuries.* London: Frank Cass, 1982.

Ketavim le-Toldot Hibbat Zion. Tel Aviv: The Institute for Zionist Research at Tel Aviv University: Vol. I, 1980–1981; Vol II, 1984–1985.

Khalidi, Rashid. *Palestinian Identity: The Construction of Modern National Consciousness.* New York: Columbia University Press, 1998.

Khalidi, Walid. *The Ownership of the U.S. Embassy Site in Jerusalem.* Jerusalem: Institute for Palestine Studies, 2000.

_____, ed. *All That Remains: The Palestinian Villages Occupied and Depopulated by Israel in 1948.* Jerusalem: Institute for Palestine Studies 1992.

_____. *From Haven to Conquest: Readings in Zionism and the Palestine Problem Until 1948.* Jerusalem: Institute for Palestine Studies, 1987.

_____. *Before Their Diaspora: A Photographic History of the Palestinians, 1876–1948.* Jerusalem: Institute for Palestine Studies, 1991.

Khalaf, Issa. *Politics in Palestine: Arab Factionalism and Social Disintegration, 1939–1948.* Albany, NY: State University of New York Press, 1991.

Kimmerling, Baruch. *The Invention and Decline of Israeliness: State, Society and the Military.* Berkeley, CA: The University of California Press, 2001.

_____, ed. *The Israeli State and Society: Boundaries and Frontiers*. Albany, NY: State University of New York Press, 1989.

Kimche, Jon. *Palestine or Israel: The Untold Story of Why We Failed*. London: Secker and Warburg, 1973.

_____. *The Second Arab Awakening*. London: Thames and Hudson, 1970.

_____. *The Unromantics: The Great Powers and the Balfour Declaration*. London: Weidenfeld and Nicolson, 1968.

_____, and David. *Both Sides of the Hill: Britain and the Palestine War*. London: Secker and Warburg, 1960.

Kiernan, Thomas. *Arafat: The Man and the Myth*. New York: W.W. Norton and Company, Inc., 1976.

Klein, Menachem. *Jerusalem: The Contested City*. New York: New York University Press, 2001.

Knee, Stuart E. *The Concept of Zionist Dissent in the American Mind, 1917–1941*. New York: Robert Speller & Sons, 1979.

Knohl, Dov, ed. *Siege in the Hills of Hebron: The Battle of the Etzion Bloc*. New York: Thomas Yoseloff, 1958.

Koestler, Arthur. *Promise and Fulfillment: Palestine 1917–1949*. London: Macmillan and Company, Ltd., 1949.

Korey, William. *The Soviet Cage: Anti-Semitism in Russia*. New York: The Viking Press, 1973.

Krammer, Arnold. *The Forgotten Friendship: Israel and the Soviet Bloc 1947–53*. Urbana, IL: University of Illinois Press, 1974.

Kretzmer, David. *The Occupation of Justice: The Supreme Court of Israel and Occupied Territories*. Albany, NY: State University of New York, 2002.

Kurzman, Dan. *Genesis 1948: The First Arab-Israeli War*. New York: The World Publishing Company, 1970.

Kymlicka, Will. *Politics in the Vernacular: Nationalism, Multiculturalism and Citizenship*. New York: Oxford University Press, 2001.

Laffin, John. *The P.L.O. Connections*. London: Transworld Publishers, Ltd., 1983.

Lall, Arthur. *The UN and the Middle East Crisis, 1967*. Revised Edition. New York: Columbia University Press, 1970.

La Guardia, Anton. *War without End: Israelis, Palestinians, and the Struggle for a Promised Land*. New York: Thomas Dunne Books, 2001.

Laqueur, Walter, and Barry M. Rubin, eds. *The Israel-Arab Reader: A Documentary History of the Middle East Conflict*. New York: Penguin, 1995.

_____. *The Road to Jerusalem: The Arab-Israeli Conflict*. New York: The Macmillan Company, 1968.

Latour, Anny. *The Resurrection of Israel: How the Modern State Was Born.* New York: The World Publishing Company, 1968.

Lazare, Bernard. *Antisemitism: Its History and Causes.* Lincoln, NE: University of Nebraska Press, 1995.

Levenberg, Haim. *The Military Preparations of the Arab Community in Palestine 1945–1948.* London: Frank Cass, 1993.

Levin, Itamar. *Confiscated Wealth: The Fate of Jewish Property in Arab Land.* Institute of the World Jewish Congress, 2000.

Levin, Kenneth. *The Oslo Syndrome: Delusions of a People Under Siege.* Hanover, NH: Smith and Kraus Global, 2005.

LeVine, Mark. *Overthrowing Geography: Jaffa, Tel-Aviv, and the Struggle for Palestine 1880–1948.* Berkeley, CA: University of California Press, 2005.

Lewis, Bernard. *The Jews of Islam.* Princeton, NJ: Princeton University Press, 1987.

_____. *Islam and the West.* New York: Oxford University Press, 1994.

_____. *The Middle East: A Brief History of the Last 2,000 Years.* New York: Touchstone Books, 1997.

_____. *Semites and Anti-Semites: An Inquiry into Conflict and Prejudice.* New York: W.W. Norton and Company, 1999.

_____. *The Multiple Identities of the Middle East.* New York: Shocken Books, 2001.

_____. *What Went Wrong: Western Impact and Middle Eastern Response.* New York: Oxford University Press, 2001.

_____. *From Babel to Dragomans.* New York: Oxford University Press, 2004.

Lie, Trygve. *In the Cause of Peace: Seven Years with the United Nations.* New York: The Macmillan Company, 1954.

Lockman, Zachary. *Comrades and Enemies: Arab and Jewish Workers in Palestine, 1906–1948.* Berkeley, CA: University of California Press, 1996.

_____, and Joel Benin, eds. *Intifada: The Palestinian Uprising Against Israel Occupation.* Cambridge, MA: South End Press, 1989.

Lorch, Netanel. *The Edge of the Sword: Israel's War of Independence 1947–1949.* New York: G. P. Putnam's Sons, 1961.

Lozowick, Yaacov. *Right to Exist: A Moral Defense of Israel's Wars.* New York: Doubleday, 2003.

Lowdermilk, Walter C. *Palestine: Land of Promise.* New York: Harper and Brother, 1944.

Lumer, Hyman, ed. *Lenin on the Jewish Question.* New York: International Publishers, 1974.

Makovsky, David. *Making Peace with the PLO: The Rabin Government's Road to the Oslo Accord.* Boulder, CO: Westview Press, 1996.

Mandel, Neville J. *The Arabs Amid Zionism before World War I*. Berkeley, CA: University of California Press, 1976.

Manor, Yohanan. *To Right a Wrong: The Revocation of the UN General Assembly Resolution 3379 Defaming Zionism*. New York: Shengold Publishers, Inc., 1996.

Mansour, Camille. *Beyond Alliance: Israel in U.S. Foreign Policy*. New York: Columbia University Press, 1994.

Manuel, Frank E. *The Realities of American-Palestine Relations*. Washington, DC: Public Affairs Press, 1949.

Ma'oz, Moshe, ed. *Studies on Palestine During the Ottoman Period*. Jerusalem: The Magnes Press, 1975.

_____, ed. *Palestinian Arab Politics*. Jerusalem: The Jerusalem Academic Press for the Harry S. Truman Research Institute of the Hebrew University of Jerusalem Mount Scopus, Jerusalem, Israel, 1975.

Masalha, Nur. *Expulsion of the Palestinians: The Concept of "Transfer" in Zionist Political Thought, 1882–1948*. Jerusalem: Institute for Palestine Studies, 1992.

_____. *A Land without a People: Israel, Transfer and the Palestinians 1946–96*. London: Faber and Faber, 1997.

_____. *Imperial Israel and the Palestinians: The Politics of Expansion*. Jerusalem: Institute for Palestine Studies, 2000.

McDonald, James G. *My Mission in Israel: 1948–1951*. New York: Simon and Shuster, 1951.

McGowan, Daniel, and Marc H. Ellis, eds. *Remembering Deir Yassin: The Future of Israel and Palestine*. New York: Olive Branch Press, 1998.

Medoff, Rafael, and Chaim I. Waxman. *Historical Dictionary of Zionism*. Lanham, MD: The Scarecrow Press, 2000.

_____. *Zionism and the Arabs: An American Jewish Dilemma, 1898–1948*. Westport, CT: Praeger, 1997.

_____. *Baksheesh Diplomacy: Secret Negotiations Between American Jewish Leaders and Arab Officials on the Eve of World War II*. Lanham, MD: Lexington Books, 2001.

_____. *Militant Zionism in America: The Rise and Impact of the Jabotinsky Movement in the United States, 1926–1948*. London and Tuscaloosa, AL: The University of Alabama Press, 2002.

Meinertzhagen, Richard. *Middle East Diary 1917–1956*. New York: Thomas Yoseloff, 1959.

Michman, Dan. *Holocaust Historiography: A Jewish Perspective*. Portland, OR: Vallentine Mitchell, 2003.

Miller, John, and Aaron Kenedi. *Inside Israel*. New York: Marlowe and Company, 2002.

Miller, Rory. *Ireland and the Palestine Question: 1948–2004.* Dublin, Ireland: Irish Academic Press, 2005.

Mills, Walter, ed. *The Forrestal Diaries.* New York: The Viking Press, 1951.

Monroe, Elizabeth. *Philby of Arabia.* London: Pitman, 1973.

_____. *Britain's Moment in the Middle East, 1914–1956.* London: Chatto and Windus, 1963.

Morris, Benny. *The Birth of the Palestinian Refugee Problem Revisited.* New York: Cambridge University Press, 2004.

_____. *The Road to Jerusalem: Glubb Pasha, Palestine and the Jews.* New York and London: I.B. Tauris, 2002.

_____. *Righteous Victims: A History of the Zionist-Arab Conflict, 1881–1999.* New York: Vintage Books, 2001.

_____. *1948 and After: Israel and the Palestinians.* New York: Oxford University Press, 1990.

_____. *The Birth of the Palestinian Refugee Problem, 1947–1949.* Cambridge: Cambridge University Press, 1987.

Mosse, George L. *Germans and Jews.* New York: Grosset and Dunlap, 1970.

Mossek, Moshe. *Palestine Immigration Policy Under Sir Herbert Samuel: British, Zionist and Arab Attitudes.* London: Frank Cass, 1978.

Motro, Helen Schary. *Maneuvering Between the Headlines: An American Lives Through the Intifada.* New York: Other Press, 2005.

Moynihan, Daniel Patrick. *A Dangerous Place.* New York: Berkley Books, 1980.

_____. *Loyalties.* New York: Harcourt Brace Jovanovich, 1984.

Muravchik, Joshua. *Covering the Intifada: How the Media Reported the Palestinian Uprising.* Washington, DC: The Washington Institute for Near East Policy, 2003.

_____. *The Future of the United Nations: Understanding the Past to Chart a Way Forward.* Washington, DC: Enterprise Institute for Public Policy Research, 2005.

Muslih, Muhammad Y. *Golan: The Road to Occupation.* Jerusalem: Institute for Palestine Studies, 2000.

_____. *The Origins of Palestinian Nationalism.* New York: Columbia University Press, 1989.

Nazzal, Nafez Y., and Laila A. Nazzal. *Historical Dictionary of Palestine.* Lanham, MD: Scarecrow Press, 1997.

Netanyahu, Benjamin. *A Durable Peace: Israel and Its Place Among the Nations.* New York: Warner Books, 2000.

_____. *Fighting Terrorism: How Democracies Can Defeat Domestic and International Terrorists.* New York: Noonday Press, 1997.

_____. *International Terrorism: Challenge and Response.* Piscataway, NJ: Transaction Publishers, 1981.

Nicosia, Francis R. *The Third Reich and the Palestine Question.* Piscataway, NJ: Transaction Publishers, 2000.

Nirenstein, Fiamma. *Terror: The New Anti-Semitism and the War Against the West.* Hanover, NH: Smith and Kraus Global, 2005.

Norman, Theodore. *An Outstretched Arm: A History of the Jewish Colonization Association.* Boston, MA: Routledge and Kegan Paul, 1985.

Nuseibeh, Hazem Zaki. *Palestine and the United Nations.* New York: Quartet Books, 1981.

O'Brien, Conner Cruise. *The Siege: The Saga of Israel and Zionism.* New York: Simon and Schuster, 1986.

Ofer, Dalia. *Escaping the Holocaust: Illegal Immigration to the Land of Israel, 1939–1944.* New York: Oxford University Press, 1990.

Orange, Wendy. *Coming Home to Jerusalem: A Personal Journey.* New York: Simon and Schuster, 2000.

Oren, Michael. *Six Days of War: June 1967 and the Making of the Modern Middle East.* New York: Oxford University Press, 2002.

Orr, Akiva. *Israel: Politics, Myths and Identity Crises.* London: Pluto Press, 1994.

Palestine: A Study of Jewish, Arab, and British Policies. New Haven, CT: Esco Foundation for Palestine, Inc. Yale University Press, 1947.

Palumbo, Michael. *The Palestinian Catastrophe: The 1948 Expulsion of a People from Their Homeland.* London and Boston: Faber and Faber, 1987.

Pappe, Ilan, ed. *Israel/Palestine Question: Rewriting Histories.* New York: Routledge, 1999.

_____. *The Making of the Arab-Israeli Conflict, 1947–1951.* New York and London: I.B. Tauris, 2001.

Parkes, James. *Whose Land? A History of the Peoples of Palestine.* New York: Penguin, 1970.

_____. *The Jewish Problem in the Modern World.* New York: Oxford University Press, 1946.

Pearlman, Moshe. *Ben Gurion Looks Back.* New York: Simon and Schuster, 1965.

Penkower, Monty Noam. *The Emergence of Zionist Thought.* Millwood, NY: Associated Faculty Press, 1986.

_____. *The Holocaust and Israel Reborn: From Catastrophe to Sovereignty.* Urbana-Champaign, IL: University of Illinois Press, 1994.

_____. *Decision on Palestine Deferred: America, Britain and Wartime Diplomacy 1939–1945.* London: Frank Cass Publishers, 2002.

Peters, Joan. *From Time Immemorial: The Origins of the Arab-Jewish Conflict Over Palestine.* New York: Harper Row, 1984.

Philby, H. St. J. B. *Arabian Jubilee.* New York: John Day, 1953.

Plascov, Avi. *The Palestinian Refugees in Jordan 1948–57.* London and Totowa, NJ: Frank Cass, 1981.

Polk, William R. *The United States and the Arab World.* Cambridge, MA: Harvard University Press, 1969.

Polish, David. *"Give Us a King": Legal-Religious Sources of Jewish Sovereignty.* Hoboken, NJ: KTAV Publishing House, 1989.

Porat, Dina, and Roni Stauber. *Antisemitism Worldwide.* Tel Aviv: The Stephen Roth Institute for the Study of Contemporary Antisemitism and Racism, 2003.

_____. *The Blue and the Yellow Stars of David: The Zionist Leadership in Palestine and the Holocaust 1939–1945.* Cambridge, MA: Harvard University Press, 1990.

Porath, Yehoshua. *The Emergence of the Palestinian Arab National Movement, 1918–1929.* London: Frank Cass, 1974.

_____. *The Palestinian Arab National Movement, 1929–1939.* London: Frank Cass, 1977.

Prior, Michael. *Zionism and the State of Israel: A Moral Inquiry.* New York: Routledge, 1999.

Prittie, Terence. *Whose Jerusalem?* London: Frederick Muller Limited, 1981.

Pryce-Jones, David. *The Closed Circle: An Interpretation of the Arabs.* Chicago, IL: Ivan R. Dee, 2002.

_____. *The Face of Defeat: Palestinian Refugees and Guerrillas.* London, Weidenfeld and Nicolson, 1972.

Quandt, William R. *Decade of Decisions: American Policy Toward the Arab-Israeli Conflict, 1967–1976.* Berkeley, CA: University of California Press, 1977.

Rabinovich. Abraham. *The Yom Kippur War: The Epic Encounter That Transformed the Middle East.* New York: Schocken Books, 2004.

Rabinovich, Itamar. *The Road Not Taken: Early Arab-Israeli Negotiations.* New York: Oxford University Press, 1991.

_____, and Jehuda Reinharz, ed. *Israel in the Middle East: Documents and Readings on Society, Politics and Foreign Relations, 1948–Present.* New York: Oxford University, 1984.

Rabinowitz, Dan, and Khawla Abu-Baker. *Coffins on Our Shoulders: The Experience of the Palestinian Citizens of Israel.* Berkeley, CA: University of California Press, 2005.

Ray, James Lee. *The Future of America-Israeli Relations: A Parting of the Ways.* Lexington, KY: University of Kentucky Press, 1985.

Reinharz, Jehuda, ed. *Living with Antisemitism: Modern Jewish Responses.* Hanover, NH: University of New England, 1987.

_____, and Anita Shapira, eds. *Essential Papers on Zionism.* New York: New York University Press, 1995.

Report by Major General Bennike, Chief of Staff of the Truce Supervision Organization in Palestine. New York: United Nations, n.d.

Rice, Michael. *False Inheritance: Israel in Palestine and the Search for a Solution*. London and New York: Kegan Paul International, 1994.

Robinson, Jacob. *Palestine and the United Nations: Prelude to Solution*. Westport, CT: Westport Press Publishers, 1947.

Rodinson, Maxime. *Cult, Ghetto, and State: The Persistence of the Jewish Question*. London: Al Saqi Books, 1983.

Rogan, Eugene L., and Avi Shlaim, eds. *The War for Palestine: Rewriting the History of 1948*. Cambridge, MA: Cambridge University Press, 2001.

Rose, N.A., ed. *Baffy: The Diaries of Blanche Dugdale 1936–1947*. London: Vallentine, Mitchell, 1973.

_____. *The Gentile Zionists: A Study in Anglo-Zionist Diplomacy 1929–1939*. London: Frank Cass, 1973.

Rose, Norman, ed. *From Palmerston to Balfour: Collected Essays of Mayir Verete*. Portland, OR: F. Cass, 1992.

Rosenbaum, Eli M. *Betrayal: The Untold Story of the Kurt Waldheim Investigation and Cover-Up*. New York: St. Martin's Press, 1993.

Rotenstreich, Nathan. *Essays on Zionism and the Contemporary Jewish Condition*. New York: Herzl Press, 1980.

Rubin, Barry. *The Arab States and the Palestine Conflict*. Syracuse, NY: Syracuse University Press, 1981.

Rubinstein, Amnon. *From Herzl to Rabin: The Changing Image of Zionism*. New York: Holmes & Meier Publishers, Inc., 2000.

Rubinstein, Danny. *The Mystery of Arafat*. South Royalton, VT: Steerforth Press, 1995.

Rosenthal, Steven T. *Irreconcilable Differences: The Waning of the American Jewish Love Affair with Israel*. Hanover, NH: Brandeis University Press, 2001.

Rubin, Barry, and Judith Colp Rubin. *Yasir Arafat: A Political Biography*. New York: Oxford University Press, 2003.

Sachar, Howard M. *A History of Israel from the Rise of Zionism to Our Time*. New York: Alfred A. Knopf, 1998.

Safran, Nadav. *Israel: The Embattled Ally*. Cambridge, MA: Belknap Press, 1978.

_____. *From War to War: The Arab-Israeli Confrontation, 1948–1967*. Indianapolis, IN: Pegasus, 1969.

Said, Edward. *End of the Peace Process: Oslo and After*. New York: Pantheon Books, 2000.

_____. *Out of Place: A Memoir*. New York: Vintage Books, 2000.

_____. *Covering Islam: How the Media and the Experts Determine How We See the Rest of the World*. New York: Vintage Books, 1997.

_____. *Peace and Its Discontents: Essays on Palestine in the Middle East Peace Process*. New York: Vintage Books, 1996.

_____. *The Politics of Dispossession*. New York: Random House, 1994.

_____. *The Question of Palestine*. New York: Vintage Books, 1992.

_____, and Christopher Hitchens, eds. *Blaming the Victims: Spurious Scholarship and the Palestinian Question*. New York: Verso, 1988.

Sanders, Ronald. *The High Walls of Jerusalem: A History of the Balfour Declaration and the Birth of the British Mandate for Palestine*. New York: Holt, Rinehart and Winston, 1983.

Scham, Paul, Walid Salem, and Benjamin Pogrund, eds. *Shared Histories: A Palestinian Dialogue*. Palestinian Center for the Dissemination and Community Development (Panorama) and the Yakar Center for Social Concern. Jerusalem: Modern Arab Press, 2005

Segev, Tom. *One Palestine, Complete: Jews and Arabs Under the British Mandate*. New York: Metropolitan Books, 2000.

_____. *1949, The First Israelis*. New York: Henry Holt, 1998.

_____. *The Seventh Million: The Israelis and the Holocaust*. New York: Hill and Wang, 1993.

Schechtman, Joseph B. *The United States and the Jewish State Movement: The Crucial Decade, 1939–1949*. New York: Herzl Press, 1966.

_____. *The Refugees in the World*. New York: A.S. Barnes and Company, 1963.

_____. *The Mufti and the Fuehrer*. New York: Thomas Yoseloff, 1965.

_____. *The Arab Refugee Problem*. New York: Philosophical Library, 1952.

Schiff, Ze'ev, and Ehud Ya'ari. *Intifada*. New York: Simon and Schuster, 1990.

Schiff, Zeev, and Raphael Rothstein. *A History of the Israeli Army (1870–1974)*. San Francisco, CA: Straight Arrow Books, 1974.

_____. *Guerrillas Against Israel*. New York: David McKay Company, Inc., 1972.

Schoenbaum, David. *The United States and the State of Israel*. New York: Oxford University Press, 1993.

Schoenberg, Harris O. *A Mandate for Terror: The United Nations and the PLO*. New York: Shapolsky Publishers, Inc., 1989.

Schoenfeld, Gabriel. *The Return of Anti-Semitism*. San Francisco, CA: Encounter Books, 2003.

Shahak, Israel. *Jewish History, Jewish Religion: The Weight of Three Thousand Years*. London: Pluto Press, 1994.

Shanks, Hershel. *The City of David: A Guide to Biblical Judaism*. Washington, DC: The Biblical Archeology Society, 1975.

Shalom, Zaki. *David Ben-Gurion: The State of Israel, and the Arab World, 1949–1956*. Brighton and Portland: Sussex University Press, 2002.

Shapira, Anita. *Land and Power: The Zionist Resort to Force 1881–1948*. New York: Oxford University Press, 1992.

Shapiro, Yonathan. *Leadership of the American Zionist Organization, 1897–1930*. Urbana, IL: University of Illinois, Press, 1971.

Sharabi, Hisham. *Palestine and the Israelis: The Lethal Dilemma*. New York: Pegasus, 1969.

Sharansky, Natan. *The Case for Democracy: The Power of Freedom to Overcome Tyranny and Terror*. Green Forest, AR: Balfour Books, Inc., 2006.

Sharef, Zeev. *Three Days*. London: W.H. Allen, 1962.

Sharif, Regina S., ed. *United Nations Resolutions on Palestine and the Arab-Israeli Conflict. Volume II: 1975–1981*. Washington, DC: Institute of Palestine Studies, 1988.

Sharon, Ariel, with David Chanoff. *Warrior: The Autobiography of Ariel Sharon*. New York: Simon & Schuster, 1989.

Segel, Binjamin W., and Richard S. Levy, eds. *A Lie and a Libel: The History of the Protocols of the Elders of Zion*. Lincoln, NE: University of Nebraska Press, 1996.

Shepherd, Naomi. *Ploughing Sand: British Rule in Palestine 1917–1948*. New Brunswick, NJ: Rutgers University Press, 2000.

Shermer, Michael, and Alex Grobman. *Denying History: Who Says the Holocaust Never Happened and Why Do They Say It?* Berkeley, CA: University of California Press, 2000.

Shimoni, Gideon. *The Zionist Ideology*. Hanover: Brandeis University Press/University Press of New England, 1995.

Shipler, David K. *Arab and Jew: Wounded Spirits in a Promised Land*. New York: Penguin, 1987.

Shulewitz, Malka Hillel. *The Forgotten Millions: The Modern Jewish Exodus from Arab Lands*. London and New York: Continuum International, 2000.

Silberstein, Laurence J. *The Postzionism Debates: Knowledge and Power in Israeli Culture*. New York: Routledge, 1999.

Sicker, Martin. *Between Hashemites and Zionists: The Struggle for Palestine, 1908–1988*. New York: Holmes and Meier, 1989.

Simons, Chaim. *International Proposals to Transfer Arabs from Palestine 1895–1947*. Hoboken, NJ: KTAV Publishing House, Inc., 1988.

Slonim, Shlomo. *Jerusalem in America's Foreign Policy, 1947–1997*. New York: Kluwer Law International, 1999.

Smith, Charles D. *Palestine and the Arab-Israeli Conflict*. New York: Bedford/St. Martin's, 1995.

Sofer, Sasson. *Zionism and the Foundations of Israeli Diplomacy*. New York: Cambridge University Press, 1998.

Sohar, Ezra. *A Concubine in the Middle East: American-Israeli Relations.* Jerusalem: Gefen Publishing House, 1999.

Sprinzak, Ehud. *Brother Against Brother: Violence and Extremism in Israeli Politics from Altalena to the Rabin Assassination.* New York: Free Press, 1999.

_____. *The Ascendance of Israel's Radical Right.* New York: Oxford University Press, 1991.

Stanislawski, Michael. *Zionism and the Fin de Siècle: Cosmopolitanism and Nationalism from Nordau to Jabotinsky.* Berkeley, CA: University of California Press, 2001.

Stein, Kenneth W. *The Land Question in Palestine, 1917–1939.* Chapel Hill, NC: University of North Carolina Press, 1984.

Stein, Leonard. *The Balfour Declaration.* London: Valentine Mitchell, 1961.

_____. *The Palestine White Paper of October 1930.* London: Jewish Agency For Palestine, 1930.

Stern, Kenneth S. *Anti-Zionism: The Sophisticated Antisemitism.* New York: The American Jewish Committee, 1990.

Sternhell, Zeev. *The Founding Myths of Israel.* Princeton, NJ: Princeton University Press, 1997.

Stone, Julius. *Israel and Palestine: Assault on the Law of Nations.* Baltimore, MD: The Johns Hopkins University Press, 1981.

Sultan, Cathy. *Israeli and Palestinian Voice: A Dialogue with Both Sides.* iUniverse, Inc., 2003.

Symonds, Richard, and Michael Carder. *The United Nations and the Population Question: 1945–1970.* New York: McGraw Hill Book Company, 1973.

Syrkin, Marie, ed. *A Land of Our Own: An Oral Autobiography by Golda Meir.* New York: G.P. Putnam's Sons, 1973.

Szereszewski, Robert. *Essays on the Structure of the Jewish Economy in Palestine and Israel.* Jerusalem, Israel: The Maurice Falk Institute For Economic Research in Israel, 1968.

Takkenberg, Alex. *The Status of Palestinian Refugees in International Law.* Oxford and New York: Clarendon Press, 1998.

Talmon, Jacob L. *Israel Among the Nations.* London: Weidenfeld and Nicolson, 1970.

Tamari, Salmi, ed. *Jerusalem 1948: The Arab Neighbourhoods and Their Fate in the War.* Jerusalem: Institute of Jerusalem Studies and Badil Resource Center, 1999.

_____. *Palestinian Refugee Negotiations: From Madrid to Oslo II.* Jerusalem: Institute for Palestine Studies, 1996.

Tekoah, Yosef. *In the Face of the Nations: Israel's Struggle For Peace.* New York: Simon and Shuster, 1976.

Teitelbaum, Joshua. *The Rise and Fall of the Hashimite Kingdom of Arabia.* Washington Square, NY: New York University Press, 2001.

Tessler, Mark A. *A History of the Israeli-Palestinian Conflict.* Bloomington, IN: Indiana University Press, 1994.

Teveth, Shabtai. *Ben-Gurion and the Palestinian Arabs: From Peace to War.* New York: Oxford University Press, 1985.

_____. *Moshe Dayan: The Soldier, the Man, the Legend.* London and Jerusalem: Weidenfeld and Nicolson, 1972.

Tiller, Charles. *The Politics of Collective Violence.* New York: Cambridge University Press, 2003.

Touval, Saadia. *The Peace Brokers: Mediators in the Arab-Israeli Conflict, 1948–1979.* Princeton, NJ: Princeton University Press, 1982.

Trachtenberg, Joshua. *The Devil and the Jews: The Medieval Concept of the Jew and Its Relation to Modern Antisemitism.* Philadelphia, PA: Jewish Publication Society, 1989.

Trevor, Daphne. *Under the White Paper: Some Aspects of British Administration in Palestine from 1939 to 1947.* Jerusalem: The Jerusalem Press, Ltd., 1948.

Troen, Ilan S. *Imagining Zion: Dreams, Designs, and Realities in a Century of Jewish Settlement.* New Haven, CT: Yale University Press, 2003.

Troy, Gil. *Why I am a Zionist: Israel Jewish Identity and the Challenges of Today.* Montreal, Canada: Bronfman Jewish Education Centre, 2002.

Turki, Fawaz. *The Disinherited: Journal of a Palestinian Exile.* New York: Monthly Review Press, 1972.

Urofsky, Melvin. *American Zionism from Herzl to the Holocaust.* Garden City, NY: Anchor Press/Doubleday, 1975.

Victor, Barbara. *Army of Roses: Inside the World of Palestinian Women Suicide Bombers.* Emmaus, PA: Rodale Books, 2003.

_____. *A Voice of Reason: Hanan Ashrawi and Peace in the Middle East.* New York: Harcourt Brace, 1994.

Vital, David. *The Origins of Zionism.* New York: Oxford University Press, 1975.

_____. *Zionism: The Formative Years.* New York: Oxford University Press, 1988.

_____. *The Future of the Jews: A People at the Crossroads?* Cambridge, MA: Harvard University Press, 1990.

Vogel, Lester I. *To See a Promised Land: Americans and the Holy Land in the Nineteenth Century.* University Park, PA: Pennsylvania State University Press, 1993.

Usher, Graham. *Dispatches from Palestine: The Collapse of the Oslo Agreement.* London: Pluto Press, 1999.

_____. *Palestine in Crisis: The Struggle for Peace in Political Independence After Oslo.* London: Pluto Press, 1995.

Wallach, Janet, and John Wallach. *Arafat: In the Eyes of the Beholder.* New York: Carol Publishing Group, 1990.

Walzer, Michael. *Just and Unjust Wars: A Moral Argument With Historical Illustrations.* New York: Basic Books, 2006.

Wasserstein, Bernard. *Israelis and Palestinians: Why Do They Fight? Can They Stop?* New Haven, CT: Yale University Press, 2003.

_____. *Divided Jerusalem: The Struggle for the Holy City.* New Haven, CT: Yale University Press, 2001.

Watson, Geoffrey R. *The Oslo Accords: International Law and the Israeli-Palestinian Peace Agreements.* New York: Oxford University Press, 2000.

Weizmann, Chaim. *Trial and Error: The Autobiography of Chaim Weizmann.* New York: Harper and Brothers, 1949.

Wheatcroft, Geoffrey. *The Controversy of Zion: Jewish Nationalism, the Jewish State, and the Unresolved Jewish Dilemma.* Reading, MA: Addison-Wesley, 1996.

Weisbord, Robert G., and Richard Kazarian Jr. *Israel in the Black American Perspective.* Westport, CT: Greenwood Press, 1985.

Weisgal, Meyer. *So Far: An Autobiography.* New York: Random House, 1971.

Whitelam, Keith W. *The Invention of Ancient Israel: The Silencing of Palestinian History.* New York: Routledge, 1997.

Wisse, Ruth R. *If I Am Not for Myself: The Liberal Betrayal of the Jews.* New York: The Free Press, 1992.

Wistrich, Robert S., and David Ohana, eds. *The Shaping of Israeli Identity: Myth, Memory and Trauma.* London: Frank Cass & Company, 1995.

_____. *Muslim Anti-Semitism: A Clear and Present Danger.* New York: The American Jewish Committee, 2001.

_____. *Terms of Survival: The Jewish World Since 1945.* New York: Routledge, 1995.

_____. *Antisemitism: The Longest Hatred.* New York: Schocken Books, 1991.

_____. *Anti-Zionism and Antisemitism in the Contemporary World.* New York: New York University Press, 1990.

_____, ed. *The Left Against Zion: Communism, Israel and the Middle East.* Totowa, NJ: Biblio Distribution Center, 1979.

Yaari, Ehud. *Strike Terror: The Story of Fatah.* New York: Sabra Books, 1970.

Yablonka, Hanna. *The State of Israel vs. Adolf Eichmann.* New York: Schocken Books, 2004.

Ye'or, Bat. *Eurabia: The Euro-Arab Axis.* Madison, NJ: Fairleigh Dickinson University Press, 2005.

_____. *Islam and Dhimmitude: Where Civilizations Collide.* Madison, NJ: Fairleigh Dickinson University Press, 2002.

Yodfat, Aryeh Y., and Yuval Arnon-Ohanna. *PLO Strategy and Tactics.* New York: St. Martin's Press, 1981.

Zaar, Isaac. *Rescue and Liberation: America's Part in the Birth of Israel*. New York: Bloch, 1954.

Zenner, Walter P. *Minorities in the Middle: A Cross Cultural Analysis*. Albany, NY: State University of New York Press, 1991.

Zertal, Idith. *From Catastrophe to Power: Holocaust Survivors and the Emergence of Israel*. Berkeley, CA: University of California Press, 1978.

_____. *Israel's Holocaust and the Politics of Nationhood*. Cambridge, UK and New York, NY: Cambridge University Press. 2005.

Zisser, Eyal. *Assad's Legacy: Syria in Transition*. New York: NYU Press, 2001.

ARTICLES

Abramov, S.Z. "Was the Conflict Unavoidable?" *Midstream* (December 1964): p. 63–73.

Albin, Cecilia. "Securing the Peace of Jerusalem: On the Politics of Unifying and Dividing." *Review of International Studies* 23 (1997): p. 117–142.

"An Interview with Lord Caradon." *Journal of Palestine Studies* vol. 5, issue 3/4 (Spring–Summer 1976): p. 142–152.

"Anti-Zionism at British Universities." *Patterns of Prejudice* vol. 11, no. 4 (July–August 1977): p. 1–3.

"The Arab Refugees." *The Economist* (October 2, 1948): p. 540–542.

Arendt, Hannah. " To Save the Jewish Homeland: There Is Still Time." *Commentary* (May 1948): p. 398–406.

Avineri, Shlomo. "Zionism as a National Liberation Movement." *Jerusalem Quarterly* number 10 (Winter 1979): p. 133–144.

_____. "The Palestinians and Israel." *Commentary* vol. no. 6 (June 1940): p. 31–44.

Banki, Judith Hershcopf. "The UN's Anti-Zionism Resolution: Christian Responses." New York, The American Jewish Committee (1976).

Bar-Joseph, Uri. "Rotem: The Forgotten Crisis on the Road to the 1967 War." *Journal of Contemporary History* vol. 3, no. 3 (1996): p. 547–566.

Barsamian, David. "Edward Said." *Progressive* (April 1999): http: www.progressive /0901/intv1101.html.

Baumel, Judith Tydor. "Bridging Myth and Reality: The Absorption of She'erit Hapletah in Eretz Yisrael, 1945–48." *Middle East Studies* vol. 33, no. 2 (April 1997): p. 362–382.

Bayefsky, Anne. "The UN and the Jews." *Commentary* (February 2004): p. 42–46.

_____. "Discrimination and Double Standards — Anti-Israeli Past Is Present at the U.N.'s Human Rights Council." *National Review Online* (July 5, 2006).

_____. "Had Enough? The U.N. Handicaps Israel, Along with the Rest of Us." *NationalReviewOnline* (July 17, 2004): Online.

_____. "One Small Step: Is the U.N. Finally Ready to Get Serious about Anti-Semitism?" *Wall Street Journal* (June 21, 2004): Online.

_____. "The U.N.'s Dirty Little Secret: The International Body Refuses to Condemn Anti-Semitism." *Wall Street Journal* (December 8, 2003): Online.

_____. "Terrorism and Racism: The Aftermath of Durban." Jerusalem Center For Public Affairs Number 468 (December 16, 2001).

Ben Gurion, David. "Ben-Gurion and De Gaulle: An Exchange of Letters." *Midstream* (February 1968): p. 11–26.

Bialer, Uri. "Top Hat, Tuxedo and Cannons: Israeli Foreign Policy from 1948 to 1956 as a Field Study." *Israel Studies* vol. 7, no. 1 (Spring 2002): http:/iupjournals. org/Israel/iss7-1.html.

Blum, Yehuda. "The Missing Reversioner: Reflections on the Status of Judea and Samaria." *Israel Law Review* vol. 3, no. 2 (1968): p. 279–301.

Brailsford, H.N. "Solution for Palestine: A British View." *Commentary* (February 1946): p. 51–55.

Brecher, Michael. "Jerusalem: Israel's Political Decisions, 1947–1977." *Middle East Journal* vol. 32, no. 1 (Winter 1978): p. 13–34.

Bruck, Connie. "The Wounds of Peace." *New Yorker* (October 1996): p. 64–90.

Brynen, Rex. "The Funding of Palestinian Refugee Compensation." FOFOGNET (March 1996): Online.

Caldwell, Christopher. "The Fallaci Affair." *Commentary* (October 2002): p. 34–43.

Caplan, Neil. " Arab-Jewish Contacts in Palestine After the First World War." *Journal of Contemporary History* 12 (1977): p. 635–668.

Carmichael, Joel. "On Again, Off Again." *Midstream* (Summer 1960): p. 56–64.

Cohen, Michael J. "British Strategy and the Palestine Question 1936–39." *Journal of Contemporary History* vol. 7, issues 3 and 4 (July–October 1972): p. 157–183.

_____. "Truman, the Holocaust and the Establishment of the State of Israel." *Jerusalem Quarterly* no. 23 (Spring 1982): p. 79–94.

Cohen, Roberta. "United Nations' Stand on Antisemitism: Principles, Priorities, Prejudices." *Patterns of Prejudice* vol. 2, no. 2 (March/April 1968): p. 21–24.

Cotler, Irwin. "The Legitimacy of Israel." *Middle East Focus* (January 1981): p. 9–14.

Crossman, Richard H.S. "The Balfour Declaration 1917–1967." *Midstream* (December 1967): p. 21–28.

_____. "Gentile Zionism and the Balfour Declaration." *Commentary* (June 1962): p. 487–494.

_____. "Framework for the Jewish State: The New Boundaries of Zionist Aspirations." *Commentary* (November 1947): p. 401–407.

Curtis, Michael. "The UN and the Middle East Conflict: 1967–75." *Middle East Review* (Spring/Summer 1975): p. 18, 27–28.

Dan, Joseph. "Jewish Sovereignty as a Theological Problem." *Azure* (Winter 2004): Online.

Dayan, Arie. "The Debate Over Zionism and Racism: An Israeli View." *Journal of Palestine Studies* 22, no. 3 (Spring 1993): p. 96–105.

De St. Aubin, W. "Peace And Refugees in the Middle East." *Middle East* vol. 3, no. 3 (July 1949): p. 249–259.

Dowty, Alan. "Is Israel Democratic? Substance and Semantics in the 'Ethnic Democracy' Debate." *Israel Studies* vol 4, no. 2.

Eban, Abba. "Israel, Anti-Semitism and the UN." *Jerusalem Quarterly* no. 1 (Fall 1976): p. 110–120.

Eisenstadt, S.N. "Portrait of the Yishuv." *Jerusalem Quarterly* no. 1 (Fall, 1976): p. 28–35.

Elmer, Jon. "Uri Avnery." *Progressive* (April 2004): http:// www.progressive.org/april04/ intv0404.html.

El-Najjar. "Zionism: The Highest Stage of Imperialism." *Aljazeerah* (May 15, 2002).

Ettinger, Shmuel. "Anti-Semitism in Our Time." *Jerusalem Quarterly* no. 23 (Spring 1982): p. 95–113.

Feiden, Douglas. "His Golden Years." *New York Daily News* (October 14, 2002): http:// www.dailynews.com/front/v-pfriendly/story/26865p-25537c.html.

Fletcher, George P. "Should One Nation Be Able to Judge the Entire World?: Belgium's Prosecution of Ariel Sharon, and Other Invocations of 'Universal Jurisdiction.' " *Find Law's Legal Commentary* (March 4, 2003): http://writ.newsfindlaw. com/scripts.

_____. "Annan's Careless Language." *New York Times* (March 21, 2002): http:// www.soci.niu.edu/~phildept/Kapitan/IPC40.html.

Friedman, Isaiah. "Lord Palmerston and the Protection of Jews in Palestine 1839–1851." *Jewish Social Studies* vol. 30, no. 1 (January 1968): p. 23–41.

_____. "The McMahon-Hussein Correspondence and the Question of Palestine." *Journal of Contemporary History* vol. 5, issue 2 (1970): p. 83–122.

Friedman, Saul S. "The Myth of Arab Toleration." *Midstream* (January 1970): p. 56–59.

Ganin, Zvi. "Activism Versus Moderation: The Conflict between Abba Hillel Silver and Stephen Wise during the 1940s." *Studies in Zionism* 5 (Spring 1984): p. 71–95.

Gavison, Ruth. "Ruth Gavison Offers a Vision of a Democratic, Jewish Israel." Los Angeles, California: UCLA Ronald W. Burkle Center For International Relations. (February 12, 2004): Online.

_____. "The Jews' Right to Statehood: A Defense." *Azure* issue no. 15 (Summer 5763/2003).

_____. "A Constitution for Israel: Lessons from the American Experiment." *Azure* issue no.12 (Winter 5672/2002).

Gazit, Mordechai. "The Israel-Jordan Peace Negotiations (1949–51): King Abdallah's Lonely Effort." *Journal of Contemporary History* vol. 23 (1988): p. 409–424.

Gerstenfeld, Manfred. "Rewriting Germany's Past — A Society in Moral Decline." Jerusalem Center for Public Affairs, no. 530 (May 1, 2005): Online.

_____. "Jews against Israel." Jerusalem Center for Public Affairs, no. 30 (March 1, 2005): Online.

_____. "An Interview with Meir Litvak: The Development of Arab Anti-Semitism." Jerusalem Center for Public Affairs, no. 5 (February 2003): Online.

Gitelson, Susan Aurelia. "UN-Middle East Voting Patterns of the Black African States, 1967–1974." *Middle East Review* (Spring/Summer 1975): p. 33–51.

Glennon, Michael J. "Why the Security Council Failed." *Foreign Affairs* (May/June 2003): http://www.foreignaffiars.org/2003050faessay11217/michael-j-glennon/why-the-security-com.

Goldberg, Arthur J. "Resolution 242 After Twenty Years." National Committee On American Foreign Policy. http://www.mefacts.com/cache/htmle/arab-countries/10159.htm.

Golan, Galia. "The Soviet Union and the Arab-Israeli Conflict." *Jerusalem Quarterly* no. 1 (Fall 1976): p. 8–17.

Gottheil, Fred M. "The Smoking Gun: Arab Immigration into Palestine, 1922–1931." *Middle East Quarterly* (Winter 2003): http://www.meforum.org/pf.php?id=522.

Green, Elliot A. "The Land of Israel and Jerusalem in 1900." *Midstream* (September–October 2000): p. 28–30.

Groiss, Arnon. "Jews, Israel and Peace in the Palestinian Authority Textbooks: The New Textbooks for Grades 4 and 9." Jerusalem: Center for Monitoring the Impact of Peace (October 2004).

Gutmann, David. "The Palestinian Myth." *Commentary* (October 1975): p. 43–47.

Haim, Sylvia. "Arabic Antisemitic Literature." *Jewish Social Studies* vol. 17, no. 4 (October 1955): p. 307–312.

Halkin, Hillel. "Was Zionism Unjust?" *Commentary* (November 1999): p. 29–35.

_____. "Why the Settlements Should Stay." *Commentary* (June 2002): p. 21–27.

_____. "Does Sharon Have a Plan?" *Commentary* (June 2004): p. 17–22.

Halberstam, Malvina. "The General Assembly Resolution, ICJ Decision, Another General Assembly Resolution Condemning Israel's Construction of the 'Fence': A Tragi-Comedy in Three Acts." n.d.: Online.

_____. "The Myth That Israel's Presence in Judea and Samaria Is Comparable to Iraq's Presence In Kuwait." *Syracuse Journal of International Law and Commerce* (Spring 1993).

Halevi, Jonathan D. "Understanding Arafat Before His Attempted Rehabilitation." *Jerusalem Issue Brief,* Jerusalem Center for Public Affairs, vol. 3, no. 32 (August 16, 2004).

Harper, Malcolm. "Comparison of the United Nations Member States' Language in Relation to Israel and Palestine as Evidenced by Resolutions in the UN Security Council and UN General Assembly." United Nations Association of the United Kingdom (August 2004).

Hazony, Yoram. "Did Herzl Want a 'Jewish' State?" *Azure* (Spring 5760/2000): p. 37–73.

Heller, Joseph. "Failure of a Mission: Bernadotte and Palestine, 1948." *Journal of Contemporary History* vol. 14 (1979): p. 515–534.

Helmreich, Jeffrey. "Diplomatic and Legal Aspects of the Settlement Issue." *Institute for Contemporary Affairs* vol. 2, no. 16 (January 19, 2003).

Henkin, Yagil. "Urban Warfare and the Lessons of Jenin." *Azure* no. 15 (Summer 2003): Online.

Hertzberg, Arthur. "A Small Peace for the Middle East." *Foreign Affairs* vol. 80, no. 1 (January/February 2001): p. 139–147.

Higgins, Rosalyn. "The June War: The United Nations and Legal Background." *Journal of Contemporary History* vol. 3, issue 3 (July, 1968): p. 253–273.

Human Rights Council, Special Session, July 5–6, 2006, "The Human Rights Council." Office of the U.N. High Commissioner for Human Rights, Online.

Idinopulos, Thomas A. "The Zionism and Racism Controversy: Historical Perspective on the Issues." *Christian Century* (January 28, 1976): p. 68–72.

Johnson, Paul. "The Resources of Civilisation," *New Statesman* vol. 90, no. 2328, p. 531–533.

_____. "The Miracle." *Commentary* (May 1998): Online.

Kahn, Mizra. "The Arab Refugees — A Study in Frustration." *Midstream* (Spring 1956): p. 31–48.

Khalidi, Walid. "The Fall of Haifa." *Middle East Forum* vol. 35, no. 10 (December 1959).

_____. "Why Did the Palestinians Leave? An Examination of the Zionist Version of the Exodus '48." *Middle East Forum* vol. 35, no. 7 (July 1959): p. 21–24, 35.

Karsh, Efraim. "Revisiting Israel's 'Original Sin.' " *Commentary* (September 2003): p. 46–50.

_____. "What Occupation?" *Commentary* (July–August 2002): p. 46–51.

_____. "Were the Palestinians Expelled?" *Commentary* (July–August 2000): p. 29–34.

_____. "The Collusion That Never Was: King Abdalla, the Jewish Agency and the Partition of Palestine." *Journal of Contemporary History* vol. 34, no. 4 (1999): p. 569–585.

_____. "Myth in the Desert, or Not the Great Arab Revolt," *Middle East Studies* vol. 2 (April 1997): p. 267–312.

_____. "Peace Despite Everything." *Israel Affairs* vol. 3, nos. 3–4 (Spring/Summer 1997): p. 117–132.

_____. "Introduction: From Rabin to Netanyahu." *Israel Affairs* vol. 3, nos. 3–4 (Spring/Summer 1997): p. i–vii.

_____, and Inari Karsh. "Reflections on Arab Nationalism." *Middle East Studies* vol. 32, no. 4 (October 1996): p. 367–392.

Katz, Jacob. "Zionism vs. Anti-Semitism." *Commentary* (April 1979): p. 46–52.

Kedourie, Elie. "Where Arabism and Zionism Differ." *Commentary* (June 1986): p. 32–36.

Kerstein, Benjamin. "What Noam Chomsky Really Wants." *Frontpagemagazine* (November 9, 2004).

Khalidi, Walid. "Thinking the Unthinkable: A Sovereign Palestine State." *Foreign Affairs* vol. 56, no. 4 (July 1978): p. 695–713.

_____. "The Jewish-Ottoman Company: Herzl's Blueprint for the Colonization of Palestine." *Journal of Palestine Studies* 22, no. 2 (Winter 1993): p. 30–47.

Kimche, Jon. "British Labor's Turnabout on Zionism." *Commentary* (December, 1947): p. 510–517.

Klein, Menachem. "From a Doctrine-Oriented to a Solution-Oriented Policy: The PLO's 'Right of Return,' 1964–2000," in *The Palestinian Refugees: Old Problems — New Solutions*, Joseph Ginat and Edward J. Perkins, eds. Norman, Oklahoma: University of Oklahoma Press, 2001.

Kochavi, Arieh J. "Britain's Image Campaign Against the Zionists." *Journal of Contemporary History* vol. 36, no. 2 (April 2001): p. 293–307.

Kollat, Israel. "The Zionist Movement and the Arabs." *Studies in Zionism* no. 5 (1982): p. 129–157.

Korey, William. "Is the Worst Over?" *Hadassah Magazine* (January 1986): p. 14–16.

Kushner, David. "Zealous Towns in Nineteenth-Century Palestine." *Middle Eastern Studies* vol. 33, no. 3 (July 1997): p. 597–612.

Landes, David S. "Palestine Before the Zionists." *Commentary* (February 1976): p. 47–56.

Lapidoth, Ruth. "UN Resolution 242." *Weiner Library Bulletin* vol. 26, nos. 1/2 new series nos. 26/7 (1972): p. 2–8.

Lasensky, Scott B. "How to Help Palestinian Refugees Today." *Jerusalem Center For Public Affairs* no. 491 (February 2003): Online.

Lehrman, Hal. "Three Weeks in Cairo: A Journalist in Quest of Egypt's Terms for Peace." *Commentary* (February 1956): p. 101–111.

_____. "Is An Arab-Israeli War Inevitable? A Challenge to American Leadership." *Commentary* (March 1956): p. 210–221.

Lewis, Bernard. "The Palestinians and the PLO: A Historical Approach." *Commentary* (January 1975): p. 32–48.

_____. "The Anti-Zionist Resolution." *Foreign Affairs* (November 1976): p. 54–64.

_____. "The Decline and Fall of Islamic Jewry." *Commentary* (June 1984): p. 44–54.

_____. "The Arab World Discovers Anti-Semitism." *Commentary* (May 1986): p. 30–34.

Lewis, Samuel. "The United States and Israel: Evolution of an Unwritten Alliance." *Middle East Journal* vol. 53, no.3 (Summer 1999): p. 364–378.

Lichtheim, George. " Winston Churchill and Zionism." *Midstream* (1959): p. 19–29.

_____. "Behind Bevin's Hostility to Israel: Britain Is Not Yet Reconciled to the Realities. *Commentary* (March 1949): p. 246–251.

Linowitz, Sol. "Analysis of a Tinderbox: The Legal Basis for the State of Israel." *American Bar Association Journal* vol. 43 (June 1957): p. 523–525.

Luft, Gal. "Who Is Winning the Intifada?" *Commentary* (July–August 2001): p. 28–33.

Lustick, Ian. "To Build and to Be Built By: Israel and the Hidden Logic of the Iron Wall." *Israel Studies* vol. 1, no. 1 (Spring 1996): http:/iupjournals.org/Israel/iss1-1.html

Makovsky, David. "Middle East Peace Through Partition." *Foreign Affairs* (March/April 2001): p. 28–45.

Mandel, Neville. "Attempts at an Arab Entente: 1913–1914." *Middle Eastern Studies* (April 1965): p. 238–267.

Manor, Yohanan. "Contemporary Anti-Zionism." *Encyclopaedia Judaica Year Book 1983–1985* (1985): p. 128–137.

_____. "The New Anti-Zionism." *Jerusalem Quarterly* (Spring 1985): p. 125–144.

Marucs, Itamar, and Barabara Crook. "Visual Hate Messages in the PA Media — May 2005." *PMW* (June 15, 2005).

Marx, Emanuel, and Nitza Nachmias. "Dilemmas of Prolonged Humanitarian Aid Operations: The Case of UNRWA (UN Relief and Work Agency for the Palestinian Refugees)." *Journal of Humanitarian Assistance* (June 22, 2004): http://www.jha.ac/articles/a135.htm

Marlowe, John. "How to Deal with Arab Nationalism? Enforcement of Partition Will Strengthen Progressive Forces." *Commentary* (April 1948): p. 317–333.

Mayer, Thomas. "The UN Resolution Equating Zionism with Racism: Genesis and Repercussions." London, Institute of Jewish Affairs (April 1985): p. 1–11.

Medoff, Rafael. "Herbert Hoover's Plan for Palestine: A Forgotten Episode in American Middle East Diplomacy." *American Jewish History* 79 (Summer 1990): p. 449–76.

_____. "The Influence of Revisionist Zionism in America during the Early Years of World War Two." *Studies in Zionism* 13 (Autumn 1992): p. 187–90.

Miller, Aaron David. "The Arab-Israeli Conflict, 1967–1987: A Retrospective." *Middle East Journal* vol. 41, no. 3 (Summer 1987): p. 349–360.

Milson, Menachem. "Countering Arab Antisemitism." Jerusalem, Institute of the World Jewish Congress (2003): p. 3–17.

Morris, Benny. "The Harvest of 1948 and the Creation of the Palestinian Refugee Problem." *Middle East Journal* vol. 40, no. 4 (Autumn 1986): p. 671–685.

Mosse, George. "Can Nationalism Be Saved? About Zionism, Rightful and Unjust Nationalism." *Israel Studies* vol. 2, no. 1 (Spring 1997): p. 156–173.

Moynihan, Daniel P. "The Politics of Human Rights." *Commentary* (August 1977): p. 19–26.

_____. " 'Joining the Jackals:' The U.S. at the UN 1977–1980." *Commentary* (February 1981): p. 23–31.

_____. "Telling the Truth About the Lie." *Moment* (March 20, 1985): p. 20–21.

Muravchik, Joshua. "The Case Against the UN." *Commentary* (November 2004): p. 36–42.

_____. "The UN on the Loose." *Commentary* (July–August 2002): p. 29–32.

"Neo-Nazi Pro-Arab and Arab Antisemites." *Patterns of Prejudice* (March–April 1968): p. 13–14, 28.

Nevo, Joseph. " The Arabs of Palestine 1947–48: Military and Political Activity." *Middle Eastern Studies* vol. 23, no. 1 (January 1987): p. 3–38.

Nevo, Yosef. "How Many Palestinians?" *New Outlook* vol. 12, no. 4 (May 1969): p. 28–31.

Niebuhr, Reinhold. "Our Stake in the State of Israel." *New Republic* (February 4, 1957): p. 9–12.

Nordbruch, Goetz. "The Socio-Historical Background of Holocaust Denial in Arab Countries: Reactions to Roger Garaudy's *The Founding Myths of Israeli Politics*." The Vidal Sassoon International Center for the Study of Antisemitism (2001).

Oded, Aryeh. "Slaves and Oil: The Arab Image in Black Africa." *Wiener Library Bulletin* vol. 27, new series no. 32 (1974): p. 34–47.

Odeh, Adnan Abu. "Two Capitals in Undivided Jerusalem." *Foreign Affairs* vol. 71, no. 2 (Spring 1992): p. 183–188.

Oren, Michael B. "The 'USS Liberty': Case Closed." *Azure* (Spring 5760/2000): p. 74–93.

_____. "Escalation to Suez: The Egypt-Israel Border War, 1946–56." *Journal of Contemporary History* vol. 24, issue 2 (April 1999): p. 347–373.

_____. "Did Israel Want the Six-Day War?" *Azure* (Spring 5759/1999): http://www.shalem.org.il/azure/7-Oren.html

_____. "Ambivalent Adversaries: David Ben-Gurion and Israel vs. the United Nations and Dag Hammarskjold, 1956–57." *Journal of Contemporary History* vol. 27 (1992): p. 90–127.

Penkower, Monty Noam. "In Dramatic Dissent: The Bergson Boys." *American Jewish History* 70 (March 1981): p. 281–309.

_____. "American Jewry and the Holocaust: From Biltmore to the American Jewish Conference." *Jewish Social Studies* 47 (Spring 1985): p. 95–114.

Peretz, Don. "Refugee Compensation: Responsibility, Recipients, and Forms and Sources," in *The Palestinian Refugees: Old Problems — New Solutions,* Joseph Ginat and Edward J. Perkins, eds. (Norman, Oklahoma: University of Oklahoma Press, 2001).

Perlmann, Moshe. "Chapters of Arab-Jewish Diplomacy, 1918–22." *Jewish Social Studies* vol. 66, no. 2 (April 1944): p. 123–153.

_____. "Arabic Antisemitic Literature: Comment on Sylvia G. Haim's Article." *Jewish Social Studies* vol. 17, no. 4, p. 313–314.

Pipes, Daniel. "Lessons from the Prophet Muhammad's Diplomacy." *Middle East Quarterly* (September 1999): www.Danielpipes.org/article/316.

_____. "The Politics of Muslim Anti-Semitism." *Commentary* (August 1981): p. 39–45.

_____. "Arab vs. Arab Over Palestine." *Commentary* (July 1987): p. 17–25.

_____. "Israel, America and Arab Delusions." *Commentary* (March 1991): p. 26–31.

_____. "Israel's Moment of Truth." *Commentary* (February 2000): p. 19–25.

Podhoretz, Norman. "The State of World Jewry." *Commentary* (December 1983): p. 37–45.

Polisar, Daniel. "Yasser Arafat and the Myth Legitimacy." *Azure* no. 13 (Summer 2002): Online edition.

Porath, Yehoshua. "The Land Problem in Mandatory Palestine." *Jerusalem Quarterly* no. 1 (Fall 1976): p. 18–35.

_____. "Mrs. Peter's Palestine." *New York Review of Books* vol. 32, no. 21 and 22 (January 1986): www.nybooks.com/articles/5249.

_____. "Tom Segev's New Mandate." *Azure* (Spring 5760/2000): p. 23–36.

Prittie, Terrence. "The UN and the Palestinian Refugees." *Middle East Review* (Spring/Summer 1975): p. 52–56.

Reichman, Shalom, Yossi Katz, and Yair Paz. "The Absorptive Capacity of Palestine 1882–1948." *Middle Eastern Studies* vol. 33, no. 2 (April, 1997): p. 338–361.

Ro'i, Yaacov. "Relations Between Rehovot and Its Arab Neighbors, 1890–1914," in *Zionism: Studies in the History of the Zionist Movement and of the Jewish Community in Palestine* (Tel-Aviv: Massada Publishing Company, Ltd., 1975), p. 337–88.

Rostow, Eugene V. "Resolved: Are the Settlements Legal? Israeli West Bank Policies." *New Republic* (October 21, 1991).

_____. "Bricks and Stones: Settling for Leverage; Palestinian Autonomy." *New Republic* (April 23, 1990).

Rotberg, Robert. "Anti-Semitism and Victimhood in Waldheim's Vienna." *Newsletter of the Eastern Europe Anthropology Group* vol. 8, nos. 1 and 2 (Autumn 1989): Online.

Rubenstein, Danny. "The People of Nowhere." *Palestine-Israel Journal* no. 2 (Spring 1994): p. 79–85.

Rubinstein, Amnon. "Zionism's Compatriots." *Azure* no. 16 (Winter 56764/2004): Online.

Salam, Nawaf A. "Between Repatriation and Resettlement: Palestinian Refugees in Lebanon." *Journal of Palestine Studies* 24, no. 1 (Autumn 1994): p. 18–27.

Sayigh, Rosemary. "The Palestinian Identity Among Camp Residents." *Journal of Palestine Studies* vol. 6, no. 3, issue 23 (Spring 1977): p. 3–23.

Schoenberg, Harris O. "The World Conference Against Racism: The Adoption and Repeal Of the Z=R Resolution and the Implications for UN Reform." Monograph 18 (Wayne, NJ: The Center for UN Reform Education, 2001).

Schoenfeld, Gabriel. "Israel and the Anti-Semites." *Commentary* (June 2002): p. 13–20.

Scholch, Alexander. "Britain in Palestine, 1838–1882: The Roots of the Balfour Policy." *Journal of Palestine Studies* 22 no. 1 (Autumn 1992): p. 38–53.

Schvindlerman, Julian. "Yerushalayim versus Al-Quds." *Midstream* (September/October 2000): p. 26–28.

Shapira, Anita. "Ben Gurion and the Bible: The Forging of an Historical Narrative?" *Middle Eastern Studies* vol. 33, no. 4 (October 1997): p. 645–674.

Sharansky, Natan. "On Hating Jews." *Commentary* (November 2003): p. 26–34.

Sharett, Moshe. "Israel's Position and Problems." *Middle East Affairs* vol. 3, no. 5 (May 1952): p. 133–149.

Shemesh, Moshe. "Did Shuqayri Call for 'Throwing the Jews into the Sea'?" *Israel Studies* vol. 8, no. 2 (Summer 2003): p. 70–81.

Shlaim, Avi. "Interview with Abba Eban, 11 March 1976." *Israel Studies* vol. 8, no. 1 (Spring 2003): p. 153–177.

Shneiderman, S.L. "Russia's Anti-Zionist Campaign: Jews vs. Zionists." *Midstream* (June/July 1970): p. 66–75.

Shwadran, Benjamin. "The Palestine Conciliation Commission." *Middle Eastern Affairs*, vol. 1, no. 10 (October 1950): p. 271–282.

_____. "Jordan Annexes Arab Palestine." *Middle Eastern Affairs* vol. 4 (April 1950): p. 99–111.

Smith, Charles D. "The Invention of a Tradition: The Question of Arab Acceptance of the Zionist Right to Palestine during World War I." *Journal of Palestine Studies* 22, no. 2 (Winter 1993): p. 48–61.

Sprinzak, Ehud. "Anti-Zionism: From Delegitimation to Dehumanization." *Forum-53* (Fall 1984): p. 1–12.

_____. "The Damage of Anti-Zionism: A preliminary Analysis." Jerusalem, World Zionist Organization (1984): p. 1–9.

Stein, Kenneth W. "Palestine's Rural Economy, 1917–1939." *Studies in Zionism* vol. 8, no. 1 (1987): p. 25–49.

_____. "The Intifada and the 1936–39 Uprising: A Comparison." (Summer 1990): p. 64–85.

Steinberg, Gerald M. "Abusing the Legacy of the Holocaust: The Role of the NGOs in Exploiting Human Rights to Demonize Israel." *Jewish Political Studies Review* 16:3–4 JCPA (Fall 2004): Online.

_____. "Zionism as Affirmative Action" (April 20, 2001): Online.

Syrkin, Marie. "The Arab Refugees: A Zionist View." *Commentary* (January 1966): p. 23–30.

Tagliabue, John. "Files Show Kurt Waldheim Served Under War Criminal." *New York Times* (March 4, 1986): p. A1, A6.

Talmon, J.L. "The New Anti-Semitism." *New Republic* (September 18, 1976): p. 18–23.

Teachout, Terry. "The Riddle of Yehudi Menuhin." *Commentary* (June 2001): p. 52–56.

Tell, David. "The UN's Israel Obsession." *Weekly Standard* vol. 007, issue 33 (May 6, 2002): http://www the weeklystandard.com/Utilities.

Teller, J.L. "Behind Palestine's Arab 'Armies.' " *Commentary* (March 1947): p. 243–249.

Tovy, Jacob. "Negotiating the Palestinian Refugees." *Middle East Quarterly* (Spring 2003): Online.

Trevor-Roper, H.R. "Jewish and Other Nationalisms." *Commentary* (January 1963): p. 15–21.

Turki, Fawaz. "To Be a Palestinian." *Journal of Palestine Studies* vol. 3, issue 3 (Spring 1974): p. 3–17.

"The UN Resolution on Zionism." *Journal of Palestine Studies* vol. 5, issue 1/2 (Autumn 1975–Winter 1976): p. 252–254.

Weltsch, Robert. "What Chance for Arab-Jewish Accord?: The Basic Issues Must Be Resolved." *Commentary* (July 1948): p. 8–17.

Williamson, Richard S. "Serpents in the UN" *Midstream* vol. 35, issue 1 (January, 1989): p. 8–10.

Wisse, Ruth R. "The Brilliant Failure of Jewish Foreign Policy." *Azure* (Winter 5761/2001): p. 118–145.

_____. "The UN's Jewish Problem: Antisemitism Has Found a Comfortable Home on the East River." *Weekly Standard* vol. 007, issue no. 29 (April 8, 2002): http://www.mideasttruth.com/tws2.html.

_____. "On Ignoring Anti-Semitism." *Commentary* (October 2002): p. 26–33.

Wodak, Ruth, "The Waldheim Affair and Antisemitic Prejudice in Austrian Public Discourse." *Patterns of Prejudice* vol. 24, nos. 2–4 (Winter 1990): p. 18–33.

Wurtele, Zivia, and Morton G. Wurtele. "De Facto Population Exchange Between Arabs and Oriental Jews, 1922–1972." *Middle East Review* (Spring/Summer 1975): p. 57–59.

Wyman, David S. "The Bergson Group, America and the Holocaust: A Previously Unpublished Interview with Hillel Kook/Peter Bergson." *American Jewish History* 89

(March 2001): p. 3–34.

Ya'ari, Ehud. "The Israeli-Palestinian Confrontation: Toward a Divorce." *Jerusalem Issue Brief,* Jewish Center for Public Affairs, vol. 2, no. 2 (June 30, 2002).

Yisraeli, David. "The Third Reich and the Transfer Agreement." *Journal of Contemporary History* vol. 6, issue 2 (1971): p. 129–148.

Young, Lewis. "American Blacks and the Arab-Israeli Conflict." *Journal of Palestine Studies* vol. 2, issue 1 (Autumn 1972): p. 70–85.

Zayyad, Ziad Abu. "The Palestine Right of Return: A Realistic Approach." *Palestine-Israel Journal* no. 2 (Spring 1994): p. 74–78.

Zimmerman, John. "Radio Propaganda in the Arab-Israeli War 1948." *Weiner Library Bulletin* vol. 27, new series nos. 30/31 (1973/74): 2–8.

Zimmerman, Moshe. "From Radicalism to Anti-Semitism." *Jerusalem Quarterly* no. 23 (Spring 1982): p. 114–128.

Zureik, Elia. "Palestinian Refugees and Peace." *Journal of Palestine Studies* 24, no. 1 (Autumn 1994): p. 5–17.

INDEX

Other books by Alex Grobman

Battling for Souls: The Vaad Hatzala Rescue Committee in Post-War Europe (Jersey City, NJ: KTAV Pub. House, 2004).

Denying History: Who Says the Holocaust Never Happened and Why Do They Say It? (Berkeley, CA: University of California Press, 2000).

In Defense of the Survivors: The Letters and Documents of Oscar A. Mintzer, AJDC Legal Advisor, Germany 1945–1946 (Berkeley, CA: Judah L. Magnes Museum, 1998).

Anne Frank in Historical Perspective (Los Angeles, CA: Martyrs Memorial and Museum of the Holocaust of the Jewish Federation Council, 1995).

Those Who Dared: Rescuers and Rescued (Los Angeles, CA: Martyrs Memorial and Museum of the Holocaust of the Jewish Federation Council, 1995).

Rekindling the Flame: American Jewish Chaplains and the Survivors of European Jewry, 1944–1948 (Detroit MI: Wayne State University Press, 1993).

Genocide: Critical Issues of the Holocaust (Los Angeles, CA: Simon Weisenthal Center; Chappaqua, NY: Rossel Books, 1983).